575+ Practice Questions for the

DIGITAL PSAT/ NMSQT®

3rd Edition

The Staff of The Princeton Review

PrincetonReview.com

Penguin
Random
House

The Princeton Review
110 East 42nd Street, 7th Floor
New York, NY 10017

Terms of Service: The Princeton Review Online Companion Tools ("Student Tools") for retail books are available for only the two most recent editions of that book. Student Tools may be activated only once per eligible book purchased for a total of 24 months of access. Activation of Student Tools more than once per book is in direct violation of these Terms of Service and may result in discontinuation of access to Student Tools Services.

ISBN: 978-0-593-51663-8
ISSN: 2333-9322

PSAT/NMSQT is a registered trademark of the College Board and the National Merit Scholarship Corporation, which are not affiliated with, and do not endorse, this product.

The Princeton Review is not affiliated with Princeton University.

The material in this book is up-to-date at the time of publication. However, changes may have been instituted by the testing body in the test after this book was published. If there are any important late-breaking developments, changes, or corrections to the materials in this book, we will post that information online in the Student Tools. Register your book and check your Student Tools to see if there are any updates posted there.

Editor: Aaron Riccio
Production Editors: Emma Parker and Emily Epstein White
Production Artist: Deborah Weber

Printed in the United States of America.

10 9 8 7 6 5 4 3 2 1

3rd Edition

The Princeton Review Publishing Team
Rob Franek, Editor-in-Chief
David Soto, Senior Director, Data Operations
Stephen Koch, Senior Manager, Data Operations
Deborah Weber, Director of Production
Jason Ullmeyer, Production Design Manager
Jennifer Chapman, Senior Production Artist
Selena Coppock, Director of Editorial
Orion McBean, Senior Editor
Aaron Riccio, Senior Editor
Meave Shelton, Senior Editor
Chris Chimera, Editor
Patricia Murphy, Editor
Laura Rose, Editor
Isabelle Appleton, Editorial Assistant

Penguin Random House Publishing Team
Tom Russell, VP, Publisher
Alison Stoltzfus, Senior Director, Publishing
Emily Hoffman, Associate Managing Editor
Patty Collins, Executive Director of Production
Mary Ellen Owens, Assistant Director of Production
Suzanne Lee, Designer
Eugenia Lo, Publishing Assistant

For customer service, please contact **editorialsupport@review.com**, and be sure to include:

- full title of the book

- ISBN

- page number

Acknowledgments

A lot of work goes into making sure that the questions in this book provide you with the necessary practice for the PSAT/NMSQT. For this latest edition, wholly revised to reflect the new digital format of the test, we are thankful to authors Kenneth Brenner, Sara Kuperstein, and Scott O'Neal, as well as the many contributors who helped these questions shine: Aleksei Alferiev, Tania Capone, Paul Christiansen, Remy Cosse, Stacey Cowap, Wahzma Daftanai, Harrison Foster, Kyle Fox, Beth Hollingsworth, Adam Keller, Kevin Keogh, Ali Landreau, Christine Lindwall, Jomil London, Sweena Mangal, Sionainn Marcoux, Valerie Meyers, Amy Minster, Acaia Nawrocik-Madrid, Gabby Peterson, Robert Otey, Elizabeth Owens, Denise Pollard, Kathy Ruppert, and Jess Thomas.

You would also not have a book of this quality without the time and attention given to each page by Emma Parker and Emily Epstein White, and would be holding nothing at all if not for the dedicated production skills of Deborah Weber.

Finally, a word of thanks to our students. Your focus and commitment to the work has in turn inspired our own and helped us to make this PSAT/NMSQT book as useful as possible.

Contents

Math

Practice Test 1

Get More (Free) Content
at **PrincetonReview.com/prep**

As easy as 1·2·3

1 Go to PrincetonReview.com/prep or scan the **QR code** and enter the following ISBN for your book: **9780593516638**

2 Answer a few simple questions to set up an exclusive Princeton Review account. *(If you already have one, you can just log in.)*

3 Enjoy access to your **FREE** content!

Once you've registered, you can...

- Access and print out one more full-length practice test as well as the corresponding answers and explanations

- Use our online tools to take your practice test digitally or use our online proctor to time you while you take the test in the book, then enter your answers online

- Enter your answers in our online bubble sheet to get an approximate scaled score with explanations (manual conversion table also available)

- Get valuable advice about the college application process

- If you're still choosing between colleges, use our searchable rankings of *The Best 390 Colleges* to find out more information about your dream school

- Access printable resources, including additional bubble sheets and the Math Formula Sheet

- Check to see if there have been any corrections or updates to this edition

Need to report a potential **content** issue?

Contact **EditorialSupport@review.com** and include:

- full title of the book
- ISBN
- page number

Need to report a **technical** issue?

Contact **TPRStudentTech@review.com** and provide:

- your full name
- email address used to register the book
- full book title and ISBN
- Operating system (Mac/PC) and browser (Chrome, Firefox, Safari, etc.)

Chapter 1
Introduction

WHAT DOES THE PSAT TEST?

As you begin your prep, it's useful to remember that the PSAT is not a test of how capable you are academically, how good of a person you are, or how successful you will be in life. The PSAT simply tests how well you take the PSAT. That's it. And performing well on the PSAT is a skill that can be learned like any other. The Princeton Review was founded over 40 years ago on this very simple idea, and—as our students' test scores show—our approach is the one that works. Any standardized test is a coachable test. A beatable test. We'll coach you to ensure you have the tools you need to beat it.

> **The PSAT doesn't measure the stuff that matters.** It measures neither intelligence nor the depth and breadth of what you're learning in high school. It doesn't predict college grades as well as your high school grades do. Colleges know there is more to you as a student—and as a person—than how you do on a single test.

HOW IS THE PSAT STRUCTURED AND SCORED?

Category	PSAT/NMSQT
Time Overall	134 minutes plus break
Components	• Reading and Writing section • Math section
Number of Questions	• Reading and Writing: 54, including 4 experimental questions • Math: 44, including 4 experimental questions
Answer Choices	• Reading and Writing: all multiple-choice with 4 answers per question • Math: 75% multiple-choice with 4 answers per question, 25% student-produced responses
Time by Section	• Reading and Writing: 64 minutes in two 32-minute modules • Math: 70 minutes in two 35-minute modules
Relationship Between Modules	• Module 1 has a broad mix of levels of difficulty. • Performance on Module 1 determines the difficulty of Module 2. • Students who do well on Module 1 will get a Module 2 that is harder, on average. • Students who do less well on Module 1 will get a Module 2 that is easier, on average.
Scoring	• The score is based on the number of questions correct and the difficulty of the questions seen. • Students who do well on Module 1 are put into a higher bracket of possible scores. • Students who do less well on Module 1 are put into a lower bracket of possible scores. • Section scores range from 160 to 760. • Total score is the sum of the section scores and ranges from 320 to 1520.

With the move to a digital PSAT starting in fall of 2023, College Board took the opportunity to alter not just the delivery format but the content of the test from its previous version. All Reading and Writing questions are now attached to short passages, with one question per passage. There will be a wide range of text complexities presented, and the passages will cover a variety of topics ranging from history to science and literature (even some poetry).

The Math content is fairly similar to the form it took on paper tests in 2022 and earlier. There is a strong focus on algebra, problem-solving, and analytical topics, and it includes some high-level content such as trigonometry. Some questions require student-produced responses, and these will be scattered throughout the Math modules. Calculator use will be allowed on all Math questions.

As you can see from the preceding table, both sections (Reading-Writing and Math) are divided into two modules. On the Digital PSAT, your performance on the first module in each section will determine the makeup of your second module. Do well on the first module, and you will see a harder (on average) mix of questions on the second module. Miss more questions in the first module, and you will get an easier (on average) difficulty for the second module. You always want to do as well as possible, of course, but it's worth keeping in mind that you will need to get the hard second module on each section in order to earn a top score.

To help you do your best, we recommend that you review the explanations for the questions in the drills and the practice tests, even if you answer a question correctly. You may discover techniques that help to shave seconds from the time it takes you to solve a question. A large part of what's being tested is your ability to use the appropriate tools in a strategic fashion, and while there may be multiple ways to solve a given problem, you'll want to focus on the most efficient path to a solution.

HOW TO USE THIS BOOK

The Digital PSAT offers savvy solvers a variety of ways to earn points. By capitalizing on the higher-value harder questions, you can improve your score—but to even see those questions on the adaptive test, you need to perform well on the first set of questions.

That's where this book comes in. We've taken all eight Reading question types, eight of the most commonly tested Writing subject areas, and six of the most commonly tested Math subject areas and provided drills for each one. By practicing each topic one at a time, you can identify where you still need the most practice and which types of questions are strong areas for you. This will be useful if you're running short on time during the actual test. The questions in each drill increase in difficulty, with the first being easiest and last being hardest. Additionally, the biggest Math content areas have been broken into drills of varying difficulty. You can build up your strengths in each category, working through the easier questions first and establishing proficiency in those before moving on to the tougher ones in that category.

Diagnostic Drills

Whether you want to start working on your verbal or your math skills, your first step is to take the diagnostic drill for that subject, which includes one or two questions from each topic covered in this book. Though that doesn't cover the full range of questions you may see on the Digital PSAT, it does reflect the most commonly tested topics. Use this like a tutorial for the exam and familiarize yourself with the kinds of questions you are likely to encounter and the ways in which these questions are presented, such as the differences between a multiple-choice question and a fill-in question in the Math section.

Practice Drills

Now that you've got a feel for the Digital PSAT content, move on to the drills in this book. How you performed on each question type in the Diagnostic Drills will help you determine how to engage with the following drills. You may want to begin with topics you are close to proficient in or those with which you struggled the most.

If you still don't know where to begin, we recommend going through them in order within a section. In both the Reading and Writing drills that follow, content is organized roughly in the order it will appear on the exam. All Reading questions appear first in each verbal module in a set order, though Charts and Claims may be mixed together. Writing questions follow the Reading ones, with all Rules questions such as those on punctuation, verbs, and pronouns coming first but mixed together. After Rules questions, you will see Rhetoric questions, which include the topics of Transitions and Rhetorical Synthesis. Knowing where to find certain questions on the verbal modules will help you jump to those in your areas of strength.

On the Math modules of the PSAT, the questions are presented in a rough order of difficulty. Since different people have different strengths and weaknesses, we've presented the Math content so that the drills are arranged by the frequency of the topic on the test. If you don't know where to start with Math, start with Algebra, as it is a big part of the test.

Regardless of which drill you choose, we suggest beginning with the first question in the set and proceeding in order, as the difficulty builds throughout each drill. You want to ensure you can get the easier ones right before moving on to the harder content.

We encourage you to revisit these drills as many times as necessary (letting time pass in between) until you've gotten every question right and you feel comfortable with the material. For this reason, you may want to do your work and mark your answers on your scratch paper as opposed to on the page, so that you can look at a question with fresh eyes when you return to it. This is, however, your book and your study time, so use whatever method works for you. Ultimately, the extra time you spend understanding and correcting your own work in this book can save you time and energy when you're taking the actual Digital PSAT.

Practice Tests

Once you have fully grasped the content in the drills, you will be ready to apply your new skills to a full-length practice test. One appears in this book with instructions on how to determine which modules to take. When you are ready to try out the Digital PSAT in all its online glory, you can take Test 2 online and put all the pieces together.

Answers and Explanations

This section is split into two parts, an answer key and then a detailed set of explanations that breaks down things such as the type of question, our recommended method for tackling that type, and the correct answer. By reading the explanations, you'll learn not only why the correct answer is right but, when applicable, what makes the wrong answers incorrect. Begin by checking off the questions that you got right; for each one you got wrong, take the time to read the explanation and understand where you went wrong in order to learn from those mistakes. Don't just rush to the next section. Take your time to not only analyze what you got wrong and why, but to be sure that you completely understand why you got each question *right*. This is what will truly give you the experience necessary to improve your skills and be as prepared as possible for the Digital PSAT.

> **Common Acronyms**
> Some strategies are explained with the terms FOIL, SOHCAHTOA, and FANBOYS. If you're unfamiliar with these and need more help understanding how these work, our *PSAT/ NMSQT Prep* book offers more practice tests and a guide to the test's content.

Common Trap Answers for Reading

In the explanations for the two practice tests (one at the end of this book, one online), you may see some bolded terms. These refer to common traps that the test-writers use, and you can use them to help eliminate wrong answers. Here's a quick guide to them:

- **Recycled Language:** These answer choices repeat exact words and phrases from the text but put the words together to say something that the text didn't actually say. They often establish relationships between the words and phrases that do not exist in the text.

- **Beyond the Text:** These answers might initially look good because they make sense or seem logical based on outside reasoning, but they lack support within the text itself.

- **Extreme Language:** These answers look just about perfect except for a word or phrase that goes too far beyond what the text can support. This also includes answers that could be called insulting or offensive to a person or a group.

- **Right Answer, Wrong Question:** These answer choices are true based on the text, but they don't answer the question that was asked. For example, they might state *what* the author said when the question was asking *why* the author said it.

- **Opposite:** These answer choices use a single word or phrase that make the answer convey a tone, viewpoint, or meaning not intended by the author. This can include a word such as *not* in the answer or a negative vocabulary word when the tone of the text was positive.

- **Half-Right:** These answers address part of but not the entire question task. They can also have one half of the answer address the question perfectly and the other half contain at least one of the traps mentioned previously.

Scratch Paper

Though the Digital PSAT is on a computer, you will have access to physical scratch paper on test day. Most of what you will need to tackle Reading and Writing questions can be done using online tools, but the scratch paper will be an essential tool for solving many Math questions. Because this is a timed test, don't waste time trying to do something in the digital environment that you can accomplish more quickly on your scratch paper. Though this paper will be collected, it won't affect your score. Therefore, either on the space provided in this book or on a spare piece of paper from your home, experiment with how writing or drawing something can save time and improve accuracy.

Online Tools

Be sure to register your book, as in your free online student tools you can download a detailed PDF on how to make the most of the Desmos calculator.

Online Tools

On the Reading and Writing modules of the Digital PSAT, you will be able to highlight text as well as make annotations (i.e., type notes into a box) to any text that you highlight. As you work through the Reading and Writing drills in this book, practice highlighting text and writing annotations that you think may help you answer each question. The explanations in this book will reference several different ways in which you can use highlighting and annotating to improve your accuracy.

On the Math modules of the Digital PSAT, you will have access to a built-in graphing calculator powered by Desmos. Although you are still free to use your own approved calculator, many features of the Desmos calculator make it very easy to use to answer Digital PSAT Math questions. As such, we strongly recommend that you practice using the Desmos calculator before test day to make the best use of it. You can access a free version of the calculator very similar to the one built into College Board's Bluebook app on the Desmos website at https://www.desmos.com/calculator.

Another useful tool to help you manage both sections of the Digital PSAT is the Mark for Review button. In the testing app, you can click the flag icon to save questions you want to return to later. At any time during the Digital PSAT, you can see a review screen that shows which ones were marked and allows you to jump easily to any question. In this book, you can use the Mark for Review icon to similarly indicate any questions you want to revisit before finishing the drill or any questions you want to review in depth as you read the explanations.

More Great Books

If you're looking for further help in a specific subject area, check out our SAT Prep book. Because this SAT is so similar to the PSAT/NMSQT, you can use the lessons and additional practice tests to help build expertise in the content you're struggling with.

Those are our recommendations for getting the most out of these PSAT practice questions. But now and on test day, it's up to you how to actually work through the questions, so find the method that works for you and dive in!

Chapter 2
Reading Diagnostic Drill

Reading Diagnostic Drill

A founding member of the American Library Association, Melvil Dewey began work on his library classification system in 1867. It was the first of its kind to organize books by similar subjects, and its utility became so apparent that over a century later it had become _____, used by libraries throughout the world.

Which choice completes the text with the most logical and precise word or phrase?

(A) nationalized

(B) commonplace

(C) united

(D) forgotten

The following text is adapted from Susan Glaspell's 1921 play *Inheritors*. Smith, a young businessman, is speaking with the grandmother of Silas Morton, a well-known farmer in the area.

GRANDMOTHER: The boy's my grandson. The little girl is Madeline Fejevary—Mr Fejevary's youngest child.

SMITH: The Fejevary place adjoins on this side?

GRANDMOTHER: Yes. We've been neighbours ever since the Fejevarys came here from Hungary after 1848. He was a count at home— and he's a man of learning. But he was a refugee because he fought for freedom in his country. Nothing Silas could do for him was too good. Silas sets great store by learning—and freedom.

As used in the text, what does the word "adjoins" most nearly mean?

(A) Connects

(B) Divides

(C) Clashes

(D) Expands

3 Mark for Review

The following text is from Henry James's 1869 short story *A Light Man*. The narrator, Max, recounts meeting Mr. Sloane at his house.

> He was waiting to receive me. We found him in his library—<u>which, by the way, is simply the most delightful apartment that I have ever smoked a cigar in</u>—a room arranged for a lifetime.

Which choice best describes the function of the underlined portion in the text as a whole?

(A) It conveys the narrator's growing envy for the opulence of his host.

(B) It shows the embarrassment the narrator feels for his own inadequate lodging.

(C) It suggests that the narrator is surprised to encounter his host in such a lavish setting.

(D) It demonstrates the narrator's admiration for the exceptional taste of his host.

4 Mark for Review

The 1937 Brazilian coup d'état saw Getúlio Vargas rise to power with military support. Vargas was already president, but he was not eligible to run for reelection to extend his term and power. He led a self-coup to change how term limits were enforced and to allow himself a longer period of time in power. Some historians identify the new regime as strict but democratic, while others claim it was totalitarian and represented a dictatorship. US ambassadors of the time agreed with the latter, citing the lack of a vote on the new constitution and incomplete news reports coming out of the region.

Which choice best describes the overall structure of the text?

(A) It discusses the circumstances surrounding Vargas's ascension to power and then cites two opposing viewpoints regarding the aftermath of that ascension.

(B) It outlines the history of an event and then laments the direct consequences that occurred in Brazil after the event occurred.

(C) It synopsizes two views of government and then compares and contrasts their pros and cons.

(D) It provides a rationale for choosing one type of government based on the historical context and then introduces other examples of similar situations.

Text 1

Utilizing a method employed by the Environmental Protection Agency (EPA), Stanford researcher William Mitch and his team measured the toxicity levels in bottled water and tap water by injecting water samples into hamster cells, which show a common vulnerability to the harmful pathogens that can be found in untreated or minimally treated water. Mitch concluded that not only is the perceived additional health benefit from drinking bottled water overstated, as both tap and bottled water had similar effects on the hamster cells, but also that the EPA method may be inadequate for assessing water safety, because the contaminants the test scans for comprised less than 1% of the damage done to the hamster cells in the study.

Text 2

While the Stanford team's study may have revealed little difference in how the contaminants in tap and bottled water affect hamster cells, it's relevant to consider the origins of these water sources. An independent team of researchers has suggested that the lack of discrepancy in the quality of bottled water and tap water may indicate that each was sourced from a lake or spring in the same region, which, if verified, would explain the similar results demonstrated by the two water types in the study.

---

5 ☐ Mark for Review

Which choice best describes a difference in how the author of Text 1 and the author of Text 2 view the Stanford team's study?

- (A) The author of Text 2 focuses only on EPA regulations, while the author of Text 1 focuses primarily on the health benefits of bottled water and tap water.

- (B) The author of Text 2 offers a possible alternative explanation for the results discussed in Text 1, while the author of Text 1 appears dissatisfied with the focus of the EPA's method.

- (C) The author of Text 2 believes that using hamster cells is inadequate when testing for water pathogen levels, while the author of Text 1 maintains that the study used appropriate methods.

- (D) The author of Text 2 believes that the Stanford team should have used methods from multiple agencies, while the author of Text 1 agrees that there is little difference between the health benefits of tap water and bottled water.

Text 1

Professor Lee Ju-hyuck and Dr. Cho Han-cheol may have found a way to filter out microplastics by combining their research. Ju-hyuck's team developed a nanogenerator, a device that creates electrical energy from physical sources. Han-cheol's team developed a technique to remove small particles using electrophoresis. By combining these technological advances, it appears that microplastics could be removed from water sources without creating more waste or requiring large sources of energy to power the process.

Text 2

Microplastics are plastics under five millimeters in size that accumulate in the human body and cause health concerns by disrupting critical functions. These microplastics typically enter the human body after being consumed by marine life, which commonly serves as a food source for humans. When filtration without the use of electrophoresis has been attempted to remove microplastics from water, the microplastics often clog the more traditional filters, which causes the filters to fail and waste material to accumulate.

6 Mark for Review

Based on the texts, what would the author of Text 2 most likely say about the process described in Text 1?

(A) It proves that it is ineffective to attempt to remove microplastics, as there are no processes that are able to do so efficiently and effectively.

(B) It represents a simple way to fix the problem of microplastics entering the human body and causing issues.

(C) It offers a potential solution to the traditional challenges associated with filtering out microplastics.

(D) It is based on a flawed premise that microplastics do not cause any harm to the human body and do not need to be removed from water sources.

7 ☐ Mark for Review

To help plants maximize their food resources, a group of researchers sought to create synthetic genetic circuits that could steer the plants' roots to grow in optimal directions. The initial circuits developed by the researchers failed to send accurate signals to the plants' root systems, but the researchers were initially unable to ascertain what could be contributing to the failure of the circuit. After experimenting with over 1,000 potential circuits in tobacco plants, the researchers discovered a glowing protein usually found in jellyfish. When overlaid into the plants' DNA, this protein acted as a gatekeeper, directing plants to grow roots in more favorable environments.

According to the text, what challenge did the researchers have to overcome to redirect the plants' root systems?

(A) Climate change had reduced available water for the plants, causing them to adapt.

(B) The tobacco plants couldn't be overlaid with DNA from other plants.

(C) The plants required fertilizer synthesized from a protein found only in jellyfish.

(D) The circuits were unable to perform the function for which they had been designed.

8 ☐ Mark for Review

The following text is adapted from Arthur Conan Doyle's 1879 short story "The Mystery of Sasassa Valley."

Do I know why Tom Donahue is called "Lucky Tom"? Yes; I do; and that is more than one in ten of those who call him so can say. I have knocked about a deal in my time, and seen some strange sights, but none stranger than the way in which Tom gained that sobriquet, and his fortune with it. For I was with him at the time.—Tell it? Oh, certainly; but it is a longish story and a very strange one; so fill up your glass again, and light another cigar, while I try to reel it off.

Based on the text, what is true about the origin of Tom Donahue's nickname?

(A) The narrator knows the story as well as most people.

(B) Most people don't know the story as well as the narrator does.

(C) Most people know the story better than the narrator does.

(D) The narrator and most people know little about the story.

9 ☐ Mark for Review

Professor Jeremy Niven wanted to test how increasing ambient light affects insects such as glowworms. He explored the behavior of glowworms at various light intensities, placing the males in a Y-shaped maze with an LED to simulate a glowing female at one end and a white light at the other. Initially, in complete darkness, the males easily found the "female" light. But the brighter the white light became, the less motivated the males were to pursue the female light, and they even tucked their heads inside their bodies' head shields to protect themselves from the white light.

Which choice states the main idea of the text?

(A) Scientists believe that glowworms are unable to navigate in Y-shaped mazes.

(B) An experiment showed that male glowworms will shield themselves from female glowworms when facing intense light.

(C) Scientists think that insects are fundamentally unable to distinguish between real and fake lights.

(D) An experiment demonstrated that artificial light can negatively affect certain insects.

10 ☐ Mark for Review

The following text is adapted from John Milton's 1667 poem "Paradise Lost." The poem retells the story of Adam and Eve as represented in the Bible.

A mind not to be chang'd by place or time.
The mind is its own place, and in itself
Can make a heav'n of hell, a hell of heav'n.
What matter where, if I be still the same,
And what I should be, all but less than he
Whom thunder hath made greater?

What is the main idea of the text?

(A) A person's perspective can change his or her reaction to circumstances and experiences.

(B) Someone's mind can be changed based on where and when the thoughts occur.

(C) Good and bad situations can be altered based on the actions of a higher power.

(D) A person's individual opinions are more important than those of a higher power.

11 ☐ Mark for Review

The New Zealand lizard known as the tuatara is considered a living link to over 200 million years of evolution in the lizard species. Recently, Smithsonian researchers discovered a fossil in Wyoming of an extinct lizard-like creature that may share lineage with the tuatara. The researchers claim that this creature, *Opisthiamimus gregori*, is part of the rhynchocephalian family that roamed the planet until about 230 million years ago and that it shares some genetic markers with the modern tuatara.

Which finding, if true, would most directly support the researchers' claim?

Ⓐ Numerous fossils of lizards in New Zealand were of a similar small size to that of the one found in Wyoming.

Ⓑ Members of the rhynchocephalian family have an extra joint in their feet bones, which the tuatara and the *Opisthiamimus gregori* fossil both possess.

Ⓒ Fossil evidence of the tuatara dates back only 50 million years, revealing that it is a relatively young species.

Ⓓ Most species of reptiles were initially confined to the Southern Hemisphere, shifting only after major climate changes.

12 ☐ Mark for Review

The Yellow Wallpaper is an 1892 short story by Charlotte Perkins Gilman. The narrator has been brought to a summer home and told not to exert herself too strongly because of her illness, but she expresses optimism regarding having something to occupy her time: _____

Which quotation from *The Yellow Wallpaper* most effectively illustrates the claim?

Ⓐ "If a physician of high standing...assures friends and relatives that there is really nothing the matter with one but temporary nervous depression...what is one to do?"

Ⓑ "Personally, I believe that congenial work, with excitement and change, would do me good."

Ⓒ "My brother is also a physician, and also of high standing, and he says the same thing."

Ⓓ "So I take phosphates or phosphites—whichever it is,—and tonics, and journeys, and air, and exercise, and am absolutely forbidden to 'work' until I am well again."

13 ☐ Mark for Review

Difference in Average Number of Years Between Subjective Age and Actual Age

Birth year range	Age at time of survey			
	38–45 years old	46–54 years old	55–63 years old	64–78 years old
1917–1925	8	8	9	12
1926–1941	10	11	14	15
1942–1953	15	16	17	17

In the field of longevity, "subjective age" is defined as the difference between how old a person feels and how old they actually are. Previous studies have shown that feeling younger was a reliable marker for longevity. A German research group aggregated a series of cross-generational studies drawing conclusions about how subjective age could change over someone's lifetime. By surveying individuals at different times in their lives, they concluded that people's subjective ages become younger in relation to their actual ages as they grow older.

Which choice uses data from the table to most effectively support the researchers' conclusion?

(A) People born between 1917 and 1925 experienced little change in their subjective age until they reached an age of 64 years.

(B) People who were surveyed when they were between 64 and 78 years old reported greater subjective ages the later that they were born.

(C) Regardless of when they were born, people reported a greater difference between their subjective age and their actual age as they grew older.

(D) The greatest subjective ages were reported by the group born between 1942 and 1953.

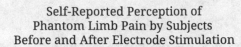

Self-Reported Perception of
Phantom Limb Pain by Subjects
Before and After Electrode Stimulation

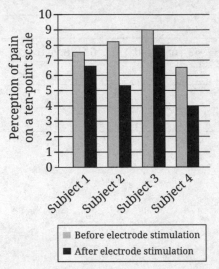

To determine whether phantom limb pain could be treated while restoring somatic sensations, neuroscientist Gurgen Soghoyan et al. implanted electrodes that could stimulate the nervous system into four amputee patients. Peripheral nerves were targeted, and participants used a 1–10 scale to self-report their levels of phantom limb pain both before and after stimulation. Soghoyan discovered that the electrode treatment reduced the perception of phantom limb pain in all subjects but to different degrees: _____

14 ☐ Mark for Review

Which choice most effectively uses data from the graph to complete the assertion?

Ⓐ Subjects 2 and 4 experienced greater reduction of perception of phantom limb pain than did Subjects 1 and 3.

Ⓑ Subject 2 self-reported a higher degree of phantom limb pain before electrode treatment than did Subject 3.

Ⓒ Subject 1 experienced a greater reduction in phantom limb pain after the electrode treatment than did Subject 2.

Ⓓ Subject 3 experienced the greatest reduction in phantom limb pain of all four subjects after electrode treatment.

15 ▢ Mark for Review

Building on an earlier study of adolescent behavior by Catherine Hartley and Aaron Heller that examined how teens explore more new places as they get older, researcher Natalie Saragos-Harris wanted to rule out the possibility of human error. In the initial study, teens were asked to self-report their own locations and actions, which allowed for mistakes based on inaccurate recollections. Saragos-Harris's study utilized a geo-tracking system, making it more _____

Which choice most logically completes the text?

(A) interactive by integrating interviews and video shoots.

(B) expansive by tracing the actions across time zones and regions.

(C) accurate by relying less on biased perceptions of the subjects' own behavior.

(D) thorough by following family members through home and school encounters.

16 ▢ Mark for Review

Researchers at the University of Melbourne set up a study to determine whether participants who received rewards for completing a task were willing to give up part of the reward in order to discover what future rewards would include. After winning a small financial reward in a game of chance, participants in their study were almost universally willing to give up a portion of the money already won in order to learn the value of a larger prize offered in a potential second game of chance, even though learning this information didn't affect the outcome of the second game in any way. Therefore, based on the decisions of the participants in the study, _____

Which choice most logically completes the text?

(A) the risk offered by games of chance is too great to warrant participation in the game by an average person.

(B) games of chance are always more interesting if they offer possibilities of additional prizes.

(C) games of chance, the perception of monetary rewards, and human behavior are all fields that demand further research.

(D) the knowledge of a future reward may be more valuable than a reward one has already obtained.

Chapter 3
Reading Diagnostic
Drill Explanations

WHAT'S NEXT

Now that you have warmed up with many different types of Digital PSAT Reading questions, review the explanations (especially for questions that you got wrong), and choose where to go next. The list below will tell you which drill to go to for more questions from that topic. You decide if that's based on the questions you missed or if it's for more practice in a topic for which you are close to achieving proficiency. Use the list below to pick your next drills.

Answer Key

Diagnostic Reading Drill							
Q #	Ans.	✔	Drill	Q #	Ans.	✔	Drill
1	B		Vocabulary	9	D		Main Idea
2	A		Vocabulary	10	A		Main Idea
3	D		Purpose	11	B		Claims
4	A		Purpose	12	B		Claims
5	B		Dual Texts	13	C		Charts
6	C		Dual Texts	14	A		Charts
7	D		Retrieval	15	C		Conclusions
8	B		Retrieval	16	D		Conclusions

READING DIAGNOSTIC DRILL EXPLANATIONS

1. **B** This is a Vocabulary question, as it asks for a *logical and precise word or phrase*. The blank describes what became of Dewey's classification system, so look for and highlight clues in the text about the system. The text states that *its utility became so apparent*, which implies that many people started using it. Therefore, a good word to enter in the annotation box would be "widespread" or "used by many."

    • (A), (C), and (D) are wrong because *nationalized*, *united*, and *forgotten* don't match "widespread."

    • (B) is correct because *commonplace* matches "widespread."

2. **A** This is a Vocabulary question, as it asks what "adjoins" *most nearly means*. Treat "adjoins" as if it were a blank—the blank describes the Fejevary place, so look for and highlight clues in the text about this house. The grandmother in the text says that *We've been neighbours ever since the Fejevarys came here*, so the Fejevary place is probably next to the grandmother's property. Therefore, a good word to enter in the annotation box would be "attaches" or "is next to."

    • (A) is correct because *Connects* matches "attaches."

    • (B), (C), and (D) are wrong because *Divides*, *Clashes*, and *Expands* don't match "attaches."

3. **D** This is a Purpose question, as it asks for the *function of the underlined portion in the text as a whole*. Read the text and highlight clues in the lines before after the underlined phrase to understand its function. The lines before mention the *library* and in the underlined phrase the narrator calls it *the most delightful apartment that I have ever smoked a cigar in*. A good function of the underlined portion to enter in the annotation box would be "describes the library positively."

    • (A) and (B) are wrong because they go beyond what the text can support—just because the narrator likes his host's library does not mean he feels *envy* or that he feels *embarrassment* regarding his own lodging.

    • (C) is wrong because the narrator is not described as *surprised* by the library—he merely comments upon it positively.

    • (D) is correct because it's consistent with the highlighting and annotation.

4. **A** This is a Purpose question, as it asks for the *overall structure of the text*. Read the text and highlight the connections between ideas in the text. The passage is an informational text about Getúlio Vargas, who staged a coup d'état *to extend his term and power*. The text goes on to discuss how some view the regime as *democratic* and others view it as a *dictatorship*. Therefore, a good overall structure of the text to enter in the annotation box would be "describe Vargas's regime and reactions to it."

    • (A) is correct because it's consistent with the highlighting and annotation.

    • (B) is wrong because the text does not claim that its author *laments* or feels sorrowful towards anything that happened in Brazil, even if the *lack of a vote* and *incomplete news reports* sound negative.

- (C) and (D) are wrong because the text neither discusses the *pros and cons* of two government systems nor introduces *other examples of similar situations* to the context given in the text.

5. **B** This is a Dual Texts question, as it asks for a *difference in how the author of Text 1 and the author of Text 2 view the Stanford team's study*. Read Text 1 and highlight its view on the study, which is that *the perceived additional health benefit from drinking bottled water* may be *overstated, as both tap and bottled water had similar effects on the hamster cells*. The author of Text 1 says nothing to dispute these findings. Then, read Text 2 and highlight what its author says about the same topic. Citing an independent team of researchers, the author of Text 2 states that *the lack of discrepancy in the quality of bottled water and tap water may indicate that each was sourced from a lake or spring in the same region*. Therefore, the author of Text 2 is offering an explanation for the results of Text 1. Enter "Text 2 agrees but gives explanation about water similarity" into the annotation box.

    - (A) is wrong because it's Text 1, not Text 2, that mentions the EPA in its argument.

    - (B) is correct because it's consistent with the relationship between the texts—in the final sentence of Text 1, the author seems *dissatisfied* with the EPA's method, as the author cites Mitch calling the test *inadequate*. In Text 2, the author cites an *independent team of researchers* that indicated the *similar results demonstrated by the two water types* in the study may have been because the water was sourced from *the same region,* which is a *possible alternative explanation* for the results seen in Text 1.

    - (C) is wrong because it misuses *inadequate* from Text 1—Text 2 never comments on whether *hamster cells* were acceptable for the test or not.

    - (D) is wrong because *multiple agencies* are not referenced or recommended by Text 2.

6. **C** This is a Dual Texts question, as it asks what *the author of Text 2* would say about *the process described in Text 1*. Read Text 1 and highlight the description of the process, which indicates that with electrophoresis, *microplastics may be able to be removed from water sources without creating more waste or requiring large sources of energy to power the process*. Then, read Text 2 and highlight what its author says about the same topic. The author states that *filtration without the use of electrophoresis…causes the filters to fail and waste material to accumulate*. Therefore, the author of Text 2 is highlighting a problem that the process in Text 1, which uses electrophoresis, may be able to avoid. Enter "Text 2 explains what happens without electrophoresis, which may be needed" into the annotation box.

    - (A) is wrong because Text 2 only comments on *filtration without the use of electrophoresis*. It does not claim that there are *no processes* that can remove microplastics *efficiently and effectively*.

    - (B) is wrong because this answer goes beyond what can be supported by the text—the process of electrophoresis is not defined in either text as *simple*.

    - (C) is correct because it's consistent with the relationship between the texts—Text 2 focuses on the *challenges* associated with filtering out microplastics, and Text 1 proposes at least a possible method for addressing one of those challenges.

- (D) is wrong because the author of Text 1 makes no comment on whether *microplastics* cause *harm to the human body*, nor does the author discuss if there's a *need* to remove these microplastics.

7. **D** This is a Retrieval question, as it asks for a detail *According to the text*. Look for and highlight information about the *challenge* that the researchers had to *overcome*. The text states that *The initial circuits developed by the researchers failed to send accurate signals…but the researchers were initially unable to ascertain what could be contributing to the failure of the circuit.* The correct answer should be as consistent as possible with these details.

   - (A), (B), and (C) are wrong because the text does not discuss *climate change, DNA from other plants*, or *fertilizer* as challenges faced by the team.

   - (D) is correct because it's consistent with the highlighted challenge faced by the team—if the circuit *were unable to perform the function for which they had been designed,* this could be the same as the circuits failing *to send accurate signals to the plants' root system.*

8. **B** This is a Retrieval question, as it asks for a detail *Based on the text*. Look for and highlight information about *the origin of Tom Donahue's nickname*. The narrator states that he knows why Tom is called "Lucky Tom" *and that is more than one in ten of those who call him so can say.* In other words, the narrator believes that very few other people know the origin of the nickname. The correct answer should be as consistent as possible with these details.

   - (A), (C), and (D) are wrong because they're each the opposite of what's stated in the text—the narrator knows the story better than most people, not *equally well* or less well than most people.

   - (B) is correct because it's consistent with the highlighted details.

9. **D** This is a Main Idea question, as it asks for the *main idea of the text*. Look for and highlight information that can help identify the main idea. The text notes that *the brighter the white light became, the less motivated the males were to pursue the female light.* Since other sentences describe the background and setup of the experiment and this last sentence is the experiment's conclusion, the last sentence serves as the main idea. The correct answer should be as consistent as possible with this portion of the text.

   - (A) and (C) are wrong because the text doesn't include what scientists believed or thought that glowworms could or could not do.

   - (B) is wrong because it misuses *shields* and *female light* from the text to create an unsupported conclusion regarding the reaction of the male glowworms to light.

   - (D) is correct because it's consistent with the highlighted portion of the text.

10. **A**   This is a Main Idea question, as it asks for the *main idea of the text*. Look for and highlight information that can help identify the main idea. The text states that *The mind is its own place, and in itself / Can make a heav'n of hell, a hell of heav'n*. These lines talk about the power of the mind to affect one's perception of experiences, and the rest of the poem continues this description. Therefore, these two lines can serve as the main idea. The correct answer should be as consistent as possible with this portion of the text.

- (A) is correct because it's consistent with the highlighted portion of the text.

- (B) is wrong because it's the opposite of what's claimed in the first sentence of the text, which states that a mind cannot be changed by *place or time*, or *where* and *when*.

- (C) and (D) are wrong because while a *higher power* seems to be included in the lines, *he Whom thunder hath made greater*, it's not claimed in the text that this being can alter *good and bad situations* or that a person's opinions are *more important* than the higher power's.

11. **B**   This is a Claims question, as it asks which choice would *directly support the researchers' claim*. Look for and highlight the claim in the text, which is that *Opisthiamimus gregori* is a member of the *rhynchocephalian family* and *shares some genetic markers with the modern tuatara*. The correct answer should address and be consistent with each aspect of this claim.

- (A) is wrong because similarly sized fossils discovered in two different locations would not be enough to establish a genetic link between species.

- (B) is correct because it's consistent with the highlighted claim—both species discussed in the text possessing *an extra joint in their feet bones* could be a shared *genetic marker*.

- (C) and (D) are wrong because the length of time that the tuatara has existed and the location that certain reptiles had been confined to are not discussed in the text or relevant to the claim.

12. **B**   This is a Claims question, as it asks which quotation would *most effectively illustrate the claim*. Look for and highlight the claim in the text, which is that the narrator *expresses optimism regarding having something to occupy her time*. The correct answer should address and be consistent with this claim.

- (A), (C), and (D) are wrong because there is nothing in these quotations that could be *optimism* on behalf of the narrator.

- (B) is correct because the belief that *work, with excitement and change, would do me good* is an expression of optimism.

13.   **C**   This is a Charts question, as it asks for *data from the table to most effectively support the researchers' conclusion*. Read the title and variables from the table. Then, read the text and highlight the researchers' conclusion. The researchers concluded that *people's subjective ages become younger in relation to their actual ages as they grow older*. The correct answer should offer accurate information from the table that supports this conclusion.

- (A) is wrong because it's consistent with the table but contradictory to the claim—an age group showing little change in subjective age as they grow older would be the opposite of their subjective age getting younger in relation to their actual age.

- (B) and (D) are wrong because they're not relevant to the claim—the text does not claim that a person's birth year affects their subjective age.

- (C) is correct because it's consistent with the table and the claim—the greater the difference between subjective and actual age, the younger a person feels in relation to their current age.

14.   **A**   This is a Charts question, as it asks for *data from the graph* that will *complete the assertion*. Read the title, key, and variables from the graph. Then, read the text and highlight the assertion, which is that *the electrode treatment reduced the perception of phantom limb pain in all subjects but to different degrees*. The correct answer should offer accurate information from the graph that supports this assertion.

- (A) is correct because it's consistent with the graph and relevant to the claim—all subjects show a decrease in pain perception, but some experienced a greater decrease than others.

- (B), (C), and (D) are wrong because they're each inconsistent with the graph—Subject 2 does not have a higher degree of phantom limb pain before electrode treatment than Subject 3, Subject 1 does not experience a greater reduction in perception of pain than Subject 2, and Subject 3 experiences a small reduction in phantom limb pain, not the greatest reduction.

15.   **C**   This is a Conclusions question, as it asks what *most logically completes the text*. Look for and highlight the main focus of the text, which is *the possibility of human error* in a study of adolescent behavior. Then, highlight the main point made regarding this focus, which is *Saragos-Harris's study utilized a geo-tracking system* rather than the previous method of teen self-reporting. Therefore, Saragos-Harris's study tried to account for the possibility that teens may not always exactly remember where they went. The correct answer should be as consistent as possible with this conclusion.

- (A) and (D) are wrong because *interviews*, *video shoots*, and *home and school encounters* are not discussed in the text as relevant to the studies.

- (B) is wrong because it's not relevant to the focus of the study—while a geo-tracking system may trace actions across time zones and regions, the focus should be on its accuracy, not its scope.

- (C) is correct because it's consistent with what the highlighted sentences say about the possibility of human error and how Saragos-Harris wanted to address it.

16. **D** This is a Conclusions question, as it asks what *most logically completes the text*. Look for and highlight the main focus of the text, which is that *participants…were willing to give up part of the reward in order to discover what future rewards would include*. Then, highlight the main point made regarding this focus, which is that participants *were almost universally willing to give up a portion of the money already won in order to learn the value of a larger prize offered in a potential second game of chance, even though learning this information didn't affect the outcome of the second game in any way*. Therefore, at least most of the participants valued the information about the second game's prize more than the reward they already had. The correct answer should be as consistent as possible with this conclusion.

- (A) is wrong because it's the opposite of what's implied by the text—the participants were willing to participate and even risk the reward they already had for the chance to learn about additional rewards.

- (B) is wrong because it's too extreme—it's not stated by the text that games of chance are *always* more interesting with additional prizes.

- (C) is wrong because while this may be true, the text does not advocate for *further research* into any of these areas.

- (D) is correct because it's consistent with what the highlighted sentences say about what the participants seemed to value more.

Chapter 4
Vocabulary Drill

Vocabulary Drill

1   Mark for Review

In 2020, Emmanuelle Charpentier and Jennifer Doudna won the Nobel Prize in Chemistry for their research on and expansion of the CRISPR-Cas9 genome editing process. In addition to being able to _____ the genome, the CRISPR technique has also been used to study fungus and to modify yeasts and crop strains.

Which choice completes the text with the most logical and precise word or phrase?

(A) access

(B) replicate

(C) categorize

(D) alter

2   Mark for Review

Yinshan zhengyao is a 14th-century Chinese cookbook by Hu Sihui, an official court dietitian and therapist during the Yuan dynasty. In addition to recipes, the tome contains articles about foods to seek out during pregnancy and other _____ recommendations.

Which choice completes the text with the most logical and precise word or phrase?

(A) healthful

(B) savory

(C) cautionary

(D) harmless

3   Mark for Review

The yellow-spotted emerald dragonfly *Somatochlora flavomaculata* made headlines in wildlife journals in 2018 after being spotted by insect enthusiast Andrew Easton in Suffolk, England, a locale beyond its normal range. The species is named for its _____ coloring, which sets it apart from the monochromatic green dragonflies of other families.

Which choice completes the text with the most logical and precise word or phrase?

(A) beautiful

(B) simple

(C) diverse

(D) decorative

4 ☐ Mark for Review

"Urban camouflage," or "fake buildings," are structures designed to resemble houses or edifices congruent to a residential area but that actually _____ electronic transformers, oil rigs, or other structures that could be considered eyesores. Their purpose is to blend into an existing urban or suburban environment in order to preserve its ambiance, rather than to deter thieves or vandals.

Which choice completes the text with the most logical and precise word or phrase?

- (A) disguise
- (B) mimic
- (C) showcase
- (D) reshape

5 ☐ Mark for Review

American businessman Timothy Dexter was a wealthy but eccentric iconoclast who touted his own importance in his self-published volume *A Pickle for the Knowing Ones*. In the book, Dexter makes _____ claims about himself, including his declarations that he should be Emperor of the United States and that the day he was born a great storm arose and Mars and Jupiter signaled he would be a great man.

Which choice completes the text with the most logical and precise word or phrase?

- (A) literary
- (B) exaggerated
- (C) unusual
- (D) credible

6 ☐ Mark for Review

In 2016, by analyzing millions of protein-coding genes, a team headed by Madeline C. Weiss identified a subset of protein clusters that were probably shared by the last universal common ancestor (LUCA). Should this discovery be verified, it may mean that this most recent protein group is _____ of all of the planet's current living organisms, whose history can each be traced back to LUCA.

Which choice completes the text with the most logical and precise word or phrase?

- (A) a responsibility
- (B) an amalgamation
- (C) a component
- (D) a harbinger

7 ☐ Mark for Review

Isabel Cooper, a zoological artist in the 1920s, was quite comfortable handling live snakes and diving into reefs in order to trap the subjects of research studies. Indeed, Cooper, along with illustrator Helen Damrosch Tee-Van and writer Ruth Rose, became famous after reports that they had sought out and _____ an enormous rainbow boa constrictor.

Which choice completes the text with the most logical and precise word or phrase?

- (A) identified
- (B) captured
- (C) documented
- (D) defeated

8 🔖 Mark for Review

In 1984, Tim DuBois, a record producer and songwriter in Nashville, Tennessee, assembled five experienced session musicians to record demos of songs he had written. Despite having signed a contract, the musicians failed to arrive at _____ for their band name, so DuBois locked the five in an office, only releasing them seven hours later when they agreed to be called Restless Heart.

Which choice completes the text with the most logical and precise word or phrase?

Ⓐ a consensus

Ⓑ an argument

Ⓒ a thesis

Ⓓ a justification

9 🔖 Mark for Review

In the "Betamax case," the United States Supreme Court ruled that consumers recording videotape copies of television shows for later viewing constitutes fair use rather than copyright infringement. Ironically, the movie studios which had originally brought the lawsuit against the recording devices _____ realized a new source of revenue by opening up videotape divisions.

Which choice completes the text with the most logical and precise word or phrase?

Ⓐ accidentally

Ⓑ vengefully

Ⓒ subsequently

Ⓓ unfairly

10 🔖 Mark for Review

The following text is adapted from the 1842 novel *Windsor Castle*, by William Harrison Ainsworth.

The youthful earl made no attempt to join his followers, but having gazed on the ancient pile before him, till its battlements and towers grew dim in the twilight, he <u>struck</u> into a footpath leading across the park, towards Datchet, and pursued it until it brought him near a dell filled with thorns, hollies, and underwood, and overhung by mighty oaks, into which he unhesitatingly plunged, and soon gained the deepest part of it.

As used in the text, what does the word "struck" most nearly mean?

Ⓐ Attacked

Ⓑ Collided

Ⓒ Stumbled

Ⓓ Ventured

Chapter 5
Vocabulary Drill
Explanations

ANSWER KEY

1.	D		6.	C
2.	A		7.	B
3.	C		8.	A
4.	A		9.	C
5.	B		10.	D

VOCABULARY DRILL EXPLANATIONS

1. **D**   This is a Vocabulary question, as it asks for a *logical and precise word or phrase*. The blank describes what the CRISPR technique is used for, so look for and highlight clues in the text about the technique's uses. The text says that the technique is a *genome editing process* and it's used to *modify* things, so a good word to enter in the annotation box would be "edit" or "modify."

    - (A), (B), and (C) are wrong because *access*, *replicate*, and *categorize* don't match "edit."

    - (D) is correct because *alter* matches "edit."

2. **A**   This is a Vocabulary question, as it asks for a *logical and precise word or phrase*. The blank describes the contents of the *Yinshan zhengyao* cookbook, so look for and highlight clues in the text about what the cookbook offers. The text says that *the tome contains articles about foods to seek out during pregnancy* and calls the author a *dietitian and therapist*, so a good phrase to enter in the annotation box would be "good for health" or "beneficial."

    - (A) is correct because *healthful* matches "good for health."

    - (B) is wrong because while cookbooks do often include *savory* recipes, the blank focuses on what it offers *In addition to recipes*.

    - (C) and (D) are wrong because *cautionary* and *harmless* don't match "good for health."

3. **C**   This is a Vocabulary question, as it asks for a *logical and precise word or phrase*. The blank describes the coloring of the yellow-spotted emerald dragonfly, so look for and highlight clues in the text about these insects. The text says that the dragonfly's coloring *sets it apart from the monochromatic green dragonflies of other families*, so a good word to enter in the annotation box would be "varied" or "multiple."

    - (A) and (D) are wrong because while the dragonfly's coloring could be viewed as *beautiful* or *decorative* by an observer, the text does not include any similar adjectives.

    - (B) is wrong because *simple* doesn't match "varied."

    - (C) is correct because *diverse* matches "varied."

4. **A** This is a Vocabulary question, as it asks for a *logical and precise word or phrase*. The blank describes the function of *urban camouflage*, so look for and highlight clues in the text about these "fake buildings." Since the text says that the purpose of these structures is to *blend into an existing urban or suburban environment*, an action they could do to *electronic transformers, oil rigs, or other structures that could be considered eyesores* would be to hide them. Enter "hidc" or "cover" into the annotation box.

    • (A) is correct because *disguise* matches "hide."

    • (B), (C), and (D) are wrong because *mimic, showcase,* and *reshape* don't match "hide."

5. **B** This is a Vocabulary question, as it asks for a *logical and precise word or phrase*. The blank describes the claims that Dexter makes about himself, so look for and highlight clues in the text about these claims. The text says that Dexter believes *he should be Emperor of the United States and that the day he was born a great storm arose and Mars and Jupiter signaled he would be a great man*, so a good word to enter in the annotation box would be "outrageous" or "over the top."

    • (A) is wrong because *literary* doesn't match "outrageous."

    • (B) is correct because *exaggerated* matches "outrageous."

    • (C) is wrong because *unusual* doesn't go far enough to match "outrageous."

    • (D) is wrong because *credible* (believable) would be the opposite of "outrageous."

6. **C** This is a Vocabulary question, as it asks for a *logical and precise word or phrase*. The blank describes the protein group discovered in LUCA, so look for and highlight clues in the text about this group. The text says that these protein clusters *were probably shared by* LUCA, and since LUCA is the last universal common ancestor, it's likely that *all of the planet's current living organisms* may contain this protein group, Therefore, a good word to enter into the annotation box would be "a part of" or "common to."

    • (A) and (D) are wrong because *a responsibility* and *a harbinger* (an omen) don't match "a part of."

    • (B) is wrong because *an amalgamation* (a blend) represents a whole rather than "a part."

    • (C) is correct because *a component* matches "a part of."

7. **B** This is a Vocabulary question, as it asks for a *logical and precise word or phrase*. The blank describes the interaction between Cooper's team and the boa constrictor, so look for and highlight clues in the text about this interaction. The text says that Cooper handled live snakes and dove into reefs *in order to trap the subjects of research studies*. Therefore, a good word to enter in the annotation box would be "caught" or "found."

    • (A), (C), and (D) are wrong because *identified, documented,* and *defeated* don't match "caught." For (C), while identifying the species is something that the writer and illustrator may have done, trapping it is the focus of Cooper's work given in the first sentence of the text.

    • (B) is correct because *captured* matches "caught."

8. **A** This is a Vocabulary question, as it asks for a *logical and precise word or phrase*. The blank describes the five musicians' interaction with a band name, so look for and highlight clues in the text about this interaction. The text says that *DuBois locked the five in an office, only releasing them seven hours later when they agreed to be called Restless Heart*, so it's likely that the group struggled to agree on a band name initially. Therefore, a good word to enter in the annotation box would be that they initially failed to come to "an agreement."

    - (A) is correct because *a consensus* matches "an agreement."

    - (B) and (C) are wrong because *an argument* and *a thesis* don't match "an agreement."

    - (D) is wrong because *a justification* implies that the band name has been decided upon and the band is only trying to justify why they picked that name, which is not supported in the text.

9. **C** This is a Vocabulary question, as it asks for a *logical and precise word or phrase*. The blank describes a realization had by movie studios after the Betamax lawsuit, so look for and highlight clues in the text about this realization. Because the text states that the *movie studios originally brought the lawsuit*, this realization occurred as a result of the lawsuit. Therefore, a good word to enter in the annotation box would be "afterwards" or "soon."

    - (A) is wrong because while the idea of a new source of revenue may not have been the original goal of the lawsuit, this does not mean the movie studios realized that videotape divisions could be a revenue source *accidentally*.

    - (B) and (D) are wrong because *vengefully* and *unfairly* don't match "afterwards."

    - (C) is correct because *subsequently* matches "afterwards."

10. **D** This is a Vocabulary question, as it asks what "struck" *most nearly* means. Treat "struck" as if it were a blank that describes the earl's movements, and look for and highlight clues in the text about this behavior. The speaker in the text says that *The youthful earl made no attempt to join his followers*, but the transition word "but" indicates that he likely attempted to go elsewhere instead. Therefore, a good word to enter in the annotation box would be "traveled" or "went towards."

    - (A) is wrong because *Attacked* misuses the reference to *battlements* in the text.

    - (B) is wrong because *Collided* doesn't match "traveled."

    - (C) is wrong because *Stumbled* goes beyond what the text can support—it uses the word *dim* to create an unsupported conclusion that the earl only accidentally discovered the path because of bad lighting.

    - (D) is correct because *Ventured* means "traveled."

Chapter 6
Purpose Drill

Purpose Drill

1 ⬜ Mark for Review

In many ecosystems, pollinators such as bees are necessary for the growth and spread of plant life, but globally, bee populations are in decline despite many conservation efforts. To explain this, biologist Sheila Colla analyzed conservation plans enacted by Canadian municipalities, focusing specifically on the species each plan was targeted towards. Colla found that a disproportionately high number of plans focused exclusively on non-endangered honeybees, while almost none of them focused on wild bees, the native pollinators who do most of the pollinating work and whose populations are the ones actually at risk.

Which choice best states the main purpose of the text?

(A) It details an analysis that disputes a commonly held belief regarding the way honeybees that pollinate plants in many ecosystems place themselves at risk.

(B) It establishes the differences between bee conservation plans enacted by Canadian municipalities and bee conservation plans enacted by biologists.

(C) It describes an analysis that partially explains why bee populations may be in decline despite conservation efforts.

(D) It references an analysis that is intended to resolve an environmental crisis without any further damage to bee populations.

2 ⬜ Mark for Review

Researchers examined roughly 9,000-year-old remains of 27 individuals who were each found buried with hunting tools. Of those 27 individuals, 11 were female and 16 were male, challenging a long-held assumption regarding hunter-gatherer societies. Prior to these discoveries, researchers generally assumed that only males participated in activities such as hunting or combat, but this new data suggests that both sexes may have hunted and fought alongside one another.

Which choices best states the function of the underlined portion in the text as a whole?

(A) It calls into question the assumption made in the previous sentence.

(B) It introduces a form of categorization that is used in the remainder of the sentence.

(C) It explains the principal motivations that the researchers had for conducting the study.

(D) It offers background information that helps explain the importance of the suggestion made in the remainder of the sentence.

3 ☐ Mark for Review

Painter Georgia O'Keeffe was well-known for her modernist style. Her paintings of natural scenes were not meant to depict the scenes exactly as they looked in real life. Rather, O'Keeffe focused on the feelings a natural scene created within her, sacrificing exact replication for the sake of emotion. While O'Keeffe's early works are more in line with her formal art education in Chicago, her eventual incorporation of distinct shapes and bold colors made her style truly unique.

Which choice best describes the overall structure of the text?

(A) It discusses a painter and then details some features present in works by that painter.

(B) It offers a perspective on a painter and then provides several possibilities as to why the painter's work proved unpopular with critics.

(C) It introduces a specific art style and then references several other painters who utilized that style.

(D) It describes a famous work of art and then contrasts its influence with lesser-known works by that same painter.

4 ☐ Mark for Review

The following text is adapted from Mark Twain's 1889 novel *A Connecticut Yankee in King Arthur's Court*. The narrator has just encountered a woman during his journey through a forest.

She was going by as indifferently as she might have gone by a couple of cows; but when she happened to notice me, then there was a change! Up went her hands, and she was turned to stone; her mouth dropped open, her eyes stared wide and timorously, she was the picture of astonished curiosity touched with fear. And there she stood gazing, in a sort of stupefied fascination, till we turned a corner of the wood and were lost to her view.

Which choice best states the main purpose of the text?

(A) To explain how the anxiety of the woman makes it difficult for people to converse with her

(B) To claim that the dangers of the forest contribute to the woman's fear

(C) To describe the specific reaction given by the woman upon seeing the narrator

(D) To contrast the personality of the narrator with that of the woman

5 ☐ Mark for Review

The following text is adapted from Percy Bysshe Shelley's 1840 essay "On Life."

<u>What is life?</u> Thoughts and feelings arise, with or without our will, and we employ words to express them. We are born, and our birth is unremembered, and our infancy remembered but in fragments; we live on, and in living we lose the apprehension of life. How vain is it to think that words can penetrate the mystery of our being! Rightly used they may make evident our ignorance to ourselves, and this is much. For what are we? Whence do we come? and whither do we go? Is birth the commencement, is death the conclusion of our being? What is birth and death?

Which choices best states the function of the underlined question in the text as a whole?

(A) It predicts that many readers will agree with the concerns expressed in the text regarding using words to define aspects of existence.

(B) It warns readers that the text's discussion of how to live a meaningful life may confuse them.

(C) It acknowledges that the description of birth made by the text is negative.

(D) It introduces the text's doubt regarding the likelihood that words alone can define certain aspects of existence.

6 ☐ Mark for Review

Political treatises such as Thomas Hobbes's *Leviathan* and John Locke's *Two Treatises of Government* largely focus on the idea of a "social contract" in which individuals consent to being governed. However, author Jean-Jacques Rousseau argued that the concentrated power held by the rich could not have been gained by consent of the people—the rich must have been able to use their wealth and influence to subjugate the common man against his will. Some political writers attempt to reconcile this by claiming that the common man will revolt if rule by the rich and wealthy becomes truly intolerable, therefore implying a degree of consent on the part of the common man, at least up to a point.

Which choice best describes the overall structure of the text?

(A) It offers a description of a political idea by referencing two works on the subject and then explains how some authors and writers have explored the idea further.

(B) It references two acclaimed works and then states that the idea focused on by the works is appealing but impractical in the real world.

(C) It summarizes the development of a political idea by referencing two works and then suggests an evolution of the idea that political experts should examine more closely.

(D) It discusses two important political works and then explains why one of them created more controversy than the other.

7 ☐ Mark for Review

Typically, ants and aphids have a mutualistic relationship in which the ants feed on a sugary waste product, called honeydew, from the aphids and, in turn, protect the aphids from predators. *Paracletus cimiciformis*, a species of aphid discovered in Europe in 1837, has been observed taking advantage of this relationship. Through a series of studies, it was noted that while some members of *P. cimiciformis* participate in the ant-aphid relationship normally, other members will disguise themselves as larval ants to trick the ants into bringing the aphids into their ant nurseries. Once inside the nursery, the aphids will feed on the true ant larvae and therefore effectively reduce the population of the ant colony, creating a notable exception to the normally positive ant-aphid relationship.

Which choice best describes the function of the third sentence in the text as a whole?

(A) It offers background that explains how ants and aphids developed their mutualistic relationship over time.

(B) It notes a similarity between how *P. cimiciformis* and other aphids each attempt to deceive ant species.

(C) It introduces a deviation that is explored later in the text regarding the ant-aphid relationship.

(D) It details how *P. cimiciformis* was initially discovered in Europe.

8 ☐ Mark for Review

The following text is from Anton Chekhov's 1890 short story "The Horse-Stealers." Kalashnikov is speaking with his fellow patrons at a local tavern.

Kalashnikov had the dignified manners of a sedate and sensible man; he spoke weightily, and made the sign of the cross over his mouth every time he yawned, and no one could have supposed that this was a thief, a heartless thief who had stripped poor creatures, who had already been twice in prison, and who had been sentenced by the commune to exile in Siberia, and had been bought off by his father and uncle, who were as great thieves and rogues as he was.

Which choice best describes the function of the underlined phrase in the text as a whole?

(A) It describes a particular outcome that Kalashnikov desires.

(B) It compares Kalashnikov to his father and uncle.

(C) It mentions an external conflict Kalashnikov avoids.

(D) It continues the previous description of Kalashnikov.

9 ▢ Mark for Review

Astronaut Steve Swanson and his colleagues grew a crop of *Lactuca sativa* (red romaine lettuce) on the International Space Station, where gravity is lower and radiation is higher than on Earth. At the same time, a team of NASA researchers grew a crop of *L. sativa* on Earth as a control. Both groups harvested their respective lettuce crops over a series of trials and measured the crops' nutritional values. The researchers found that in all trials, when compared to the Earth-grown lettuce, the space-grown lettuce exhibited higher levels of sodium, phosphorus, sulfur, and zinc—all of which are important nutrients for the body to regulate its functions and repair itself.

Which choice best states the main purpose of the text?

(A) It discusses two different metrics for determining the nutritional value of lettuce crops grown in space.

(B) It details a series of trials that indicated the possible benefits of growing a crop in space.

(C) It offers findings that support the theory that lettuce crops grown in space will not be a sustainable food source.

(D) It describes a series of trials that confirmed an unverified theory regarding how resilient *L. sativa* is to different environments.

10 ▢ Mark for Review

In 1791, Austrian Franz Joseph Haydn, already an accomplished composer, wrote his *Symphony No. 94*, also known as the "Surprise Symphony." The "surprise" in the composition was a sudden crescendo, or increase in volume, in the middle of an otherwise peaceful, quiet movement within the work. This unexpected burst of sound proved quite popular with audiences, who would often demand that section of the symphony to be replayed. Some music historians, however, criticize the timing of the composition's release, claiming that it was intentional to draw attention away from new works published by Ignaz Pleyel, Haydn's greatest professional rival.

Which choice best describes the overall structure of the text?

(A) It details the process undertaken to compose a particular symphony, discusses the early life of a composer, and then theorizes on a connection between the composer's life and composition process.

(B) It references a particular symphony, emphasizes one movement as being paramount to the symphony, and then summarizes the impact of all of the symphony's movements when taken as a whole.

(C) It introduces a particular musical composition, explains one of the central features of the composition, and then provides a critical viewpoint regarding one aspect of the composition.

(D) It mentions the composer of a particular musical composition, explains one of the features included by that composer in his composition, and then offers an overview of that composer's rivalry with another composer.

Chapter 7
Purpose Drill
Explanations

ANSWER KEY

1.	C	6.	A
2.	D	7.	C
3.	A	8.	D
4.	C	9.	B
5.	D	10.	C

PURPOSE DRILL EXPLANATIONS

1. **C** This is a Purpose question, as it asks for the *main purpose of the text*. Read the text and highlight who or what the text focuses on: why bee populations are in decline despite conservation efforts. The passage states that *a disproportionately high number of plans focused exclusively on non-endangered honeybees, while almost none of them focused on wild bees…whose populations are the ones actually at risk.* Therefore, a good main purpose of the text to enter in the annotation box would be "explain why populations are dropping despite efforts."

   - (A) and (B) is wrong because they're **Recycled Language**—(A) misuses *honeybees* and *at risk* from different parts of the text, while (B) misuses *Canadian municipalities* and *biologist* from different parts of the text.

   - (C) is correct because it's consistent with the highlighting and annotation.

   - (D) is wrong because it's **Extreme Language**—the text does not claim that Colla's work will *resolve* an environmental crisis.

2. **D** This is a Purpose question, as it asks for the *function of the underlined portion in the text as a whole*. Read the text and focus on the lines before and after the underlined portion to understand its function. The sentence before references an assumption that the underlined portion explains, that *only males participated in activities such as hunting or combat*. The rest of the text, however, states that the *new data suggests that both sexes may have hunted and fought alongside one another*. Therefore, a good function of the underlined portion to enter in the annotation box would be "explain what people thought about hunters before discovery."

   - (A) is wrong because it's the **Opposite** of what happens in the text—the underlined portion doesn't call the assumption from the previous sentence *into question*, it instead explains exactly what that assumption was.

   - (B) and (C) are wrong because no new *categorization* is introduced in the underlined portion, nor are the researchers' *motivations* ever offered in the text.

   - (D) is correct because it's consistent with the highlighting and annotation—without the previous assumption that only a single sex fought and hunted, the suggestion that it was actually both sexes would be less relevant.

3. **A** This is a Purpose question, as it asks for the *overall structure of the text*. Read the text and highlight the connections between ideas in the text. The passage is a descriptive text about Georgia O'Keeffe, who was known for her modernist style that *focused on the feelings a natural scene created within her.* The text goes on to note that *her eventual incorporation of distinct shapes and bold colors made her style truly unique.* Therefore, a good overall structure of the text to enter in the annotation box would be "describe O'Keeffe's style as unique."

- (A) is correct because it's consistent with the highlighting and annotation.

- (B) and (C) are wrong because they're **Half-Right**—both answers begin with a supported statement, but the text does not claim O'Keeffe's work was *unpopular with critics*, nor does it discuss any *other painters.*

- (D) is wrong because no specific works of art are discussed in the text.

4. **C** This is a Purpose question, as it asks for the *main purpose of the text*. Read the text and highlight who or what the text focuses on: a description of the woman encountered by the narrator. The narrator states that *when she happened to notice me, then there was a change* and that *she was turned to stone; her mouth dropped open, her eyer stared wide and timorously, she was the picture of astonished curiosity touched with fear.* Therefore, a good main purpose of the text to enter in the annotation box would be "describe how woman froze up when she saw narrator."

- (A) is wrong because it goes **Beyond the Text**—there is no discussion of anyone trying to *converse* with the woman.

- (B) is wrong because it's **Recycled Language**—it misuses *forest* and *fear* from different parts of the text.

- (C) is correct because it's consistent with the highlighting and annotation.

- (D) is wrong because the *personality of the narrator* is never discussed in the text.

5. **D** This is a Purpose question, as it asks for the *function of the underlined question in the text as a whole*. Read the text and focus on the lines after the underlined question to understand its function. The lines after attempt to further define the lines before by claiming that it is *vain* to *think that words can penetrate the mystery of our being.* The remainder of the text reinforces this point and offers examples of other ideas that are tough to define by words alone. Therefore, a good function of the underlined question to enter in the annotation box would be "give an example of how words can't define certain things."

- (A) is wrong because it goes **Beyond the Text**—the author does not comment on whether *many readers will agree* with his conclusion.

- (B) is wrong because the text does not offer any advice on *how to live a meaningful life* nor indicate that its readers may be confused.

- (C) is wrong because it's **Right Answer, Wrong Question**—stating that our *birth is unremembered* could be interpreted as a negative, but the underlined question in the text is not about birth.

- (D) is correct because it's consistent with the highlighting and annotation—*life* is the first of several examples that the author uses to make his point that it's hard to express certain concepts with words alone.

6. **A** This is a Purpose question, as it asks for the *overall structure of the text*. Read the text and highlight the connections between ideas in the text. The passage is an informational text about a political idea called the social contract, which states that *individuals consent to being governed*. The text goes on to offer both the perspective of Rousseau, who *argued that the concentrated power held by the rich could not have been gained by consent of the people*, and *political writers*, who *attempt to reconcile* this contradiction by explaining that there is *a degree of consent…up to a point*. Therefore, a good overall structure of the text to enter in the annotation box would be "discuss social contract and what others have said about it."

   - (A) is correct because it's consistent with the highlighting and annotation.

   - (B) is wrong because it's **Extreme Language**—the text never states that either work is *acclaimed* or that the ideas in those books are *appealing but impractical*.

   - (C) is wrong because the text neither *summarizes* how the idea of the social contract developed nor suggests an *evolution of the idea* that anyone *should examine more closely*.

   - (D) is wrong because it's **Half-Right**—while two works are discussed, neither is mentioned to have caused *controversy*.

7. **C** This is a Purpose question, as it asks for the *function of the third sentence in the text as a whole*. Read the text and focus on the lines before and after the underlined portion to understand its function. The sentence before indicates that a certain species of aphid, *Paracletus cimiciformis*, has been observed *taking advantage* of a mutually beneficial relationship between ants and aphids. The underlined lines explain that this species sometimes will *trick the ants into bringing the aphids into their ant nurseries*, while the lines after explain how the aphids feeding on the ant larvae is a *notable exception* to the usually positive relationship between the species. Therefore, a good function of the underlined portion to enter in the annotation box would be "introduce an exception to the relationship."

   - (A) is wrong because the text does not discuss how the ant-aphid relationship *developed over time*, only that there is such a relationship.

   - (B) is wrong because it's **Half-Right**—while some members of *P. cimiciformis* do deceive ants, no *other aphids* are stated to do so in the text.

- (C) is correct because it's consistent with the highlighting and annotation—a *deviation* can be the same as an *exception*.

- (D) is wrong because it's **Right Answer, Wrong Question**—the discovery of the ants is noted in the second sentence of the text, not the third, and even so, no detail is given besides the location and date.

8. **D** This is a Purpose question, as it asks for the *function of the underlined phrase in the text as a whole*. Read the text and focus on the lines before and after the underlined phrase to understand its function. The lines before state that Kalashnikov *was a thief, a heartless thief who had stripped poor creatures, who had already been twice in prison* and the phrase itself states that he *had been sentenced by the commune to exile in Siberia*. The end of the sentence continues and concludes this negative description, so a good function of the underlined portion to enter in the annotation box would be "continue to list negatives about Kalashnikov."

- (A) and (C) are wrong because they're the **Opposite** of what's stated or implied in the text—it's not stated or likely based on the text that Kalashnikov *desires* exile in Siberia or that the exile was something he was able to *avoid*.

- (B) is wrong because it's **Right Answer, Wrong Question**—the final phrase of the sentence compares Kalashnikov to his father and uncle, not the underlined phrase.

- (D) is correct because it's consistent with the highlighting and annotation.

9. **B** This is a Purpose question, as it asks for the *main purpose of the text*. Read the text and highlight who or what the text focuses on: the trials conducted on *Lactuca sativa*, or lettuce. The passage indicates that *in all trials, when compared to the Earth-grown lettuce, the space-grown lettuce exhibited higher levels of sodium, phosphorus, sulfur, and zinc*, which the text indicates are *important nutrients*. Therefore, a good main purpose of the text to enter in the annotation box would be "demonstrate that space lettuce had more nutrients."

- (A) is wrong because only one metric that could help determine nutritional value, levels of important nutrients, is discussed in the text.

- (B) is correct because it's consistent with the highlighting and annotation.

- (C) is wrong because it goes **Beyond the Text**—the text does not discuss how *sustainable* space-grown lettuce will be, only that it seems to contain more nutrients than Earth-grown lettuce.

- (D) is wrong because none of the trials focused on how *resilient* the lettuce is.

10.   **C**   This is a Purpose question, as it asks for the *overall structure of the text*. Read the text and highlight the connections between ideas in the text. The passage is an informational text about Franz Joseph Haydn's *Symphony No. 94*, which contains an *unexpected burst of sound* that *proved quite popular with audiences*. The text goes on to say that some historians *criticize the timing of the composition's release*, as they believe it was intentional to take away from another composer's works. Therefore, a good overall structure of the text to enter in the annotation box would be "discuss positives and negatives about the symphony."

- (A) is wrong because the text never discusses the actual *process undertaken* by Haydn to compose the symphony, Haydn's *early life*, or any *connection* between Haydn's life and work.

- (B) and (D) are wrong because they're **Half-Right**—the first two pieces of each of these answers are supported, but the final piece of each answer is not. The text does not *summarize the impact of all of the symphony's movements* nor does it give an *overview* of the rivalry with Pleyel; it only mentions the rivalry.

- (C) is correct because it's consistent with the highlighting and annotation—this answer follows the same chronology and is a paraphrase of all of the ideas in the text.

Chapter 8
Dual Texts Drill

Dual Texts Drill

<table>
<tr><td>1</td><td>☐ Mark for Review</td></tr>
</table>

Text 1

Sea otters in Alaska's kelp forests used to have no natural predators. However, orcas in the region have recently begun to prey upon the otters, as the orca's preferred prey, large whales, has had its numbers reduced by industrial whaling operations. This has resulted in reduced otter populations and a corresponding increase in population of the otter's primary prey, sea urchins. This, in turn, has led to large-scale destruction of portions of the kelp forest as the urchins eat more and more kelp.

Text 2

New research has analyzed previous data on sea otters to determine whether factors other than direct consumption of sea otters by orcas could contribute to changing kelp forest ecosystems. Researchers observed that otter populations had moved closer to land, which would put them in shallower water and therefore make it harder for orcas to attack them. It is thus likely that circumstances other than predation alone are responsible for the series of events observed in Alaskan kelp forests.

Based on the texts, both authors would most likely agree with which statement?

(A) Researchers have more advanced technology for monitoring sea otter populations more than they did previously.

(B) How sea otters care for their young is a relatively unexplored area in biology.

(C) Sea otter presence in Alaska's kelp forests has been reduced to some extent.

(D) Sea otters that live close to land often have relatives that live farther from the shoreline.

<table>
<tr><td>2</td><td>☐ Mark for Review</td></tr>
</table>

Text 1

Originally performed in 429 BCE, Sophocles's *Oedipus Rex* focuses on a man named Oedipus who rejects the wisdom of others. Sophocles uses Oedipus to demonstrate the danger of hubris, or pride—Oedipus wishes to avoid a prophecy that he will kill his own father and therefore seeks out knowledge that is forbidden to him. However, this knowledge is exactly what precipitates his father's demise. Aristotle later described the pride of Oedipus as an example of a "fatal flaw," which became a hallmark of most of the tragedies written since.

Text 2

Aristotle noted that Oedipus's problems in *Oedipus Rex* were caused by a "hamartia," which later scholars translated as "fatal flaw," akin to a personal failing or sin. However, some historians have claimed that the word is more appropriately translated as "mistake," or something caused by lack of knowledge rather than a failing. While there is little doubt among these historians that Sophocles intended Oedipus to serve as a warning of the dangers of hubris, they claim that the mistranslation casts doubt on whether or not Aristotle meant to call Oedipus a fundamentally flawed character.

Based on the texts, both the author of Text 1 and the historians in Text 2 would most likely agree with which statement?

(A) The male characters in the works of Sophocles differ greatly from the male characters in the works of Aristotle.

(B) *Oedipus Rex* should be included in any discussion of works that most clearly demonstrate the concept of the "fatal flaw."

(C) Sophocles's work contains a cautionary tale regarding a certain characteristic.

(D) Aristotle's commentary on *Oedipus Rex* is meant to be interpreted as a tribute to the talents of Sophocles.

3 ⬜ Mark for Review

Text 1

Certain critics have argued that it's not possible for a man of Shakespeare's background to have written the 38 or so plays attributed to him. It is important, however, to question the implications of attributing the works to Shakespeare in the first place. Elizabethan era plays were usually not attributed to any playwright, only being attributed if that individual had already achieved some level of renown: by the mere fact that the plays were attributed to Shakespeare in the first place, it is more likely that he was the original author of those plays than not.

Text 2

While it is understandable to focus on the attribution of Shakespeare's works as an argument in favor of Shakespeare's fame during his life, historians who focus only on the attribution argument often neglect to consider that Shakespeare would likely have had several collaborators who worked with him on some or all of his plays. Moreover, such a collaboration would explain how a single individual was able to write in such a wide diversity of styles, which was incredibly uncommon to see from a single playwright in the Elizabethan era.

Which of the following best describes a difference in how the author of Text 1 and the author of Text 2 view the works of Shakespeare?

(A) Whereas the author of Text 1 considers the attribution of Shakespeare's works to Shakespeare to be strong evidence of their authorship, the author of Text 2 believes such a conclusion to be too narrow.

(B) The author of Text 1 claims that Shakespeare's earlier works were comedies, while the author of Text 2 argues that Shakespeare's final few plays were the most comedic.

(C) Although the author of Text 1 argues that Shakespeare's works were primarily written as collaborations, the author of Text 2 claims that Shakespeare was the sole author of each of his plays.

(D) The author of Text 1 believes Shakespeare's best quality to be his ability to create memorable characters, whereas the author of Text 2 considers that Shakespeare's written dialogue is his greatest strength.

4 ⬜ Mark for Review

Text 1

The construction of the Great Pyramid of Giza in Egypt was most certainly an impressive construction for its time, but <u>researchers are uncertain as to how the ancient Egyptians overcame certain engineering obstacles.</u> For instance, the Great Pyramid of Giza was constructed from more than 2.3 million blocks of granite which came from nearly 500 miles away, and no records from the time period exist to explain how such a monumental transport would have been possible.

Text 2

Scientists have analyzed fossilized pollen samples from the Giza build site to establish how the site may once have appeared. This analysis focused on determining the pollen's origin—therefore allowing scientists to reconstruct the migration path taken by the pollen itself. The scientists claim that their reconstruction demonstrates that a tributary of the Nile must have once flown from the main river to the Giza build site, which allowed for the efficient transport of building materials.

Based on the texts, how would the scientists in Text 2 most likely respond to the underlined portion in Text 1?

(A) They would argue that pollen migration reconstruction is relevant in the case of the Great Pyramid of Giza because it was performed directly on samples from the Nile River.

(B) They would contend that their process for reconstructing the pollen migration path provides a possible answer to a previously unresolved question.

(C) They would stress that pollen samples collected from the Giza build site may be less reliable because of the passing of millennia.

(D) They would claim that if research on both Nile River pollen and building site pollen were synthesized, their reconstruction of the pollen's migration path would vary considerably.

5 ⬜ Mark for Review

Text 1

It is generally accepted that technological advancements yield a net positive for society, though it's understood that each advancement does come with a series of potential consequences. For instance, the separation of radioisotopes produces energy that could reduce society's reliance on fossil fuels, but this process also helped to produce nuclear weapons. Though regrettable, such consequences of progress are unavoidable if science is to effectively address the emerging needs of a society.

Text 2

In a 2016 interview, cosmologist Stephen Hawking warned that technological advancements pose the greatest threat to human existence. Citing such perils as laboratory-fabricated viruses and nuclear weapons, he predicted significant losses of human life within the next thousand years and opined that scientists themselves may unwittingly be a catalyst of such disasters. He argued that scientists must take a meticulous and cautious approach and work to offset the zealousness from governments and businesses, whose leaders are often the driving impetus for such rapid innovation.

Based on the texts, how would Hawking (Text 2) mostly likely respond to what is "generally accepted" in Text 1?

(A) By conceding that some technological advancements were indeed dangerous and catastrophic but arguing that such outcomes are quite uncommon

(B) By acknowledging the net positive of technological advancements but claiming that governments and businesses are more responsible for the positive outcome than scientists are

(C) By embracing the concept of technological advancement completely and suggesting that the pace of technological improvements should be accelerated rather than impeded

(D) By suggesting that the current pace of technological advancement be balanced by a careful approach on the part of scientists

Chapter 9
Dual Texts Drill
Explanations

ANSWER KEY

1. C
2. C
3. A

4. B
5. D

DUAL TEXTS DRILL EXPLANATIONS

1. **C** This is a Dual Texts question, which asks with *which statement* would *both authors* agree. Read Text 1 and highlight its main idea or conclusion, which is that *orcas in the region have recently begun to prey upon the otters*, while the rest of the text examines the consequences of this change. Then read Text 2 and highlight what Text 2 says about the same topic. The author of Text 2 states that *circumstances other than predation alone are responsible for the series of events observed in Alaskan kelp forests*. Since it's not clear upon which idea the texts agree, go right to the answers and eliminate those that are not consistent with one or both texts.

   - (A) is wrong because while Text 2 does mention *new research*, neither text mentions anything that could be *more advanced technology*.

   - (B) and (D) are wrong because while both may be true, neither text discusses how much is known about sea otter *young* nor does either text mention where *relatives* of sea otters might live.

   - (C) is correct because it's consistent with the highlighted ideas—both authors agree that *sea otter presence…has been reduced*, but they disagree as to exactly why that has happened.

2. **C** This is a Dual Texts question, as it asks for a statement that *the author of Text 1 and the historians in Text 2* would agree on. Read Text 1 and highlight the main argument made regarding Sophocles, which is that *Sophocles uses Oedipus to demonstrate the danger of hubris, or pride*. Then, read Text 2 and highlight what the historians say about the same topic. The text states that *there is little doubt among these historians that Sophocles intended Oedipus to serve as a warning of the dangers of hubris*. Enter "both agree that Oedipus was used to demonstrate danger of pride" into the annotation box.

   - (A) is wrong because only *male characters in the works of Sophocles* are mentioned—none of Aristotle's characters are discussed in the text, male or otherwise.

   - (B) is wrong because it's the opposite of what the historians in Text 2 believe—they are not convinced that Oedipus in *Oedipus Rex* was ever intended to have a "fatal flaw" at all.

   - (C) is correct because it's consistent with the relationship between the texts.

   - (D) is wrong because it misuses *commentary* from Text 1 and Sophocles, *Oedipus Rex*, and *Aristotle* from both texts—there's no evidence that Aristotle was trying to praise Sophocles in his commentary.

3. **A**   This is a Dual Texts question, as it asks for a *difference in how the author of Text 1 and the author of Text 2 view the works of Shakespeare*. Read Text 1 and highlight its main idea or conclusion, which is that *by virtue of the plays being attributed to Shakespeare, it is therefore more likely that he was the original author of those plays than not.* Then, read Text 2 and highlight what the author of Text 2 says about the same topic. The author argues that *historians who focus only on the attribution argument often neglect to consider that Shakespeare would likely have had several collaborators who worked with him.* The difference in the texts relates to how important they think it is that Shakespeare's plays were attributed to Shakespeare. Enter "texts disagree on importance of attribution" into the annotation box.

    - (A) is correct because it's consistent with the highlighting and annotation—the author of Text 2 argues that just because the works are attributed to Shakespeare does not mean Shakespeare could not have written the plays with others.

    - (B) and (D) are wrong because neither text discusses which of Shakespeare's plays were *comedies* or what Shakespeare's *best quality* was as a writer.

    - (C) is wrong because it reverses which author believes which argument—it is the author of Text 2 who believes that *Shakespeare's works were primarily written as collaborations*, not the author of Text 1. The same is true of the second half of the sentence—Text 1 believes that Shakespeare was the *sole author*, not Text 2.

4. **B**   This is a Dual Texts question, as it asks how *the scientists in Text 2* would *respond to the underlined portion in Text 1*. Read Text 1 and highlight the underlined portion, which is that *researchers are uncertain as to how the ancient Egyptians overcame certain engineering obstacles.* Then, read Text 2 and highlight what the scientists say about the same topic. They *claim that their reconstruction demonstrates that a tributary of the Nile must have once flown from the main river to the Giza build site, which allowed for the efficient transport of building materials.* Enter "scientists claim they found part of the answer" into the annotation box.

    - (A) is wrong because the pollen samples were taken from the Giza build site, not the *Nile River*.

    - (B) is correct because it's consistent with the relationship between the texts.

    - (C) is wrong because the scientists don't suggest that their samples were *unreliable*, even if that sounds like a logical conclusion because of the passage of time.

    - (D) is wrong because no research was done on *Nile River pollen*, nor is there evidence to suggest that the *pollen's migration path would vary considerably* if such data existed.

5.   **D**   This is a Dual Texts question, as it asks how *Hawking* in *Text 2* would *respond to what is "generally accepted" in Text 1*. Read Text 1 to learn what is *generally accepted*, which is that *technological advancements yield a net positive for society*. Then, read Text 2 and highlight what Hawking says about the same topic. He argues that these advancements *pose the greatest threat to human existence*. While Hawking does not want technological advancements to cease entirely, he does believe that caution is needed to avoid catastrophe. Enter "Hawking disagrees—will be a negative if we don't slow down" into the annotation box.

- (A) and (C) are wrong because they're the opposite of Hawking's argument—calling the dangerous outcomes of these advancements *quite uncommon* or *embracing the concept of technological development* completely would mean that Hawking is much more positive toward technological advancements than he actually is in Text 2.

- (B) is wrong because it's misusing *net positive* from Text 1 and *governments*, *businesses*, and *scientists* from Text 2.

- (D) is correct because it's consistent with the relationship between the texts—Hawking calls upon scientists to be *meticulous and cautious* as they pursue advancements, in order to avoid potential disasters.

Chapter 10
Retrieval Drill

Retrieval Drill

1 ☐ Mark for Review

In 1908, a figurine later named the Venus of Willendorf was discovered in Willendorf, Austria. The figurine was estimated to be nearly 30,000 years old, making it exceptionally difficult to determine its exact origin. However, the anthropological team that uncovered the figurine used tomography scans on the figurine to assess its composition. The team determined that the figurine is made of oolitic limestone and was able to trace the limestone's origin to a location in the Southern Alps, which at least provides researchers with a region to investigate further in the hopes of tracing the figurine's origin.

According to the text, what challenge did the anthropologists have to overcome regarding the figurine?

- (A) The anthropologists were not able to assess the composition of the figure.

- (B) The figurine was so old that the anthropologists couldn't easily handle it.

- (C) Some of the paint on the figurine was so old that it couldn't be analyzed.

- (D) The figurine's age posed a challenge in determining the figurine's origin.

2 ☐ Mark for Review

Though trained in many instruments, blues musician Jessie Mae Hemphill was especially drawn to percussion. Percussion instruments such as the tambourine and the drum help add a distinctive sound to blues music, and Hemphill's songs were no exception. In her debut album *She-Wolf* (1981), she not only played the drums but also sang and played lead guitar in an effort to spread her love of blues through her home region of Mississippi. Hemphill also used the album's songs to connect with other women and inspire them to pursue their own musical dreams at a time when very few women participated in blues music.

According to the text, what is significant about Hemphill's use of blues music?

- (A) Blues music required connections with producers that were easily obtained by Hemphill.

- (B) Blues music helped Hemphill inspire people, especially women musicians.

- (C) Hemphill was one of the first women to play drums on an album.

- (D) Hemphill experienced considerable success once she released her debut blues album.

3 🔖 Mark for Review

The Earth's climate is continuously placed under stress due to anthropogenic CO_2, or the release of carbon dioxide due to the consumption of fossil fuels, among other secondary factors. Anthropogenic CO_2 warms the air in the Earth's atmosphere, which causes the air to retain more moisture and therefore creates extreme amounts of rainfall and flooding. Climatologists claim that diminishing reliance on automobiles, which burn gasoline, may help lower the mean air temperature of the planet and give the climate time to recover.

According to the text, what is the main cause of anthropogenic CO_2 release?

(A) Warming of the Earth's atmosphere

(B) Automobiles powered by gasoline

(C) Expending fossil fuels

(D) Extreme amounts of flooding via rainfall

4 🔖 Mark for Review

The following text is adapted from William Blake's 1789 poem "A Poison Tree."

I was angry with my friend:
I told my wrath, my wrath did end.
I was angry with my foe:
I told it not, my wrath did grow.
And I watered it in fears
Night and morning with my tears,
And I sunnèd it with smiles
And with soft deceitful wiles.
And it grew both day and night,
Till it bore an apple bright,
And my foe beheld it shine,
And he knew that it was mine.

Based on the text, what is true of the speaker's mental state?

(A) He slowly becomes enraged when presented with evidence that someone tampered with his garden.

(B) He cannot understand his enemy's motivations as he and his enemy come from different backgrounds.

(C) He feels a strong emotion towards his enemy that grows in strength because of a lack of communication.

(D) He cannot focus on his work because of an overwhelming sense of hatred towards his enemy.

5 ▢ Mark for Review

The following text is adapted from L. Frank Baum's 1900 novel *The Wonderful Wizard of Oz*. In the story, Aunt Em has lived on a farm in Kansas for many years.

When Aunt Em came there to live she was a young, pretty wife. The sun and wind had changed her, too. They had taken the sparkle from her eyes and left them a sober gray; they had taken the red from her cheeks and lips, and they were gray also. She was thin and gaunt, and never smiled now. When Dorothy, who was an orphan, first came to her, Aunt Em had been so startled by the child's laughter that she would scream and press her hand upon her heart whenever Dorothy's merry voice reached her ears; and she still looked at the little girl with wonder that she could find anything to laugh at.

According to the text, what is true about Aunt Em?

(A) She has been changed by life on the farm.

(B) She has difficulty expressing love towards Dorothy.

(C) She is much younger than she looks.

(D) She has a more refined sense of humor than Dorothy does.

Chapter 11
Retrieval Drill
Explanations

ANSWER KEY

1. D
2. B
3. C

4. C
5. A

RETRIEVAL DRILL EXPLANATIONS

1. **D** This is a Retrieval question, as it asks for a detail *according to the text*. Look for and highlight information about the *challenge* that the anthropologists had to overcome. The text states that *The figurine was estimated to be nearly 30,000 years old, making it exceptionally difficult to determine its exact origin.* The correct answer should be as consistent as possible with this detail.

   - (A) is wrong because it's the opposite of what's stated in the text—the team was able to assess the composition of the figure.

   - (B) and (C) are wrong because they each go **Beyond the Text**—while the figure is old, it's not stated in the text that the anthropologists *couldn't easily handle* it or that it had any *paint* on it.

   - (D) is correct because it's consistent with the highlighting.

2. **B** This is a Retrieval question, as it asks for a detail *according to the text*. Look for and highlight information about *Hemphill's use of blues music*. The text states that *Hemphill also used the album's songs to connect with other women and inspire them to pursue their own musical dreams at a time when very few women participated in blues music.* The correct answer should be as consistent as possible with this detail.

   - (A) and (D) are wrong because they each go beyond what the text can support—while connections with producers are important in music and Hemphill's album may have been successful, neither idea is discussed in the text.

   - (C) is wrong because it's too extreme—we don't know that Hemphill was *one of the first women* to play drums on an album, only that she was one of the earlier female blues musicians.

   - (B) is correct because it's consistent with the highlighting.

3. **C** This is a Retrieval question, as it asks for a detail *according to the text*. Look for and highlight information about *the main cause of anthropogenic CO_2 release*. The text states that this release is *due to the consumption of fossil fuels*. The correct answer should be as consistent as possible with this detail.

   - (A) and (D) are wrong because they are results, rather than causes, of anthropogenic CO_2 release.

- (B) is wrong because although the text does advocate for *diminishing reliance on automobiles*, it doesn't claim that automobiles themselves are the *main cause* of anthropogenic CO_2 release.

- (C) is correct because it's consistent with the highlighting—*expending* could be the same as *consumption*.

4.   **C**   This is a Retrieval question, as it asks for a detail *based on the text*. Look for and highlight information about the *speaker's mental state*. The speaker focuses primarily on *wrath* and explains that *I was angry with my foe* and states that because *I told it not, my wrath did grow*. Because most of the text describes the wrath growing, those lines are the main idea of the text and the correct answer should be as consistent as possible with those lines.

- (A) and (D) are wrong because while becoming enraged or feeling hatred are similar to wrath, there is no evidence that anyone *tampered* with the speaker's garden or that *He cannot focus on his work*. Both of these answers misuse or misinterpret the discussion of watering and the apple from the text.

- (B) is wrong because it goes beyond what the text can support—none of the *enemy's motivations* or emotions are ever discussed.

- (C) is correct because it's consistent with the highlighting.

5.   **A**   This is a Retrieval question, as it asks for a detail *according to the text*. Look for and highlight information about *Aunt Em*. Since most of the text is about Aunt Em, go right to the answers and compare them back to the text. The correct answer should be as consistent as possible with the details in the text.

- (A) is correct because it's consistent with what the introduction and text say about Aunt Em—she *has lived on a farm in Kansas for many years*, and the *sun and wind had changed her, too,* having *taken the sparkle from her eyes* and *the red from her cheeks*. She also *never smiled now,* indicating a contrast between past and present.

- (B) and (D) are wrong because they each go too far beyond what the text can support—Aunt Em being *startled by the child's laughter* and wondering *that she could find anything to laugh at* do not mean that Aunt Em has difficulty *expressing love* or *has a more refined sense of humor*.

- (C) is wrong because the text makes it clear that Aunt Em has been on the farm *for many years* and has *gray* in her features. While none of this necessarily makes Aunt Em old, there is no support for her being *younger* than she looks.

Chapter 12
Main Idea Drill

Main Idea Drill

---

1 ☐ Mark for Review

The following text is from Lucy M. Montgomery's 1921 novel *Rilla of Ingleside*. The opening chapter introduces a kitten known as "Dr. Jekyll-and-Mr. Hyde," who is owned by a woman named Susan.

Dr. Jekyll loved new milk; Mr. Hyde would not touch milk and growled over his meat. Dr. Jekyll came down the stairs so silently that no one could hear him. Mr. Hyde made his tread as heavy as a man's. Several evenings, when Susan was alone in the house, he "scared her stiff," as she declared, by doing this. He would sit in the middle of the kitchen floor, with his terrible eyes fixed unwinkingly upon hers for an hour at a time. This played havoc with her nerves, but poor Susan really held him in too much awe to try to drive him out. Once she had dared to throw a stick at him and he had promptly made a savage leap towards her.

Which choices best states the main idea of the text?

- (A) Although the kitten could sometimes be easy to be live with, its owner faces occasional difficulties with it.

- (B) The kitten is temperamental and can be violent, but its owner misses it when the two are separated.

- (C) The kitten enjoys solitude much more than Susan does.

- (D) Susan admires different behaviors of the kitten depending on which mood it is in.

---

2 ☐ Mark for Review

First patented in North America by Margaret Knight, the flat-bottomed paper bag was introduced in the 1870s, allowing improving the consumer experience. This ingenious design, along with the use of sturdier kraft paper in bag construction, provided a larger and less cumbersome vessel in which to transport products from the store to the home. Patrons were able to purchase more goods each visit, avoid inconveniences such as rips and tears, and reuse bags from one trip to the next. The volume and variety of sales per consumer at markets quickly increased, with stores enjoying increased profits thanks to Knight's innovation.

Which choice best states the main idea of the text?

- (A) The invention of the flat-bottomed paper bag in the 1870s made paper bags cheaper to produce.

- (B) The sturdier paper used in the construction of the flat-bottomed paper bag became sought after by other industries.

- (C) The institution of the flat-bottomed paper bag in the 1870s helped markets turn a profit for the first time that decade.

- (D) The utilization of the flat-bottomed paper bag in the 1870s was beneficial in several ways.

---

3 🔖 Mark for Review

The following text is adapted from William Wordsworth's 1807 poem "London, 1802."

> Milton! thou shouldst be living at this hour:
> England hath need of thee: she is a fen
> Of stagnant waters: altar, sword, and pen,
> Fireside, the heroic wealth of hall and bower,
> Have forfeited their ancient English dower
> Of inward happiness. We are selfish men;
> Oh! raise us up, return to us again;
> And give us manners, virtue, freedom, power.

Which choice best states the main idea of the text?

(A) After decades of neglecting his country, the speaker is concerned that he has contributed to the country's decline.

(B) As the condition of a country continues to deteriorate, the speaker expresses confusion as to how the deterioration began.

(C) Because the speaker believes a country is in need of guidance, he wishes for the presence of an individual who has died.

(D) The speaker laments the passing of a colleague whose warnings about the country went unheeded.

4 🔖 Mark for Review

Leading one of the most successful rebellions in history, Haitian general Toussaint Louverture is generally considered to be a major contributor to the downfall of European colonialism. However, Louverture may not have joined the Haitian Revolution at all if not for the actions of French Governor Philippe François Rouxel, who allowed cruel treatment of the prisoners under his watch. Not only did Louverture prevent these prisoners from being unfairly executed, but he also fully committed to the revolution once the French colonial assembly refused to meet with him over this and other incidents.

Which choice best states the main idea of the text?

(A) The driving force behind the Haitian Revolution is a subject of debate among scholars.

(B) Rouxel may have unintentionally contributed to Louverture's participation in the Haitian Revolution.

(C) The Haitian Revolution convinced people from many other Caribbean nations to revolt against their oppressors.

(D) The majority of the injustices that sparked the Haitian Revolution were committed by Rouxel.

5 ⚑ Mark for Review

For nearly 100 years, hair transplants have been employed to cosmetically reduce the visible and emotional effects of androgenetic alopecia—or hereditary hair loss. Trichology (the study of human hair) research since then has shown that hair transplants may serve a role beyond combating androgenetic alopecia, and new research conducted by Claire Higgins and her team shows that during their active growth phase, hair follicles that are transplanted into a scar present on the body will actually remodel scar tissue, reducing the visibility and impact of scarring and therefore allowing the body greater range of motion in that area.

Which choices best states the main idea of the text?

(A) Hair transplants were initially used mainly to treat androgenic alopecia, but additional benefits of hair transplants are now being investigated by researchers.

(B) The connection between implanted hair follicles and reduced scar tissue proves what had long been assumed about the benefits of hair transplants.

(C) New research in the field of trichology has disputed commonly held viewpoints regarding the connection between hair follicles and the improvement of areas affected by scar tissue.

(D) Antiquated equipment has posed an impediment to hair transplant research, but recent improvements to the equipment have allowed for expanded understanding of the benefits of hair transplants.

Chapter 13
Main Idea Drill
Explanations

ANSWER KEY

1. A
2. D
3. C

4. B
5. A

MAIN IDEA DRILL EXPLANATIONS

1. **A**   This is a Main Idea question, as it asks for the *main idea of the text*. Look for and highlight information that can help identify the main idea. Because the text is both a description of the kitten Dr. Jekyl-and-Mr. Hyde and of Susan, a single main idea may be difficult to highlight. Instead, go right to the answer choices and compare them back to the text. The correct answer should be as consistent as possible with the ideas and details in the text.

    *   (A) is correct because it's consistent with the text—the "Mr. Hyde" mood of the kitten is described as *terrible* and *savage* at times, so these could be *difficulties*. The "Dr. Jekyll" mood is described as loving milk and not making much noise, qualities that could be *easy to live with*.

    *   (B) and (D) are wrong because they're each **Half-Right**—the kitten could be described as *temperamental and violent* when it's acting more like "Mr. Hyde," but there is no evidence that Susan ever *misses* the kitten. Similarly, Susan may or may not admire the cat's "Dr. Jekyll" mood, but she definitely does not admire any *behaviors* when the cat is acting like "Mr. Hyde."

    *   (C) is wrong because it misuses *alone* from the third sentence and the text does not compare to what extent the kitten and Susan enjoy *solitude*.

2. **D**   This is a Main Idea question, as it asks for the *main idea of the text*. Look for and highlight information that can help identify the main idea. The text talks about flat-bottomed bags and how their *ingenious design… provided a larger and less cumbersome vessel in which to transport products*. The text goes on to state that this also led to *stores enjoying increased profits*. Since the other sentences either give background information or further explain these two phrases, these two phrases together serve as the main idea. The correct answer should be as consistent as possible with these portions of the text.

    *   (A) is wrong because *cheaper to produce* is not mentioned as one of the benefits of flat-bottomed bags.

    *   (B) is wrong because it goes beyond what the text can support—it's not stated that *other industries* started to seek out the sturdier paper.

    *   (C) is wrong because it's too extreme—it's unknown whether this is the *first time* in the 1870s that markets turned a profit.

    *   (D) is correct because it's consistent with the highlighted portions of the text—both discuss benefits of the invention.

3. **C**   This is a Main Idea question, as it asks for the *main idea of the text*. Look for and highlight information that can help identify the main idea. The speaker addresses Milton and says *thou shouldst be living at this hour: England hath need of thee*. Since the rest of the poem explains why the speaker thinks England could use Milton's help, these lines serve as the main idea. The correct answer should be as consistent as possible with this portion of the text.

    - (A) and (B) are wrong because the speaker does not claim to have neglected his country, nor does he ponder how its *deterioration began* in the text.

    - (C) is correct because it's consistent with the highlighted portion of the text.

    - (D) is wrong because it goes beyond what the text can support—just because the speaker believes Milton could help the country now does not mean that Milton had given *warnings about the country* that *went unheeded* when he was alive.

4. **B**   This is a Main Idea question, as it asks for the *main idea of the text*. Look for and highlight information that can help identify the main idea. The text claims that *Louverture may not have joined the Haitian Revolution at all if not for the actions of French Governor Philippe François Rouxel*. Since the rest of the text explains either Louverture's role in the revolution or Rouxel's role in Louverture's joining of the revolution, this sentence serves as the main idea. The correct answer should be as consistent as possible with this portion of the text.

    - (A) is wrong because the *driving force* behind the Haitian Revolution is not discussed in the text, nor is there any mention of a *debate among scholars*.

    - (B) is correct because it's consistent with the highlighted portion of the text.

    - (C) and (D) are wrong because they each go beyond what the text can support—it's not known from that text that *other Caribbean nations* were inspired *to revolt* or that the *majority* of injustices *were committed by Rouxel*.

5. **A**   This is a Main Idea question, as it asks for the *main idea of the text*. Look for and highlight information that can help identify the main idea. The text states that *Trichology...research since then has shown that hair transplants may serve a role beyond combating androgenetic alopecia*. Since the rest of the text either discusses the traditional use of hair transplants or that hair transplants have indeed been shown to also improve the areas affected by scar tissue, this sentence serves as the main idea. The correct answer should be as consistent as possible with this portion of the text.

    - (A) is correct because it's consistent with the highlighted portion of the text.

    - (B) and (C) are wrong because while both mention a *connection* between hair transplants and scar tissue, that connection had not *long been assumed* or commonly held. It was discovered as part of *new research* and was demonstrated rather than *disputed* by the research.

    - (D) is wrong because there is no mention of *antiquated equipment* or improvements to such equipment in the text.

Chapter 14
Claims Drill

Claims Drill

Graffiti is a form of visual art that is increasingly being utilized in some classrooms. The most common form of classroom graffiti involves creating a central space in which students can ask questions and allowing students to add their answers to these questions in their own handwriting. For example, California teacher Kari Kerrigan's students use specifically colored markers to indicate which question from Kerrigan's graffiti board they are answering. Educators argue that in addition to expanding student comprehension of a topic, graffiti art can increase student engagement in the classroom by providing an interactive alternative to rote instruction and memorization.

Which finding, if true, would most strongly support the underlined claim?

(A) Students who are focused on comprehension of material don't generally have a preference for how much engagement there is in the classroom.

(B) Teachers who utilize classroom graffiti in their instruction are among the educators with the highest percentages of student participation and satisfaction.

(C) Teachers claim that they like working in districts that allow classroom graffiti more than working in those that do not.

(D) Students tend to be more interested in finding answers to questions than they do writing their answers on a central board.

"The Diamond Necklace" is an 1884 short story by Guy de Maupassant. In the story, the author suggests that the main character, Mathilde, is dissatisfied with her surroundings: _____

Which quotation from "The Diamond Necklace" most effectively supports the claim?

(A) "Suddenly she discovered, in a black satin box, a superb diamond necklace, and her heart throbbed with an immoderate desire."

(B) "She left the ball about four o'clock in the morning."

(C) "But she did not listen to him and rapidly descended the stairs."

(D) "She was distressed at the poverty of her dwelling, at the bareness of the walls, at the shabby chairs, the ugliness of the curtains."

3 ☐ Mark for Review

In his 1817 poem "Ozymandias," Percy Bysshe Shelley reflects on the transient nature of political power. Rather than analyzing the men who achieve power, Shelley focuses on how little of a mark those men leave upon the world: _____

Which quotation from "Ozymandias" most effectively illustrates the claim?

- (A) "My name is Ozymandias, king of kings: / Look on my works, ye Mighty, and despair!"

- (B) "Two vast and trunkless legs of stone / Stand in the desert."

- (C) "Nothing beside remains. Round the decay / Of that colossal wreck, boundless and bare."

- (D) "Near them, on the sand, / Half sunk, a shattered visage lies."

4 ☐ Mark for Review

For years, scientists assumed that only certain bird species will pretend to be injured to draw the attention of predators away from bird nests. But a series of ornithological studies have shown that hundreds of species from different taxonomic families employ this diversionary tactic, suggesting multiple independent evolutionary pathways. Researchers Clinton Francis and Wren Thompson assert that the reason for this may be geographic—the farther a species lives from the equator, the more its predators will rely on eyesight to hunt, and therefore the more likely a bird is to feign injury to protect its young.

Which finding, if true, would most directly support Francis and Thompson's assertion?

- (A) Bird species at the North and South Poles have been noted to feign injuries more frequently than any other bird species.

- (B) Birds are able to distract predators through birdsong but rarely choose to do so.

- (C) Some male birds have been noted to help their female partners in protecting their young.

- (D) Bird species who live near the equator and those who live near the poles seem to feign injuries at similar rates.

5 ☐ Mark for Review

A professor of dance and theater studies is writing a biography about Uday Shankar, an Indian-born artist and performer. The professor suggests that after Shankar's visit to Great Britain, his incorporation of Western influences in his Hindi dance performances, such as the ballet *Radha-Krishna*, demonstrates a desire to bring traditional Hindi dances into the European mainstream culture.

Which quotation from a work by a music historian would be the most effective evidence for the professor to include in support of this suggestion?

(A) "*Radha Krishna* is important for its demanding maneuvers, with Shankar executing quick jumps, full-body rotations, and dynamic flourishes with his limbs as he glides gracefully across the stage."

(B) "Unlike many of the routines Shankar developed early in his career, *Radha Krishna* features a narrative arc with a cohesive story and defined characters."

(C) "There are many talented dancers who performed alongside Shankar in *Radha Krishna*, though the most memorable of them was the famous Russian ballerina, Anna Pavlova."

(D) "*Radha Krishna*'s music is performed by a Western orchestra, which Shanka specifically requested as a means to make the ballet more accessible to European audiences during the tour."

6 ☐ Mark for Review

A human's parasympathetic nervous system becomes most active when the body goes to sleep and relaxes after a period of stress. Creating a preparatory bedtime routine helps facilitate the efficient function of this system. Some aspects of an effective preparatory bedtime routine include lowering the temperature of the bedroom, doing breathing exercises, and calming the body with reading, stretching, or meditation. Experts assert that, by adhering to a consistent preparatory bedtime routine, individuals will experience a greater sense of rejuvenation from their parasympathetic nervous system.

Which finding, if true, would most strongly support the underlined claim?

(A) Physicians often suggest preparatory bedtime routines in conjunction with other recommendations, such as daily exercise programs.

(B) Patients who utilize preparatory bedtime routines report higher energy levels during the day than those who do not utilize such routines.

(C) Doctors who advise preparatory bedtime routines are among the most highly rated doctors in their hospitals.

(D) Patients often find preparatory bedtime routines more helpful for the reduction of stress than for achieving restful sleep.

7 ☐ Mark for Review

The Secret Garden is a 1911 novel by Frances Hodgson Burnett. In the novel, Burnett's portrayal of Mary emphasizes that Mary's mother, known as the Mem Sahib, may have influenced those around Mary to be attentive to Mary's desires: _____

Which quotation from *The Secret Garden* most effectively illustrates the claim?

Ⓐ "[Mary] never remembered seeing familiarly anything but the dark faces of her Ayah and the other native servants, and...they always obeyed her and gave her her own way in everything, because the Mem Sahib would be angry if she was disturbed by her crying."

Ⓑ "When Mary Lennox was sent to Misselthwaite Manor to live with her uncle everybody said she was the most disagreeable-looking child ever seen."

Ⓒ "She had not wanted a little girl at all, and when Mary was born she handed her over to the care of an Ayah, who was made to understand that if she wished to please the Mem Sahib she must keep the child out of sight as much as possible."

Ⓓ "So when she was a sickly, fretful, ugly little baby she was kept out of the way, and when she became a sickly, fretful, toddling thing she was kept out of the way also."

8 ☐ Mark for Review

Malian artist Ali Farka Touré is best known for his unique musical synthesis of Western blues with traditional African sounds, incorporating modern blues chord progressions, Moroccan guitars, Malian lutes, and nine different African languages. In his 1988 album *Ali Farka Touré,* Touré's synthesis of blues and African music created a unique sound that could not be classified into an existing genre. Musicians, Touré argued, should always look to innovate with their compositions, while still remaining true to the cultural traditions and musical styles of their hometowns.

Which quotation from a music critic most directly challenges the underlined claim in the text?

Ⓐ "Many critics fixate on the African rhythms in *Ali Farka Touré* and other albums by Touré but ignore the impact of modern blues on the album's chord progressions."

Ⓑ "While *Ali Farka Touré* certainly deserves praise, its synthesis of Western blues and African sounds—coined "desert blues" in the 1970s—had been seen in at least a dozen albums prior."

Ⓒ "Although many traditional African compositions feature guitars, the melodies achieved in the songs present on *Ali Farka Touré* contain a distinct Moroccan sound."

Ⓓ "In *Ali Farka Touré*, the blend of Western blues and traditional African sound bears striking similarities to many experimental jazz albums from the 1980s."

9 ☐ Mark for Review

Jonathan Swift's 1726 book *Gulliver's Travels* follows Lemuel Gulliver, a traveler seeking new perspectives among non-human races such as the *Yahoo*. In the story, Gulliver is depicted in ways that imply he has begun to reject aspects of his humanity: _____

Which quotation from *Gulliver's Travels* most effectively illustrates the claim?

(A) "For these reasons, the trade of a soldier is held the most honourable of all others; because a soldier is a *Yahoo* hired to kill, in cold blood, as many of his own species, who have never offended him, as possibly he can."

(B) "At other times, the like battles have been fought between the *Yahoos* of several neighbourhoods, without any visible cause; those of one district watching all opportunities to surprise the next, before they are prepared."

(C) "When I happened to behold the reflection of my own form in a lake or fountain, I turned away my face in horror and detestation of myself, and could better endure the sight of a common *Yahoo* than of my own person."

(D) "By what I could discover, the *Yahoos* appear to be the most unteachable of all animals, their capacities never reaching higher than to draw or carry burdens."

10 ☐ Mark for Review

Many historians claim that in 1572, French queen mother Catherine de'Medici instigated the St. Bartholomew's Day Massacre, a conflict that began with the failed assassination of a French admiral and ended with the execution of thousands of Huguenots, a name for French Calvinist Protestants. Shortly after the death of her son, Charles IX, an anonymous pamphlet accused Catherine of being a "murderess" motivated by "ruthless jealousy and ambition," an accusation that further tarnished Catherine's legacy. Some researchers claim that her role in the massacre has been greatly exaggerated based on the pamphlet's failure to include any evidence and instead argue that throughout her reign, Catherine staunchly believed in religious tolerance and freedom.

Which quotation from a scholarly article best supports the claim of the researchers mentioned in the text?

(A) "The 1559 death of Henry II of France had several long-term consequences: a rift in the French court between his widow Catherine and the French nobility; the ensuing French Wars of Religion, which pitted French Catholics against French Protestants; and the St. Bartholomew's Day Massacre, which forever altered the religious and political balance in the region."

(B) "At the time of the St. Bartholomew's Day Massacre, Huguenots made up approximately ten percent of France's population; by 1600, the percentage of the French population that was Huguenot had dropped to six percent."

(C) "In 1572, two months before the St. Bartholomew's Day Massacre, Catherine de'Medici oversaw the signing of a marriage contract—the contract, signed between a French Huguenot prince and a French Catholic princess, increased tensions in the French court."

(D) "In his 1998 work *Catherine de'Medici*, biographer R. J. Knecht claims that both Catholics and Huguenot writers of the late sixteenth century were looking to blame someone for France's woes, and targeted Catherine, who could hardly be called a proponent of bloodshed."

Chapter 15
Claims Drill
Explanations

ANSWER KEY

1. B
2. D
3. C
4. A
5. D

6. B
7. A
8. B
9. C
10. D

CLAIMS DRILL EXPLANATIONS

1. **B** This is a Claims question, as it asks which choice would *most strongly support the underlined claim*. Look for and highlight the claim in the text, which is that *graffiti art can increase student engagement in the classroom by providing an interactive alternative to rote instruction and memorization*. The correct answer should address and be consistent with each aspect of this claim.

   - (A) and (D) are wrong because it would weaken, not support, the claim if students did not have a preference for *how much engagement* there was in a classroom or are not overly interested in *writing their answers on a central board*, which is an aspect of classroom graffiti.

   - (B) is correct because it's consistent with the highlighted claim.

   - (C) is wrong because it's not relevant to the claim—the claim focuses on *student engagement* due to the use of classroom graffiti, not on teachers' preferences for *districts that allow classroom graffiti*.

2. **D** This is a Claims question, as it asks which choice *most effectively illustrates the claim*. Look for and highlight the claim in the text, which is that *the main character, Mathilde, is dissatisfied with her surroundings*. The correct answer should address and be consistent with each aspect of this claim.

   - (A) is wrong because it's the opposite of the claim—Mathilde seems pleased with her discovery of the *superb diamond necklace*.

   - (B) and (C) are wrong because they go too far beyond what the text can support—while leaving a ball and descending the stairs rapidly could express dissatisfaction with one's environment, there's no evidence of Mathilde's emotions in these answers.

   - (D) is correct because it's consistent with the highlighted claim.

3. **C** This is a Claims question, as it asks which choice *most effectively illustrates the claim*. Look for and highlight the claim in the text, which is that *Shelley focuses on how little of a mark those men leave upon the world*. The correct answer should address and be consistent with each aspect of this claim.

   - (A), (B), and (D) are wrong because each is the opposite of Shelley's focus—*my works, vast and trunkless legs of stone*, and *a shattered visage* focus on things men did indeed leave behind, rather than *how little of a mark* they made.

- (C) is correct because it's consistent with the highlighted claim—stating that *Nothing beside remains...Of that colossal wreck* focuses on how *little of a mark* men leave upon the world.

4. **A** This is a Claims question, as it asks which choice would *most directly support Francis and Thompson's assertion.* Look for and highlight the claim in the text, which is that *the farther a species lives from the equator...the more likely a bird is to feign injury to protect its young.* The correct answer should address and be consistent with each aspect of this claim.

   - (A) is correct because it's consistent with the claim—the poles are farthest from the equator, so those birds having the highest frequency of feigned injuries supports the assertion.

   - (B) and (C) are wrong because neither is relevant to the claim—neither *birdsong* nor the roles of *male* and *female* birds are discussed in the text.

   - (D) is wrong because it would weaken, not support, the claim, if birds near and far from the equator had *similar rates* of feigned injuries.

5. **D** This is a Claims question, as it asks which choice would be the *most effective evidence for the professor to include in support of this suggestion.* Look for and highlight the claim in the text, which is that Shankar's *incorporation of Western influences in his Hindi dance performances...demonstrates a desire to bring traditional Hindi dances into the European mainstream culture.* The correct answer should address and be consistent with each aspect of this claim.

   - (A), (B), and (C) are wrong because they're not relevant to the claim—the text does not focus on *demanding maneuvers*, a *narrative arc*, or any other *talented dancers* besides Shankar.

   - (D) is correct because it's consistent with the highlighted claim.

6. **B** This is a Claims question, as it asks which choice would *most strongly support the underlined claim.* Look for and highlight the claim in the text, which is that *individuals will experience a greater sense of rejuvenation from their parasympathetic nervous system.* The correct answer should address and be consistent with each aspect of this claim.

   - (A) is wrong because it's not relevant to the claim—the correct answer should address something regarding a person's *sense of rejuvenation* rather than *other recommendations* a physician might make to a patient.

   - (B) is correct because it's consistent with the highlighted claim—*higher energy levels during the day* could be an example of *a greater sense of rejuvenation.*

   - (C) and (D) are wrong because they go beyond what the text can support—while doctors who give useful recommendations may be more popular than others or patients may feel one benefit of a preparatory bedtime routine over another, neither comparison is part of the claim.

7. **A** This is a Claims question, as it asks which choice *most effectively illustrates the claim*. Look for and highlight the claim in the text, which is that *Mary's mother…may have influenced those around Mary to be attentive to Mary's desires*. The correct answer should address and be consistent with each aspect of this claim.

    - (A) is correct because it's consistent with the highlighted claim—if the servants *always obeyed* Mary and *gave her her own way*, that could be consistent with being *attentive to Mary's desires*, and if the servants did so *because the Mem Sahib would be angry if she was disturbed* by Mary crying, that could be consistent with *Mary's mother* having *influenced those around Mary*.

    - (B) and (D) are wrong because they're **Half-Right**—each describes Mary negatively but does not contain anything that could be her mother being responsible for those negative qualities.

    - (C) is wrong because while it describes Mary's mother negatively, there is nothing that could be evidence of Mary's *selfish personality*.

8. **B** This is a Claims question, as it asks which choice *most directly challenges the underlined claim in the text*. Look for and highlight the claim in the text, which is that *Touré's synthesis of blues and African music created a unique sound that could not be classified into an existing genre*. The correct answer should be as contradictory to this claim as possible, suggesting an alternative explanation or offering new, conflicting data.

    - (A) is wrong because it's not relevant to the claim—whether *critics…ignore the impact of modern blues* on the album or not, this would not challenge the claim about the sound of the album being *unique*.

    - (B) is correct because it's contradictory to the highlighted claim—if there already was an established *desert blues* genre and the synthesis *had been seen in at least a dozen albums prior*, this would challenge the idea that the album's sound is *unique* and *could not be classified into an existing genre*.

    - (C) and (D) are wrong because they would strengthen, not challenge, the claim in the text—both support the text's descriptions regarding the album *Ali Farka Touré*.

9. **C** This is a Claims question, as it asks which choice *most effectively illustrates the claim*. Look for and highlight the claim in the text, which is that *Gulliver is depicted in ways that imply he has begun to reject aspects of his humanity*. The correct answer should address and be consistent with each aspect of this claim.

    - (A), (B), and (D) are wrong because they're not relevant to the claim—each depicts the *Yahoos*, the non-human race that Gulliver has encountered, rather than Gulliver himself.

    - (C) is correct because it's consistent with the highlighted claim—if *Gulliver turned away from* his *face in horror* and *could better endure the sight of a common Yahoo* than his own face, this could support that *he has begun to reject* at least one aspect of his humanity, the appearance of his face.

10. **D** This is a Claims question, as it asks which choice *best supports the claim of the researchers mentioned in the text*. Look for and highlight the claim in the text, which is that *the queen mother's role in the massacre has been greatly exaggerated* and *Catherine staunchly believed in religious tolerance and freedom*. The correct answer should address and be consistent with each aspect of this claim.

- (A) and (B) are wrong because they're not relevant to the claim—both discuss the St. Bartholomew's Day Massacre but neither discusses Catherine de'Medici's role in it.

- (C) is wrong because it weakens, not supports, the researchers' claim—since the contract that de'Medici oversaw *increased tensions in the French court*, this would be evidence towards her playing an antagonistic role in the ensuing violence, not evidence against.

- (D) is correct because it's consistent with the highlighted claim—if the writers were *looking for someone to blame*, that could mean Catherine's role was *greatly exaggerated*, and if Catherine *could hardly be called a proponent of bloodshed*, this could be evidence for her believing in *religious tolerance and freedom*.

Chapter 16
Charts Drill

Charts Drill

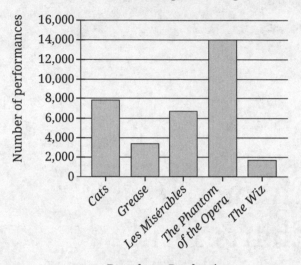

Broadway Productions by Total Number of Performances During Their Original Runs

Number of performances

Broadway Production

The Phantom of the Opera, a 1986 musical written and composed by Andrew Lloyd Weber, is one of the most famous Broadway productions of all time. It is frequently compared to both *Cats* and *Les Misérables*, the two other most successful musicals of the decade. All three productions feature sets with dark color palettes to establish a serious mood and also feature plots related to class conflict. However, *The Phantom of the Opera* _____

1 ⬚ Mark for Review

Which choice most effectively uses data from the graph to complete the text?

A) had about as many performances as *Grease*, another popular musical, which had just over 3,000 performances.

B) had more performances than both *Cats* and *Les Misérables*, as it had over 13,000 performances, while *Cats* and *Les Misérables* had about 7,800 and 6,700 performances, respectively.

C) had notably fewer performances than both *Cats* and *Les Misérables*, as it had only about 1,600 performances, while *Cats* and *Les Misérables* had about 7,800 and 6,700 performances, respectively.

D) had slightly fewer performances than *Cats*, which had about 7,800 performances, but slightly more performances than *Les Misérables*, which had about 6,700 performances.

2 🔖 Mark for Review

Demand Caused by EV Batteries

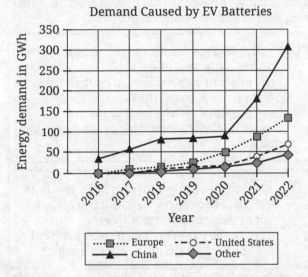

As the number of electric vehicle (EV) batteries used by consumers within a country increases, so does the energy demand, in Gigawatt hours (GWh), on that country's electrical grid. In a research paper on electric vehicles, a student claims that Europe's population distribution makes its citizens more prone to adoption of electric vehicles than those in the United States.

Which choice best describes data in the graph that support the student's claim?

(A) The energy demand in GWh from the countries that make up the "Other" category decreased every year from 2016 to 2022.

(B) In 2016, China's electrical grid saw about 40 GWh of demand from electric vehicle batteries, while countries in the "Other" category had virtually zero GWh of demand.

(C) No countries in 2016 besides China experienced an energy demand above ten GWh from electric vehicle batteries whereas multiple countries in 2022 experienced an energy demand above ten GWh.

(D) Both Europe and the United States had a negligible energy demand from electric vehicle batteries in 2016, but by 2022, Europe's demand had increased more than that of the United States.

3 🔖 Mark for Review

Parking Space Usage at City Park and Ride Locations

Location	Percentage of parking spaces utilized on Tuesday morning
Brownson Square	46%
Greenfield Park	23%
Orlando Woods	65%
Smithfield Terrace	98%
Worthington Hills	51%

A city's Transit Authority wants to encourage commuters to ride the train rather than drive to the city center. On Tuesday morning, the city examined the parking spaces utilized at five of its "Park and Ride" locations, where commuters from the suburbs can park their cars and take the train to the city center. The most utilized area, with 98 percent of parking spaces full that morning, was the "Park and Ride" location at _____

Which choice most effectively uses data from the table to complete the statement?

(A) Smithfield Terrace.

(B) Brownson Square.

(C) Orlando Woods.

(D) Worthington Hills.

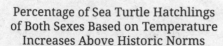

Percentage of Sea Turtle Hatchlings
of Both Sexes Based on Temperature
Increases Above Historic Norms

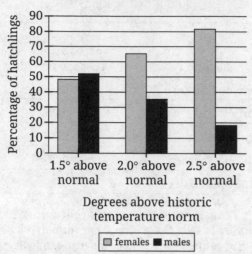

Sea turtle sex is determined by the temperature in the nest during gestation. While the internal nest temperature can be determined by a wide variety of factors, surface air temperature remains an important component of the process, rendering populations of these large ocean-going reptiles highly vulnerable to climate change. In North Carolina, researchers from project N.E.S.T. conducted a series of experiments on loggerhead sea turtles and adjusted the temperature of the nests to simulate the effects of rising temperatures on sea turtle sex. Based on the data, the N.E.S.T. team has concluded that, as global temperatures increase above historic norms, shifting sex ratios could create an imbalance in sea turtle populations that negatively affects the current breeding rate of the species.

4 ☐ Mark for Review

Which choice best describes data in the graph that support the N.E.S.T. team's conclusion?

(A) At 1.5 degrees above historic temperature norms, only 49% of sea turtle hatchlings in the experiments conducted by the team were female, but at the maximum temperature setting used in the experiments, that percentage rose to about 80%.

(B) At all three temperature settings, less than 60% of the sea turtle hatchlings were male, but at the minimum temperature setting used in the experiments, less than 60% of the sea turtle hatchlings were female.

(C) At 1.5 degrees above historic temperature norms, more than 40% of sea turtle hatchlings in the experiments conducted by the team were female, but at the maximum temperature setting used in the experiments, the percentage of sea turtle hatchlings that were female was significantly less.

(D) At 2.0 degrees above historic temperature norms, females accounted for, at most, 50% of sea turtle hatchlings, but at 2.5 degrees above historic temperature norms, more than 50% of all sea turtle hatchlings in the experiment were female.

5 ☐ Mark for Review

Building and Societal Structure Among Southeastern and Midwestern Native American Cultures

Culture	Mound type	Settlement type	Hierarchical political organization?
Woodland	Dome-shaped	Small villages	No
Mississippian	Flat-topped	Large cities	Yes
Mississippian descendants: Osage	None	Small villages	No
Mississippian descendants: Cherokee	None	Large towns	Yes

The Mississippian culture of the Midwest and Southeast was a Pre-Columbian Native American civilization. Large cities that rivaled the size of those in Europe served as hubs for political discourse, military action, religious rituals, craft production, and transcontinental trade. Unlike the smaller forest villages established by Native American tribes who called the woods home, Mississippian cities were most commonly located near a confluence of rivers to aid in the transportation of agricultural goods and manufactured items. While archaeologists are uncertain as to why Mississippian cities were abandoned, European diseases spreading along trade routes from Central America may have played a role. By the time that European colonists arrived, only remnants of the once-great Mississippian civilization remained, in the form of tribes such as the Cherokee and Osage. While the original Mississippian culture had vanished, the influence of the Mississippian legacy was apparent in _____

Which choice most effectively uses data from the table to complete the statement?

(A) the diversity of mound constructions utilized by their descendant tribes, the Cherokee and Osage, who each borrowed different aspects of Mississippian mound-building when constructing their own mounds.

(B) certain architectural and social aspects of the Cherokee tribe, whose larger town size and organized political hierarchy are consistent with those developed by their Mississippian ancestors.

(C) the Woodland tribe, which modeled the size of its settlements and organization of its political structure after the Mississippians after seeing the degree to which Mississippian settlements thrived.

(D) certain architectural and social aspects of the Osage tribe, whose small village size and lack of organized political hierarchy are consistent with those developed by their Mississippian ancestors.

Chapter 17
Charts Drill
Explanations

ANSWER KEY

1. B
2. D
3. A

4. A
5. B

CHARTS DRILL EXPLANATIONS

1. **B** This is a Charts question, as it asks for *data from the graph* that will *complete the text*. Read the title and variables from the graph. Then, read the text and highlight the text that references the information from the graph. The text states that *The Phantom of the Opera…is frequently compared to both Cats and Les Misérables*, but the final sentence utilizes the word *However*. The correct answer should offer accurate information from the graph that focuses on a difference between *Phantom* and the other two plays, rather than a similarity.

   - (A), (C), and (D) are wrong because they're inconsistent with the graph—*Phantom* had significantly more performances than *Grease*, *Cats*, and *Les Misérables*—it did not have a *similar* number of performances, nor did it have *fewer* than any of them.

   - (B) is correct because it's consistent with the graph and would show a difference between *Phantom* and the other two musicals to which it is compared.

2. **D** This is a Charts question, as it asks for *data in the graph that support the student's claim*. Read the title, key, and variables from the graph. Then, read the text and highlight the claim or argument that references the information from the graph. The last sentence states that *Europe's population distribution makes its citizens more prone to adoption of electric vehicles than those in the United States*. The correct answer should offer accurate information from the graph in support of this claim.

   - (A) is wrong because it's inconsistent with the graph—the energy demand in the "Other" category increased from 2016 to 2022 rather than *decreased*.

   - (B) and (C) are wrong because they're consistent with the graph but irrelevant to the claim—neither of these answers compares Europe to the United States as the claim does.

   - (D) is correct because it's consistent with the data in the graph and supports the highlighted claim.

3. **A** This is a Charts question, as it asks for *data from the table* that will *complete the statement*. Read the title and variables from the table. Then, read the text and highlight the statement that references the information from the table. The statement focuses on the *most utilized area, with 98 percent of parking spaces full that morning*. The correct answer should offer accurate information from the table that completes the highlighted statement.

   - (A) is correct because *Smithfield Terrace* is the location with 98% of parking spaces utilized.

- (B), (C), and (D) are wrong because none of those three locations had 98% of parking paces utilized.

4. **A** This is a Charts question, as it asks for *data in the graph that support the N.E.S.T. team's conclusion.* Read the title and variables from the graph. Then, read the text and highlight the claim or argument that references the information from the graph. The last sentence states that *as global temperatures increase above historic norms, shifting sex ratios could create an imbalance in sea turtle populations that negatively affects the current breeding rate of the species.* The correct answer should offer accurate information from the graph in support of this claim.

    - (A) is correct because it's consistent with the graph and supports the claim—at 1.5 degrees above historic norms, the ratio between females and males is almost even, but as the temperature increases to the maximum one studied, the ratio becomes 80% female, which is consistent with *shifting sex ratios.*

    - (B) is wrong because it's consistent with the graph but irrelevant to the claim—this answer does not provide support for *shifting sex ratios*, it only makes generalizations about the percentages of each sex at various points in the study.

    - (C) and (D) are wrong because they're not consistent with the data in the graph. For (C), at the maximum temperature, the percentage of female sea turtle hatchlings is significantly more than 40%, not *significantly less.* For (D), the percentage of female sea turtle hatchlings is already above 50% at 2.0 degrees above historic norms, not *at most* 50%.

5. **B** This is a Charts question, as it asks for *data from the table* that will *complete the statement.* Read the title, key, and variables from the graph. Then, read the text and highlight the claim or argument that references the information from the graph. The text says that *only remnants of the once-great Mississippian civilization remained, in the form of tribes such as the Cherokee and Osage*, but the civilization's *influence* was still *apparent* somehow. The correct answer should offer accurate information from the graph that completes the statement.

    - (A) is wrong because it's inconsistent with the graph—the Cherokee and Osage do not have diverse mound structure, as neither makes mounds at all.

    - (B) is correct because it's consistent with the graph and completes the statement—since the Cherokee tribe has both larger settlements and an organized political hierarchy as the original Mississippians did, this could be evidence of the influence of the Mississippians on their descendants.

    - (C) and (D) are wrong because they are inconsistent with the claim—the Woodland and the Osage tribe lack both the large town size and organized political hierarchy that was seen in the Mississippian culture.

Chapter 18
Conclusions Drill

Conclusions Drill

1 ☐ Mark for Review

Abby Kelley Foster was an abolitionist who delivered a series of lectures from the 1830s to the 1860s. After the Civil War, Foster shifted her focus to women's suffrage. While women did not enjoy such liberties as the right to vote, they still had to pay taxes on property. In the 1870s, Foster refused to pay taxes on her home as she declared she was being taxed without representation. Each time the government seized her home due to Foster's refusal, Foster's friends would purchase the home and return it to Foster. This act by Foster's friends could therefore serve as _____

Which choice most logically completes the text?

(A) a potential topic for future lectures by Foster.

(B) a means for Foster to continue her activism without financial hardship.

(C) an opportunity for Foster to discover how people of different backgrounds managed their finances.

(D) a chance for local governments to make money.

2 ☐ Mark for Review

A vacuum tube is an enclosed tube—with all gases removed—used in electronic devices to control the flow of electrons. Vacuum tubes could be used in electronic devices that required the amplification of voltage and the transfer of current, such as radios, televisions, and even computers. However, because vacuum tubes were often made of glass or ceramic, they could break easily during installation or during consumer use. Therefore, vacuum tubes were eventually supplanted by technology that _____

Which choice most logically completes the text?

(A) worked in similar ways but was cheaper to manufacture and store.

(B) was not so susceptible to structural damage.

(C) could be utilized for devices beyond radios, televisions, and computers.

(D) enabled the production of devices that didn't require the removal of gases.

3 🔖 Mark for Review

Archaeologists recently discovered bladed stone tools in southern India that they believe are approximately 385,000 years old. Prior research showed that African and European hominins started creating blades during independent technical revolutions that occurred 300,000 to 400,000 years ago; until now, there was no evidence of this technology from the same period found in India. Although it is possible that the stone tools came from migrating hominins from Africa, scientists believe it is more likely that

_____

Which choice most logically completes the text?

- (A) the development of bladed stone tools by Indian hominins occurred independently just as the African and European developments did.

- (B) Indian hominins learned to make bladed stone tools from migrating African hominins before perfecting these tools on their own.

- (C) Indian hominin bladed stone tools are uncommon and therefore more valued by collectors than those from Africa or Europe.

- (D) processes used to analyze bladed stone tools are not as effective on bladed tools of other materials.

4 🔖 Mark for Review

According to some art historians, Spanish still-life paintings of the seventeenth century were defined by their focus on common pantry items, such as food and cooking utensils. Some art critics, explaining that the kitchen was the heart of Spanish households, view these traditional still-life paintings as celebrations of Spanish culture. However, during this same period, painters began to portray more complex, elaborate subjects and often included human figures in the scenes. Called bodegónes—derived from the Spanish word for storehouse—these works differ from traditional still-life paintings in that they attempt to showcase a broader scope of Spanish life while still focusing on painting mastery. This development of bodegónes in the seventeenth century calls into question the idea that _____

Which choice most logically completes the text?

- (A) kitchen utensils were a more popular focal point of Spanish paintings than they were of paintings from other countries during the seventeenth century.

- (B) Spanish paintings of the seventeenth century may have depicted kitchen utensils that would not necessarily have been common in the average Spanish kitchen.

- (C) human interactions were a more important aspect of Spanish culture in the seventeenth century than food was.

- (D) Spanish still-life painting from that time should necessarily by defined by its focus on objects found in the kitchen.

5 ☐ Mark for Review

Initially, some researchers assumed that the James Webb Space Telescope (JWST) was intended as a replacement for the Hubble Space Telescope. One possibility for this assumption was that the Hubble had already been in space for 32 years when the JWST began its journey, and the Hubble's somewhat antiquated lens array could not provide accurate images of objects in deeper space. A statement released by the James Webb team sought to correct this assumption—the JWST is actually meant to be complementary to the Hubble—as both telescopes serve differing purposes in the analysis of celestial bodies. Since the JWST—with its larger, lighter mirror and more sensitive infrared instruments—is intended for viewing objects in deeper space, the James Webb team commented that _____

Which choice most logically completes the text?

(A) the data from deep space gathered by the Hubble Space Telescope will likely be more accurate than the data from nearby space gathered by the James Webb Space Telescope.

(B) celestial bodies in deep space are likely composed of different elements from those in nearby space.

(C) the Hubble Space Telescope may continue to serve a role in nearby space to complement the James Webb Space Telescope's role.

(D) getting clearer pictures of deep space through a larger, lighter mirror and more sensitive infrared equipment will help researchers determine which innovations will be necessary to explore space further.

Chapter 19
Conclusions Drill
Explanations

ANSWER KEY

1. B
2. B
3. A

4. D
5. C

CONCLUSIONS DRILL EXPLANATIONS

1. **B** This is a Conclusions question, as it asks what *most logically completes the text*. Look for and highlight the main focus of the text, which is the activism of *Abby Kelley Foster*. Then, highlight the main points made regarding this focus, which is that *Foster refused to pay taxes on her home as she declared she was being taxed without representation* and *Foster's friends would purchase the home and return it to Foster*. Therefore, not having to worry about paying to get her home back likely would have facilitated Foster continuing to refuse to pay the taxes as a means of protest. The correct answer should be as consistent as possible with this conclusion.

    - (A) is wrong because it misuses *lectures* from the first sentence, which were part of Foster's abolitionism, not her activism for women's suffrage.

    - (B) is correct because it's consistent with the highlighted sentences about Foster's activism and how her friends helped her.

    - (C) is wrong because the text does not focus on other people *managing their finances* but rather on Foster's activism.

    - (D) is wrong because it goes beyond what the text can support—while the local government would have made money each time Foster's friends paid off her house, the text doesn't support that the government viewed Foster's refusal as an opportunity in this way.

2. **B** This is a Conclusions question, as it asks what *most logically completes the text*. Look for and highlight the main focus of the text, which is the *vacuum tube*. Then, highlight the main point made regarding this focus, which is that *because vacuum tubes were often made of glass or ceramic, they could break easily during installation or during consumer use*. Therefore, any technology that would replace the vacuum tubes should likely address this issue. The correct answer should be as consistent as possible with this conclusion.

    - (A), (C), and (D) are wrong because they each go beyond what the text can support—there's no evidence in the text that the new technology would be *cheaper to manufacturer*, used in additional *devices*, or not *require the removal of gases*.

- (B) is correct because it's consistent with the highlighted sentences about the weakness of vacuum tubes—they could *break easily*, so the technology that supplants, or replaces them, would ideally be *not so susceptible to structural damage*.

3. **A** This is a Conclusions question, as it asks what *most logically completes the text*. Look for and highlight the main focus of the text, which is the discovery of *bladed stone tools in southern India*. Then, highlight the main point made regarding this focus, which is that *African and European hominins started creating blades during independent technical revolutions*, but there was *no evidence* of this in India before the discovery. Note that the text says *it is possible* that the Indian *stone tools came from migrating hominins from Africa*, but the word *Although* indicates the author disagrees with this. Therefore, based on the second sentence, it's most likely that the author thinks the Indian development of stone tools was *independent*, just like the African and European ones were. The correct answer should be as consistent as possible with this conclusion.

   - (A) is correct because it's consistent with what the highlighted sentences say about the Indian development of bladed stone tools.

   - (B) is wrong because it's the opposite of what the text concludes—the author contradicts this idea in the last sentence with the word *Although*.

   - (C) and (D) are wrong because certain tools being *more valued* or the *processes* used to analyze these tools are not discussed within the text.

4. **D** This is a Conclusions question, as it asks what *most logically completes the text*. Look for and highlight the main focus of the text, which is *traditional still-life paintings* and a variant called *bodegónes*. Then, highlight the main point made regarding this focus, which is that *during this same period, painters began to portray more complex, elaborate subjects and often include human figures in the scenes*. Therefore, some artists still did traditional still-life paintings of food and kitchen utensils, while others started doing more complex bodegónes featuring more of Spanish culture, such as its people. The correct answer should be as consistent as possible with this conclusion.

   - (A) is wrong because no *other countries* are mentioned in the text.

   - (B) and (C) are wrong because they go beyond what the text can support—it's not known from the text which *kitchen utensils* were *common* to the average kitchen, nor is it stated which *aspect of Spanish culture* was most important to Spaniards.

   - (D) is correct because it's consistent with what the highlighted sentences says about both traditional still-life paintings and bodegónes—this answer accounts for the idea that common pantry items found in a kitchen were not the only focus of Spanish still-life paintings in the seventeenth century.

5.   **C**   This is a Conclusions question, as it asks what *most logically completes the text*. Look for and highlight the main focus of the text, which is the *James Webb Space Telescope* and the *Hubble Space Telescope*. Then, highlight the main point made regarding this focus, which is that the *JWST is actually meant to be complementary to the Hubble*. Since the text goes on to say that the JWST is *intended for viewing objects in deeper space*, it's likely that the Hubble will be used for nearby space, since the two are meant to serve complementary roles. The correct answer should be as consistent as possible with this conclusion.

- (A) is wrong because it's the opposite of what's stated or implied by the text—the JWST isn't meant for *nearby* space at all, but even if it were, the text implies that its more advanced technology will provide better images than does the Hubble regardless of which region of space it observes.

- (B) is wrong because the *elements* that compose celestial bodies are not discussed in the text.

- (C) is correct because it's consistent with what the highlighted sentences imply about each telescope's roles.

- (D) is wrong because it misuses *larger, lighter mirror* and *more sensitive infrared equipment* to make an unsupported conclusion about future *innovations*.

Chapter 20
Writing Diagnostic Drill

Writing Diagnostic Drill

1 ☐ Mark for Review

German chemist Otto Hahn faced a scientific mystery. Some uranium that he had exposed to neutrons suddenly began behaving identically to barium, but _____ He sent the results to a former colleague, physicist Lise Meitner, who explained that the nuclei of the uranium atoms must have split to form barium and another lighter element, releasing a large amount of energy; thus, nuclear fission was discovered.

Which choice completes the text so that it conforms to the conventions of Standard English?

Ⓐ uranium could turn into barium?

Ⓑ how could uranium turn into barium?

Ⓒ uranium could turn into barium.

Ⓓ how could uranium turn into barium.

2 ☐ Mark for Review

Dr. Jennifer Doudna, a renowned biochemist, opened unprecedented possibilities for precision genome editing with her groundbreaking work on CRISPR-Cas9 gene editing, _____ her the Nobel Prize in Chemistry.

Which choice completes the text so that it conforms to the conventions of Standard English?

Ⓐ earned

Ⓑ will earn

Ⓒ has earned

Ⓓ earning

3° ☐ Mark for Review

Some animals display very characteristic symptoms of rabies, such as foaming at the mouth and erratic behaviors, but vampire bats are unique. A study at The Ohio State University found that rabid vampire bats _____ from other individuals and limit their typical grooming behavior.

Which choice completes the text so that it conforms to the conventions of Standard English?

Ⓐ withdraw

Ⓑ having withdrawn

Ⓒ to withdraw

Ⓓ withdrawing

4 ☐ Mark for Review

Visual artist Simon Fujiwara's installation *Hope House* is a full-scale immersive replica of the house where Anne Frank, while hiding during World War II, wrote her highly influential _____ the ways in which capitalism and media culture contort authentic reality, Fujiwara opted to base his reconstructed house on a 3D model sold in a museum gift shop rather than on the actual Anne Frank House.

Which choice completes the text so that it conforms to the conventions of Standard English?

- (A) diary. Exploring
- (B) diary, exploring
- (C) diary exploring
- (D) diary and exploring

5 ☐ Mark for Review

Unlike most birds, the common cuckoo, a widespread summer migrant to Europe and Asia that winters in Africa, does not build its own _____ it lays its eggs in the nests of other bird species, tricking the unsuspecting hosts into incubating and raising its offspring. This adaptation is called brood parasitism, a survival strategy that may have evolved due to the adult cuckoo's preference for a diet of hairy caterpillars that can irritate the guts of newborn cuckoos.

Which choice completes the text so that it conforms to the conventions of Standard English?

- (A) nest, instead,
- (B) nest; instead,
- (C) nest, instead;
- (D) nest instead,

6 ☐ Mark for Review

A group of scientists led by Sandra Gordon-Salant at the University of Maryland has found that individuals can be trained to follow fast talkers in noisy _____ the training could help restore the ability of older individuals to discriminate sounds in noisy environments to a level similar to that of young adults.

Which choice completes the text so that it conforms to the conventions of Standard English?

- (A) environments, while
- (B) environments while
- (C) environments:
- (D) environments

7 ☐ Mark for Review

Although the material cyanoacrylate was discovered in _____ wasn't until 1951 that inventor Harry Coover and his team realized that it could be used as a powerful adhesive. Originally marketed in 1958 under the name "Eastman #910," the material would eventually be known as Super Glue.

Which choice completes the text so that it conforms to the conventions of Standard English?

- (A) 1942, it
- (B) 1942 it
- (C) 1942; it
- (D) 1942. It

8 ☐ Mark for Review

Kronan was a warship in the Swedish Navy. The _____ built over four years starting in 1668, was one of the largest ships at the time. Unfortunately, it sank in 1676 during the Battle of Öland in the Scanian War.

Which choice completes the text so that it conforms to the conventions of Standard English?

(A) ship—

(B) ship;

(C) ship,

(D) ship

9 ☐ Mark for Review

Known as the *Compendium of Materia* _____ in English, the *Bencao Gangmu* is a Chinese book compiled by Li Shizhen that includes information about medicine, natural history, and Chinese herbology.

Which choice completes the text so that it conforms to the conventions of Standard English?

(A) *Medica*,

(B) *Medica*;

(C) *Medica*:

(D) *Medica*

10 ☐ Mark for Review

Renowned for her captivating portraits of musicians and celebrities, Annie _____ was the natural choice to photograph the cover images of some of *Rolling Stone* magazine's most iconic editions.

Which choice completes the text so that it conforms to the conventions of Standard English?

(A) Leibovitz—

(B) Leibovitz:

(C) Leibovitz,

(D) Leibovitz

11 ☐ Mark for Review

The Great Green Wall initiative, set up by the African Union, aims to combat desertification, land degradation, and climate change in the Sahel region of _____ planting a green belt of trees across the continent from west to east.

Which choice completes the text so that it conforms to the conventions of Standard English?

(A) Africa by

(B) Africa, by

(C) Africa; by

(D) Africa. By

12 ☐ Mark for Review

The ancient Greek cynics believed that eduaimonia, the state of flourishing and self-actualization, was the purpose of _____ the practice of abstaining from pleasures and conveniences, was the proper behavior; and that nomos, society's customs and rules, ought to be publicly disrespected.

Which choice completes the text so that it conforms to the conventions of Standard English?

Ⓐ life, that asceticism,

Ⓑ life; that asceticism,

Ⓒ life, that asceticism:

Ⓓ life; that asceticism

13 ☐ Mark for Review

After being expelled from school for violent behavior, Australian artist Lin Onus taught himself mechanical and painting skills. Eventually, Onus became a painter, sculptor, and filmmaker. He _____ credited as the sound producer on *Blackfire*, a 1972 film thought to be the first directed by an Indigenous Australian filmmaker.

Which choice completes the text so that it conforms to the conventions of Standard English?

Ⓐ were being

Ⓑ were

Ⓒ are

Ⓓ is

14 ☐ Mark for Review

The comet known as Hale-Bopp was simultaneously discovered by two individuals on July 23, 1995. It was visible to the naked eye for a record-breaking 18 months. Catching a glimpse of one of the 4,500 known comets _____ many people to become interested in astronomy and seek out other phenomena in the sky, so the Hale-Bopp comet greatly increased society's interest in astronomy.

Which choice completes the text so that it conforms to the conventions of Standard English?

Ⓐ prompts

Ⓑ prompt

Ⓒ have prompted

Ⓓ are prompting

15 ☐ Mark for Review

As snow falls each year, ice layers form on top of each other with the oldest layer at the bottom. By analyzing the physical properties of the ice and any debris found frozen within it, scientists today _____ the climate from different time periods in the Earth's past. Combined with fossil and DNA evidence, such reconstructions allow scientists to develop possible evolutionary hypotheses for different species.

Which choice completes the text so that it conforms to the conventions of Standard English?

(A) can reconstruct

(B) will reconstruct

(C) were reconstructing

(D) had reconstructed

16 ☐ Mark for Review

Oda Nobunaga, known as the "Great Unifier," was the leader of the Oda clan and _____ wars against other clans in order to unite the country of Japan.

Which choice completes the text so that it conforms to the conventions of Standard English?

(A) launches

(B) launched

(C) had launched

(D) was launching

17 ☐ Mark for Review

In his memoir, *A Long Way Gone,* Ishmael Beah describes his life as a forced child soldier in 1990s Sierra Leone. After he was rescued, Beah was invited to New York to speak at the United Nations and shared with _____ members the devastating effects that war in his country had had on children.

Which choice completes the text so that it conforms to the conventions of Standard English?

(A) their

(B) they're

(C) it's

(D) its

18 ▢ Mark for Review

According to research performed at Duke University, plants may be able to turn on defense mechanisms when threatened. When plants detect a pathogen, _____ energy to creating proteins that can help fight the infection and stop producing proteins used for everyday functions, such as photosynthesis and growth.

Which choice completes the text so that it conforms to the conventions of Standard English?

Ⓐ it devotes

Ⓑ they devote

Ⓒ those devote

Ⓓ one devotes

19 ▢ Mark for Review

The English royal charter known as Magna Carta is often viewed as one of the founding documents of modern democracy. However, it was fundamentally concerned with the balance of power between the nobility and the monarchy and had little to say about common _____ and privileges.

Which choice completes the text so that it conforms to the conventions of Standard English?

Ⓐ peoples rights

Ⓑ people's rights

Ⓒ peoples right's

Ⓓ people's rights'

20 ▢ Mark for Review

Swedish painter Hilma af Klint was one of the first to create purely abstract art: visual art with no references to the physical world. Often mistaken for works by much later artists, _____ held a deep spiritual meaning for her.

Which choice completes the text so that it conforms to the conventions of Standard English?

Ⓐ her use of geometric patterns of bright pastel colors in her paintings

Ⓑ the bright pastel colors of the geometric patterns in her paintings

Ⓒ she filled her paintings with geometric patterns of bright pastel colors, which

Ⓓ her paintings are filled with geometric patterns of bright pastel colors, which

21 ☐ Mark for Review

Many students in Germany visit *Brennender Berg*, a monument found in a deep gorge, on field trips. The natural monument includes a smoldering fire that still burns after being ignited in the mid-1600s. The exact cause of the ignition is still a mystery, and many legends have developed and gained popularity; _____ one legend states that a shepherd intentionally started the fire by lighting a tree stump.

Which choice completes the text with the most logical transition?

- Ⓐ furthermore,
- Ⓑ however,
- Ⓒ for example,
- Ⓓ eventually,

22 ☐ Mark for Review

Before the introduction of standard time, cities and towns would set their clocks based on the position of the sun. This system worked well until Britain introduced its railway system in the 1820s. The trains could travel long distances quickly, requiring clocks to be reset constantly as the trains traveled through various towns. _____ Britain established Greenwich Mean Time, and all clocks in Britain were set to the same time.

Which choice completes the text with the most logical transition?

- Ⓐ Likewise,
- Ⓑ Still,
- Ⓒ Thus,
- Ⓓ However,

23 ☐ Mark for Review

While researching a topic, a student has taken the following notes:

- Researchers recently found that fish more strongly react to motion below them than above them.

- In a 2022 study, Emma Alexander developed a computer model that combined simulations of zebrafish's brains and their native environments in India.

- She was initially uncertain why fish look down when they swim.

- She used her computer model to show that the fish use the stable riverbed below them to self-stabilize.

- Self-stabilization allows fish to swim against the current and to avoid being swept away.

The student wants to present the study and its findings. Which choice most effectively uses relevant information from the notes to accomplish this goal?

(A) A 2022 study by Alexander focused on zebrafish in India.

(B) In a 2022 study, Alexander used a computer model to show that zebrafish in India look down as they swim in order to self-stabilize and prevent themselves from being swept away.

(C) In 2022, Alexander studied zebrafish and was initially uncertain why the fish look down when they swim.

(D) In a 2022 study, Alexander used a computer model to simulate zebrafish swimming in their native environments in India.

24 ☐ Mark for Review

While researching a topic, a student has taken the following notes:

- Betelgeuse is one of the stars in the constellation Orion.

- It is a red supergiant.

- It is an M-type star and its visual magnitude (brightness) is 0.50.

- Rigel is another star in the constellation Orion.

- It is a blue supergiant.

- Its spectral type is B and its visual magnitude (brightness) is 0.13.

The student wants to compare the brightness of the two stars. Which choice most effectively uses relevant information from the notes to accomplish this goal?

(A) Two of the stars in the constellation Orion are Betelgeuse and Rigel.

(B) Betelgeuse is a red supergiant in the constellation Orion and has a visual magnitude (brightness) of 0.50.

(C) While both stars are in the constellation Orion, Betelgeuse has a visual magnitude (brightness) of 0.50 and Rigel has a visual magnitude (brightness) of 0.13.

(D) Betelgeuse is a red supergiant, and Rigel is a blue supergiant.

Chapter 21
Writing Diagnostic
Drill Explanations

WHAT'S NEXT

Now that you have warmed up with many different types of Digital PSAT Writing questions, review the explanations (especially for questions that you got wrong), and choose where to go next. The list below will tell you which drill to go to for more questions from that topic. You decide if that's based on the questions you missed or if it's for more practice in a topic for which you are close to achieving proficiency. Use the list below to pick your next drills.

Answer Key

Diagnostic Writing Drill							
Q #	Ans.	✔	Drill	Q #	Ans.	✔	Drill
1	B		Complete Sentences	13	D		Verbs
2	D		Complete Sentences	14	A		Verbs
3	A		Complete Sentences	15	A		Verbs
4	A		Connecting Clauses	16	B		Verbs
5	B		Connecting Clauses	17	D		Pronouns and Nouns
6	C		Connecting Clauses	18	B		Pronouns and Nouns
7	A		Connecting Clauses	19	B		Pronouns and Nouns
8	C		Other Punctuation Topics	20	D		Modifiers
9	D		Other Punctuation Topics	21	C		Transitions
10	D		Other Punctuation Topics	22	C		Transitions
11	A		Other Punctuation Topics	23	B		Rhetorical Synthesis
12	B		Other Punctuation Topics	24	C		Rhetorical Synthesis

WRITING DIAGNOSTIC DRILL EXPLANATIONS

1. **B** In this Rules question, periods and question marks are changing in the answer choices, so it's testing questions versus statements. The previous sentence states that *Otto Hahn faced a scientific mystery*, and the sentence after this one states that Meitner *explained* what *must have* happened. Therefore, the second part of this sentence should be a question. Eliminate answers that aren't correctly written as questions.

    - (A) is wrong because it has a question mark but is written as a statement.

    - (B) is correct because it's correctly written as a question.

    - (C) and (D) are wrong because they are statements.

2. **D** In this Rules question, verb forms are changing in the answer choices, so it's testing sentence structure. The sentence already contains an independent clause followed by a comma. Thus, the part after the comma must be a phrase that describes Doudna's work. Eliminate any answer that does not correctly form this phrase.

    - (A), (B), and (C) are wrong because each of them is in main verb form, but there is no subject for this verb.

    - (D) is correct because the *-ing* form correctly produces a describing phrase that makes it clear that her work earned her this prize.

3. **A** In this Rules question, verbs are changing in the answer choices, so it's testing consistency with verbs. In this case, the verb is part of a list of two things that vampire bats do, the second of which is *limit their typical grooming behavior*. Highlight the word *limit*, which the verb in the answer should be consistent with. Eliminate any answer that isn't consistent with *limit*.

    - (A) is correct because *withdraw* is in the same tense and form as *limit*.

    - (B), (C), and (D) are wrong because *having withdrawn, to withdraw,* and *withdrawing* aren't consistent with *limit*.

4. **A** In this Rules question, punctuation is changing in the answer choices. Look for independent clauses. The first part of the sentence says *Fujiwara's installation Hope House is a full-scale immersive replica of the house where Anne Frank...wrote her highly influential diary*, which is an independent clause. The second part says *exploring the ways in which capitalism and media culture contort authentic reality, Fujiwara opted to base his reconstructed house on a 3D model...*, which is also an independent clause. Eliminate any answer that can't correctly connect two independent clauses.

    - (A) is correct because the period makes each independent clause its own sentence, which is fine.

    - (B) is wrong because a comma without a coordinating conjunction (FANBOYS) can't connect two independent clauses.

- (C) is wrong because some type of punctuation is needed in order to connect two independent clauses.

- (D) is wrong because a coordinating conjunction (*and*) without a comma can't connect two independent clauses.

5. **B** In this Rules question, punctuation with a transition is changing in the answer choices. Look for independent clauses. The first part of the sentence says *Unlike most birds, the common cuckoo…does not build its own nest*. There is an option to add *instead* to this independent clause, but this is the first part of the text, so it's not contrasting with something that came before. The second part of the sentence does contrast with the first part, so *instead* belongs in the second part of the sentence. Eliminate options with *instead* in the first part.

- (A) and (D) are wrong because the sentence contains two independent clauses, which cannot be connected with commas alone.

- (B) is correct because it puts *instead* with the second independent clause and puts a semicolon between the two independent clauses.

- (C) is wrong because it puts *instead* with the first independent clause.

6. **C** In this Rules question, punctuation is changing in the answer choices. Look for independent clauses. The first part of the sentence says *A group of scientists…has found that individuals can be trained to follow fast talkers in noisy environments*, which is an independent clause. The second part of the sentence says *the training could help restore the ability of older individuals to discriminate sounds…*, which is also an independent clause. Eliminate any option that doesn't correctly connect two independent clauses.

- (A) and (B) are wrong because the second part of the sentence doesn't disagree with the first as *while* implies.

- (C) is correct because a colon can connect two independent clauses.

- (D) is wrong because some type of punctuation is needed in order to connect two independent clauses.

7. **A** In this Rules question, punctuation is changing in the answer choices. Look for independent clauses. The first part of the sentence says *Although the material cyanoacrylate was discovered in 1942*, which is a dependent clause. The second part of the sentence says *it wasn't until 1951 that inventor Harry Coover and his team realized that it could be used as a powerful adhesive*, which is an independent clause. Eliminate any option that doesn't correctly connect a dependent + an independent clause.

- (A) is correct because dependent + independent can be connected with a comma.

- (B) is wrong because a comma is needed to connect the dependent clause to the independent clause in this case.

- (C) and (D) are wrong because dependent + independent cannot be connected with punctuation other than a comma.

8. **C** In this Rules question, punctuation is changing in the answer choices. The main meaning of the sentence is *The ship…was one of the largest ships at the time.* The phrase *built over four years starting in 1668* has a comma after it, so it must have a comma before it to show that it is not essential to the meaning of the sentence. Eliminate answers that do not have a comma before the phrase.

    - (A), (B), and (D) are wrong because they don't use a comma.

    - (C) is correct because it uses a comma before the non-essential phrase.

9. **D** In this Rules question, punctuation is changing in the answer choices. There is an option to put punctuation before the phrase *in English*, but this phrase is essential in order to complete the introductory phrase, so there is no reason to use punctuation here. Eliminate answers that have punctuation.

    - (A), (B), and (C) are wrong because there is no reason to use punctuation after *Medica*.

    - (D) is correct because no punctuation is needed.

10. **D** In this Rules question, punctuation is changing in the answer choices. The blank gives the option to put punctuation between the subject of the sentence (*Annie Leibovitz*) and its verb (*was*), and there is no other punctuation in between. A single punctuation mark can't separate a subject and its verb, so eliminate answers with punctuation.

    - (A), (B), and (C) are wrong because a single punctuation mark can't come between a subject and its verb.

    - (D) is correct because no punctuation should be used here.

11. **A** In this Rules question, punctuation is changing in the answer choices. The punctuation appears before the phrase *by planting a green belt of trees across the continent from west to east*, but there shouldn't be punctuation before this phrase because it's used to specify the Great Green Wall initiative's method. Eliminate answers with punctuation.

    - (A) is correct because no punctuation should be used here, as the phrase is essential to the sentence's meaning.

    - (B), (C), and (D) are wrong because there isn't a reason to use punctuation.

12. **B** In this Rules question, commas and semicolons are changing in the answer choices. The sentence already contains a semicolon near the end, and the part after it is not an independent clause, which suggests that the sentence contains a list separated by semicolons. Use the third example to determine the structure of each item: "that," Greek term, comma, definition, comma, belief. Make an annotation of this pattern and eliminate any answer that doesn't follow it.

    - (A) and (C) are wrong because they don't have a semicolon after the first item, which ends with *life.*

- (B) is correct because it follows the pattern of the third item.

- (D) is wrong because a comma should follow the Greek term, *asceticism*.

13. **D** In this Rules question, verbs are changing in the answer choices, so it's testing consistency with verbs. Find and highlight the subject, *He*, which is singular, so a singular verb is needed. Write an annotation saying "singular." Eliminate any answer that is not singular.

    - (A), (B), and (C) are wrong because they are plural.

    - (D) is correct because it's singular.

14. **A** In this Rules question, verbs are changing in the answer choices, so it's testing consistency with verbs. Find and highlight the subject, *Catching*, which is singular, so a singular verb is needed. Write an annotation saying "singular." Eliminate any answer that is not singular.

    - (A) is correct because it's singular.

    - (B), (C), and (D) are wrong because they are plural.

15. **A** In this Rules question, verbs are changing in the answer choices, so it's testing consistency with verbs. Find and highlight the subject, *scientists*, which is plural, so a plural verb is needed. All of the answers work with a plural subject, so look for a clue regarding tense. This sentence contains the word *today*. Highlight the word *today* and write an annotation that says "present." Eliminate any answer not in present tense.

    - (A) is correct because it's in present tense.

    - (B) is wrong because it's in future tense.

    - (C) and (D) are wrong because they're in past tense.

16. **B** In this Rules question, verbs are changing in the answer choices, so it's testing consistency with verbs. Find and highlight the subject, *Oda Nobunaga*, which is singular, so a singular verb is needed. All of the answers work with a singular subject, so look for a clue regarding tense. This sentence uses a past tense verb: *was*. Highlight this verb and write an annotation that says "past." Eliminate any answer not in past tense.

    - (A) is wrong because it's in present tense.

    - (B) is correct because it's in past tense.

    - (C) is wrong because this form of past tense is used for an event that happened prior to some other past event, which isn't suggested here.

    - (D) is wrong because this form of past tense is used while a past event is occurring, but this sentence refers to something once it has already ended.

17. **D**   In this Rules question, pronouns and apostrophes are changing in the answer choices, so it's testing consistency with pronouns. Find and highlight the phrase that the pronoun refers back to: *the United Nations*. This phrase is singular, so in order to be consistent, a singular pronoun is needed. Eliminate any answer that isn't consistent with *the United Nations* or is incorrectly punctuated.

- (A) and (B) are wrong because they are plural.

- (C) is wrong because it means "it is."

- (D) is correct because it is singular and possessive.

18. **B**   In this Rules question, pronouns are changing in the answer choices, so it's testing consistency with pronouns. Find and highlight the word the pronoun refers back to, *plants*, which is plural, so a plural pronoun is needed. Write an annotation saying "plural." Eliminate any answer that isn't plural or doesn't clearly refer back to *plants*.

- (A) is wrong because it is singular.

- (B) is correct because *they* is plural and is consistent with *plants*.

- (C) and (D) are wrong because *those* and *one* don't refer back to a specific thing.

19. **B**   In this Rules question, apostrophes with nouns are changing in the answer choices. Determine whether each word possesses anything. The people possess the rights, but the rights don't possess anything. Eliminate any answer that doesn't match this.

- (A) and (C) are wrong because *people* should have an apostrophe.

- (B) is correct because *people* is possessive and *rights* is not.

- (D) is wrong because *rights* shouldn't be possessive.

20. **D**   In this Rules question, the subjects of the answers are changing, which suggests it may be testing modifiers. Look for and highlight a modifying phrase: *Often mistaken for works by much later artists*. Whatever is *mistaken for* later works needs to come immediately after the comma. Eliminate any answer that doesn't start with something that can be *mistaken for* later works.

- (A), (B), and (C) are wrong because *her use of geometric patterns*, *the bright pastel colors*, and *she* can't be *mistaken for works* by later artists.

- (D) is correct because *her paintings* can be *mistaken for works* by later artists.

21. **C** This is a transition question, so highlight ideas that relate to each other. The first part of the sentence says *The exact cause of the ignition is still a mystery, and many legends have developed and gained popularity,* and the second part of the sentence states what one of the legends is. These ideas agree, so a same-direction transition is needed. Make an annotation that says "agree." Eliminate any answer that doesn't match.

- (A) is wrong because this part of the sentence is not an additional point from the first part of the sentence.

- (B) is wrong because *however* is an opposite-direction transition.

- (C) is correct because this part of the sentence provides an example of one of the *legends*.

- (D) is wrong because this part of the sentence doesn't indicate something that will happen in the future.

22. **C** This is a transition question, so highlight ideas that relate to each other. The preceding sentences explain that the earlier time system *worked well until Britain introduced its railway system*, which caused *clocks to be reset constantly*, and this sentence explains what happened as a result, in order to solve the new problem. These ideas agree, so a same-direction transition is needed. Make an annotation that says "agree." Eliminate any answer that doesn't match.

- (A) is wrong because this sentence is not a description of something similar to the previous sentence.

- (B) and (D) are wrong because *Still* and *However* are opposite-direction transitions.

- (C) is correct because this sentence is a result of the previous sentence.

23. **B** This is a Rhetorical Synthesis question, so highlight the goal(s) stated in the question: *present the study and its findings*. Eliminate any answer that doesn't fulfill this purpose.

- (A), (C), and (D) are wrong because they mention the study, but not *its findings*.

- (B) is correct because it presents *the study and its findings*.

24. **C** This is a Rhetorical Synthesis question, so highlight the goal(s) stated in the question: *compare the brightness of the two stars*. Eliminate any answer that doesn't fulfill this purpose.

- (A) and (D) are wrong because they mention the two stars but don't compare their *brightness*.

- (B) is wrong because it mentions the *brightness* of only one of the two stars.

- (C) is correct because it compares *the brightness of the two stars*.

Chapter 22
Complete Sentences
Drill

Complete Sentences Drill

1 🔖 Mark for Review

Studies have shown that mindfulness-based stress reduction, or MBSR, can decrease anxiety. Researchers at Georgetown University questioned the efficacy of MBSR. If the effectiveness of MBSR were compared to that of anti-anxiety medication, _____ The researchers designed a study to find out the answer.

Which choice completes the text so that it conforms to the conventions of Standard English?

(A) MBSR would be as effective in treating anxiety?

(B) would MBSR be as effective in treating anxiety?

(C) would MBSR be as effective in treating anxiety.

(D) MBSR would be as effective in treating anxiety.

2 🔖 Mark for Review

In the late 1990s and early 2000s, the stock price of internet-based companies ballooned, with not-yet-profitable companies selling for much more than their fair valuation price. Some economists _____ that the "dot com bubble" and the following crash were the result of speculation and hype, while others contend that the regulatory environment could have prevented the economic turmoil.

Which choice completes the text so that it conforms to the conventions of Standard English?

(A) asserting

(B) assert

(C) having asserted

(D) to assert

3 ☐ Mark for Review

American ophthalmologist Patricia Bath discovered that African American people developed glaucoma leading to blindness at a rate eight times higher than that of other people. Bath pioneered the concept of "community ophthalmology" _____ combat this inequity and reduce the rate of preventable blindness in underserved communities in the United States.

Which choice completes the text so that it conforms to the conventions of Standard English?

- Ⓐ helped
- Ⓑ helping
- Ⓒ having helped
- Ⓓ to help

4 ☐ Mark for Review

Many early Greek thinkers concerned themselves with the problem of _____ Thales stated that the fundamental substance was water, while Anaximenes and Heraclitus argued in favor of air and fire, respectively. Empedocles suggested that instead of just one essential substance, there were four elements: water, air, fire, and earth.

Which choice completes the text so that it conforms to the conventions of Standard English?

- Ⓐ what the world is composed of at a fundamental level.
- Ⓑ what is the world composed of at a fundamental level.
- Ⓒ what is the world composed of at a fundamental level?
- Ⓓ what the world is composed of at a fundamental level?

5 ☐ Mark for Review

One of the earliest surviving novels of Western literature is *The Satyricon*, believed to have been written by Gaius Petronius in the late 1st century CE. The novel, which today exists only in fragments, _____ the episodic and chaotic travels of Encolpius, an educated young man, and his companions and satirized the moral decadence of ancient Rome under the reign of Emperor Nero.

Which choice completes the text so that it conforms to the conventions of Standard English?

- Ⓐ depicts
- Ⓑ to depict
- Ⓒ depicted
- Ⓓ depicting

Chapter 23
Complete Sentences
Drill Explanations

ANSWER KEY

1. B
2. B
3. D

4. A
5. C

COMPLETE SENTENCES DRILL EXPLANATIONS

1. **B** In this Rules question, periods and question marks are changing in the answer choices, so it's testing questions versus statements. The following sentence states that the researchers wanted to *find out the answer*, so the sentence with the blank must be a question. Eliminate answers that aren't correctly written as questions.

   - (A) is wrong because it has a question mark but is written as a statement.

   - (B) is correct because it's correctly written as a question.

   - (C) and (D) are wrong because they are statements.

2. **B** In this Rules question, verb forms are changing in the answer choices, so it's testing sentence structure. The subject of the sentence is *economists*, and there is no main verb, so the answer must provide the main verb. Eliminate any answer that isn't in the correct form to be the main verb.

   - (A) and (C) are wrong because an *-ing* verb can't be the main verb in a sentence.

   - (B) is correct because it's in the right form to be the main verb.

   - (D) is wrong because a "to" verb can't be the main verb in a sentence.

3. **D** In this Rules question, verb forms are changing in the answer choices, so it's testing sentence structure. The sentence already has a subject (*Bath*) and a main verb (*pioneered*), so the part of the sentence with the blank should form a phrase that elaborates on what Bath did. Eliminate any answer that does not make the phrase clear and correct.

   - (A) is wrong because it is in main verb form, but the sentence already has a main verb and there is no conjunction (such as *and*) to suggest that this verb would also apply to the subject.

   - (B) and (C) are wrong because *helping* and *having helped* are not consistent with the later verb *reduce*.

   - (D) is correct because the word *to* properly conveys that this was Bath's purpose and *to help combat…and reduce…* is consistent.

4. **A**   In this Rules question, periods and question marks are changing in the answer choices, so it's testing questions versus statements. The sentence states a *problem* that *early Greek thinkers* were concerned with, so the second part of the sentence should be a statement. Eliminate answers that aren't correctly written as statements.

-   (A) is correct because it's correctly written as a statement.

-   (B) is wrong because it has a period but is written as a question.

-   (C) and (D) are wrong because they are questions.

5. **C**   In this Rules question, verb forms are changing in the answer choices, so it's testing sentence structure. In this case, the verb is part of a list of two things that the novel did, the second of which is *satirized*. Highlight the word *satirized*, which the verb in the answer should be consistent with. Eliminate any answer that isn't consistent with *satirized*.

-   (A), (B), and (D) are wrong because they're not consistent with *satirized*.

-   (C) is correct because *depicted* is in the same tense and form as *satirized*.

Chapter 24
Connecting Clauses
Drill

Connecting Clauses Drill

1 Mark for Review

The need to remove microplastics, tiny fragments of plastic materials that pose a threat to marine ecosystems (as well as humans), is an increasingly urgent priority. Scientists are starting to experiment with a device called a triboelectric nanogenerator (TENG) and electrophoresis, a technique typically used to separate DNA molecules, to create eco-friendly filters for _____ TENG requires no external power source, so it can operate anywhere in the ocean.

Which choice completes the text so that it conforms to the conventions of Standard English?

(A) microplastics, the

(B) microplastics the

(C) microplastics. The

(D) microplastics and the

2 Mark for Review

Pablo Picasso's early Blue Period paintings are generally considered more facile and less creatively complex than his later groundbreaking _____ these paintings impressed collectors Leo and Gertrude Stein, two important champions of Picasso who helped establish him as a major figure in the art world.

Which choice completes the text so that it conforms to the conventions of Standard English?

(A) work but

(B) work

(C) work,

(D) work, but

3 Mark for Review

Though Austrian tennis player Hans Redl lost his left arm during World War _____ he continued his tennis career by developing a new serving technique, eventually competing multiple times at Wimbledon.

Which choice completes the text so that it conforms to the conventions of Standard English?

(A) II, and

(B) II;

(C) II

(D) II,

4 ☐ Mark for Review

Although relatively recently corroborated by satellite data, the mysterious occurrence of milky seas, whereby parts of the ocean seem to glow a snowy white color, has been observed and recorded by sailors for hundreds of years, even appearing in two popular works of 19th-century _____ *Moby Dick*, by Herman Melville, and *20,000 Leagues Under the Sea*, by Jules Verne.

Which choice completes the text so that it conforms to the conventions of Standard English?

Ⓐ literature:

Ⓑ literature,

Ⓒ literature;

Ⓓ literature

5 ☐ Mark for Review

The belief that tiny worms living inside one's teeth and feeding on them from the inside were responsible for various dental ailments, including cavities, gum disease, and toothaches, began as early as the 7th century BCE and persisted into the modern _____ in fact, it wasn't debunked until the 18th century.

Which choice completes the text so that it conforms to the conventions of Standard English?

Ⓐ era,

Ⓑ era;

Ⓒ era

Ⓓ era and

6 ☐ Mark for Review

Ancient Egyptians are credited with inventing the first candles, known as rushlights, from reeds and animal fat in 3,000 _____ the predecessor of today's table candles did not come into use until the Romans dipped papyrus into beeswax to create wicks.

Which choice completes the text so that it conforms to the conventions of Standard English?

Ⓐ BCE, however,

Ⓑ BCE, however;

Ⓒ BCE however,

Ⓓ BCE; however,

7 ☐ Mark for Review

While solar panels are traditionally deep black in order to absorb light _____ a team of researchers was able to use photonic glass to create blue, green, and purple solar panels that were only slightly less efficient in power generation.

Which choice completes the text so that it conforms to the conventions of Standard English?

Ⓐ effectively, but

Ⓑ effectively,

Ⓒ effectively

Ⓓ effectively but

575+ Practice Questions for the Digital PSAT/NMSQT

8 | Mark for Review

In 2020, Dutch startup Avy's solar-powered drone prototype completed its first successful test flight. The drone is equipped with a custom solar foil developed by Wattlab to reflect and absorb more sunlight without adding _____ to support nature conservation initiatives and deliver emergency medical supplies, Avy's solar-powered drone can carry payloads weighing up to 1.5 kilograms without producing any emissions.

Which choice completes the text so that it conforms to the conventions of Standard English?

(A) weight. Designed

(B) weight, designed

(C) weight and designed

(D) weight designed

9 | Mark for Review

The works of Zeuxis, an ancient Greek painter who lived during the 5th century BCE, garnered acclaim for their realism and innovative use of light and shadow, though none of his paintings have survived. Pliny the Elder, an ancient Roman author, described a contest held to determine who could paint in the most realistic _____ following Zeuxis's unveiling of his entry, a depiction of grapes, birds were said to have flown down and pecked at the painted image of the fruit.

Which choice completes the text so that it conforms to the conventions of Standard English?

(A) manner;

(B) manner,

(C) manner

(D) manner and

10 | Mark for Review

Chinese Zhusuan is a traditional method of performing mathematical calculations using an _____ it involves manipulating beads on a frame specially designed to represent numbers and perform arithmetic operations.

Which choice completes the text so that it conforms to the conventions of Standard English?

(A) abacus while

(B) abacus:

(C) abacus

(D) abacus, while

Chapter 25
Connecting Clauses
Drill Explanations

ANSWER KEY

1.	C	6.	D
2.	D	7.	B
3.	D	8.	A
4.	A	9.	A
5.	B	10.	B

CONNECTING CLAUSES DRILL EXPLANATIONS

1. **C** In this Rules question, punctuation is changing in the answer choices. Look for independent clauses. The first part of the sentence says *Scientists are starting to experiment with a device…to create eco-friendly filters for microplastic*, which is an independent clause. The second part says *the TENG requires no external power source…*, which is also an independent clause. Eliminate any answer that can't correctly connect two independent clauses.

   - (A) is wrong because a comma without a coordinating conjunction (FANBOYS) can't connect two independent clauses.

   - (B) is wrong because some type of punctuation is needed in order to connect two independent clauses.

   - (C) is correct because the period makes each independent clause its own sentence, which is fine.

   - (D) is wrong because a coordinating conjunction (*and*) without a comma can't connect two independent clauses.

2. **D** In this Rules question, punctuation is changing in the answer choices. Look for independent clauses. The first part of the sentence says *Pablo Picasso's early Blue Period paintings are generally considered more facile…than his later groundbreaking work*, which is an independent clause. The second part says *these paintings impressed collectors Leo and Gertrude Stein…*, which is also an independent clause. Eliminate any answer that can't correctly connect two independent clauses.

   - (A) is wrong because a coordinating conjunction (*but*) without a comma can't connect two independent clauses.

   - (B) is wrong because some type of punctuation is needed in order to connect two independent clauses.

   - (C) is wrong because a comma without a coordinating conjunction (FANBOYS) can't connect two independent clauses.

   - (D) is correct because it connects the independent clauses with a comma + a coordinating conjunction (FANBOYS), which is acceptable.

3. **D** In this Rules question, punctuation is changing in the answer choices. The first part of the sentence says *Though Austrian tennis player Hans Redl lost his left arm during World War II*, which is a dependent clause. The second part of the sentence says *he continued his tennis career by developing a new serving technique…*, which is an independent clause. Eliminate answers that don't properly connect a dependent clause to an independent clause.

- (A) and (B) are wrong because the first part isn't an independent clause, and a semicolon or a comma + a coordinating conjunction (FANBOYS) can only follow an independent clause.

- (C) is wrong because a comma is needed after the dependent clause in this case.

- (D) is correct because it uses a comma between the dependent clause and the independent clause.

4. **A** In this Rules question, punctuation is changing in the answer choices. Look for independent clauses. The first part of the sentence says *…the mysterious occurrence of milky seas…has been observed and recorded by sailors…even appearing in two popular works of 19th-century literature*, which is an independent clause. The second part of the sentence lists the *two popular works*. Eliminate any option that doesn't correctly connect the independent clause to the list.

- (A) is correct because a colon is used when the second part explains the first, such as by providing a list of things.

- (B) is wrong because the comma makes it look like *two popular works* is part of the list, which it isn't.

- (C) is wrong because a semicolon can only connect two independent clauses, and the list isn't an independent clause.

- (D) is wrong because some punctuation is needed to separate the independent clause from the list.

5. **B** In this Rules question, punctuation is changing in the answer choices. Look for independent clauses. The first part of the sentence says *The belief…began as early as the 7th century BCE and persisted into the modern era*, which is an independent clause. The second part says *…it wasn't debunked until the 18th century*, which is also an independent clause. Eliminate any answer that can't correctly connect two independent clauses.

- (A) is wrong because a comma without a coordinating conjunction (FANBOYS) can't connect two independent clauses.

- (B) is correct because a semicolon can connect two independent clauses.

- (C) is wrong because some type of punctuation is needed in order to connect two independent clauses.

- (D) is wrong because a coordinating conjunction (*and*) without a comma can't connect two independent clauses.

6. **D**   In this Rules question, punctuation with a transition is changing in the answer choices. Look for independent clauses. The first part of the sentence says *Ancient Egyptians are credited with inventing the first candles...from reeds and animal fat in 3,000 BCE.* There is an option to add *however* to this independent clause, but it's not contrasting with the previous idea as nothing came before. Eliminate options with *however* in the first part.

   • (A) and (C) are wrong because the sentence contains two independent clauses, which cannot be connected with commas alone.

   • (B) is wrong because it puts *however* with the first independent clause.

   • (D) is correct because it puts *however* with the second independent clause and puts a semicolon between the independent clauses.

7. **B**   In this Rules question, punctuation is changing in the answer choices. The first part of the sentence says *While solar panels are traditionally deep black in order to absorb light effectively,* which is a dependent clause. The second part of the sentence says *a team of researchers was able to use photonic glass...,* which is an independent clause. Eliminate any answer that doesn't correctly connect a dependent + an independent clause.

   • (A) and (D) are wrong because a coordinating conjunction (*but*) can't be used with a dependent clause.

   • (B) is correct because it uses a comma after the dependent clause.

   • (C) is wrong because a comma is needed after the dependent clause in this case.

8. **A**   In this Rules question, punctuation is changing in the answer choices. Look for independent clauses. The first part of the sentence says *The drone is equipped with a custom solar foil developed by Wattlab to reflect and absorb more sunlight without adding weight,* which is an independent clause. The second part says *designed to support nature conservation initiatives...Avy's solar-powered drone can carry payloads weighing up to 1.5 kilograms without producing any emissions,* which is also an independent clause. Eliminate any answer that can't correctly connect two independent clauses.

   • (A) is correct because the period makes each independent clause its own sentence, which is fine.

   • (B) is wrong because a comma without a coordinating conjunction (FANBOYS) can't connect two independent clauses.

   • (C) is wrong because a coordinating conjunction (*and*) without a comma can't connect two independent clauses.

   • (D) is wrong because some type of punctuation is needed in order to connect two independent clauses.

9. **A** In this Rules question, punctuation is changing in the answer choices. Look for independent clauses. The first part of the sentence says *Pliny the Elder…described a contest held to determine who could paint in the most realistic manner*, which is an independent clause. The second part says *following Zeuxis's unveiling of his entry…birds were said to have flown down and pecked at the painted image of the fruit*, which is also an independent clause. Eliminate any answer that can't correctly connect two independent clauses.

- (A) is correct because a semicolon can connect two independent clauses.

- (B) is wrong because a comma without a coordinating conjunction (FANBOYS) can't connect two independent clauses.

- (C) is wrong because some type of punctuation is needed in order to connect two independent clauses.

- (D) is wrong because a coordinating conjunction (*and*) without a comma can't connect two independent clauses.

10. **B** In this Rules question, punctuation is changing in the answer choices. Look for independent clauses. The first part of the sentence says *Chinese Zhusuan is a traditional method of performing mathematical calculations using an abacus*, which is an independent clause. The second part says *it involves manipulating beads on a frame specially designed to represent numbers and perform arithmetic operations*, which is also an independent clause. Eliminate any answer that can't correctly connect two independent clauses.

- (A) and (D) are wrong because there is no reason to add the word *while*, as these ideas don't contrast.

- (B) is correct because a colon is an acceptable way to connect two independent clauses if the second part elaborates on the first, which it does here.

- (C) is wrong because some type of punctuation is needed in order to connect two independent clauses.

Chapter 26
Other Punctuation
Topics Drill

Other Punctuation Topics Drill

---

1 ⚑ Mark for Review

There are several references to golf, or what seem to be precursors to golf, throughout European writings from the 13th and 14th centuries: a Middle Dutch collection of works by Flemish poet Jacob van Maerlant in _____ an edict from the council of Brussels in 1360, and a charter sealed by Albrecht of Bavaria in 1387.

Which choice completes the text so that it conforms to the conventions of Standard English?

- (A) 1261;
- (B) 1261:
- (C) 1261
- (D) 1261,

---

2 ⚑ Mark for Review

One of the first female players in a professional _____ Rebecca Clarke was internationally recognized as both a composer and a violist.

Which choice completes the text so that it conforms to the conventions of Standard English?

- (A) orchestra;
- (B) orchestra,
- (C) orchestra
- (D) orchestra:

---

3 ⚑ Mark for Review

In his two major series "Drape" and "Beveled-edge," painter Sam Gilliam explored the possibilities _____ sculptural, spatial, and three-dimensional effects of different materials, pushing the limits of what was once considered possible for painting.

Which choice completes the text so that it conforms to the conventions of Standard English?

- (A) of
- (B) of,
- (C) of—
- (D) of:

---

4 ⚑ Mark for Review

Popularized during the Ottoman period, the traditional Turkish shadow play showcases two main _____ and the conflicts that arise during their interactions.

Which choice completes the text so that it conforms to the conventions of Standard English?

- (A) characters
- (B) characters;
- (C) characters:
- (D) characters,

---

5 ☐ Mark for Review

In a 2022 study, researchers at the University of Maryland found that people of different age groups could be trained to differentiate subtle changes in the speed of sound. According to Sandra _____ an author of the study, these auditory improvements are driven by neuroplasticity, the process by which the brain alters its neural network.

Which choice completes the text so that it conforms to the conventions of Standard English?

(A) Gordon-Salant

(B) Gordon-Salant:

(C) Gordon-Salant,

(D) Gordon-Salant—

6 ☐ Mark for Review

Ghanaian neuropharmacologist Priscilla Kolibea Mante researches plant-based therapies to manage drug-resistant epilepsy. _____ Mante has said, "The more women push for senior roles, the harder it will be to ignore them."

Which choice completes the text so that it conforms to the conventions of Standard English?

(A) Additionally, regarding the place of women in science

(B) Additionally regarding the place of women in science

(C) Additionally, regarding the place of women in science,

(D) Additionally, regarding the place, of women in science

7 ☐ Mark for Review

Justin Dart Jr. was an American disability rights activist and advocate who played a significant role in the passage of the Americans with Disabilities _____ landmark piece of legislation that prohibits discrimination against people with disabilities in employment, transportation, public accommodations, and other areas of daily life.

Which choice completes the text so that it conforms to the conventions of Standard English?

(A) Act (ADA). A

(B) Act (ADA); a

(C) Act (ADA) a

(D) Act (ADA), a

8 ☐ Mark for Review

After the Migratory Bird Treaty Act of 1918 was passed in the United States, _____ was given the responsibility of mapping out flyways, the flight paths used by birds during migration.

Which choice completes the text so that it conforms to the conventions of Standard English?

(A) ornithologist, Frederick Charles Lincoln,

(B) ornithologist Frederick Charles Lincoln

(C) ornithologist Frederick Charles Lincoln,

(D) ornithologist, Frederick Charles Lincoln

9 ☐ Mark for Review

Spanish artist Cristina Iglesias's sculptures contain latticed panels that invite viewers to experience the tension between openness and enclosure. Her sculpture *Untitled [Jealousy II]*, for instance, is constructed with multiple panels that can be viewed only from the outside, while her 2005 sculpture *Pavilion Suspended in a Room* _____ allows observers to step among the panels and view the outside world through them.

Which choice completes the text so that it conforms to the conventions of Standard English?

Ⓐ *I*

Ⓑ *I*:

Ⓒ *I*—

Ⓓ *I*,

10 ☐ Mark for Review

In 1975, India's prime minister Indira Gandhi launched her Twenty Point Program in which she laid out her goals for eradicating poverty in accordance with her *Garibi Hatao* (Remove Poverty) campaign. The program consisted of goals such as the protection of the _____ socio-economic groups officially recognized by the government as highly disadvantaged; and the improvement of water irrigation.

Which choice completes the text so that it conforms to the conventions of Standard English?

Ⓐ environment, the establishment of rights for SC/ST (Scheduled Castes and Scheduled Tribes),

Ⓑ environment, the establishment of rights for SC/ST (Scheduled Castes and Scheduled Tribes);

Ⓒ environment the establishment of rights for SC/ST (Scheduled Castes and Scheduled Tribes),

Ⓓ environment; the establishment of rights for SC/ST (Scheduled Castes and Scheduled Tribes),

Chapter 27
Other Punctuation Topics Drill Explanations

ANSWER KEY

1.	D		6.	C
2.	B		7.	D
3.	A		8.	B
4.	A		9.	A
5.	C		10.	D

OTHER PUNCTUATION TOPICS DRILL EXPLANATIONS

1. **D** In this Rules question, commas are changing in the answer choices. The sentence mentions *several references* and contains the word *and* towards the end, so look for a list. The list consists of 1) *a Middle Dutch collection of works by Flemish poet Jacob van Maerlant in 1261*, 2) *an edict from the council of Brussels in 1360*, and 3) *a charter sealed by Albrecht of Bavaria in 1387*. Eliminate any answer that doesn't put commas between the list items.

   - (A) and (B) are wrong because they put other punctuation after the first item, not a comma.

   - (C) is wrong because there is no punctuation after the first item.

   - (D) is correct because it has a comma after the first item.

2. **B** In this Rules question, punctuation is changing in the answer choices. The first part of the sentence says *One of the first female players in a professional orchestra*, which is an introductory phrase that is non-essential to the meaning of the sentence. It should therefore be followed by a comma to separate it from the rest of the sentence. Eliminate answers that do not have a comma.

   - (A), (C), and (D) are wrong because they don't use a comma.

   - (B) is correct because it uses a comma after the non-essential phrase.

3. **A** In this Rules question, punctuation is changing in the answer choices. The punctuation follows a preposition, *of*, but prepositions shouldn't be followed by punctuation, so eliminate answers with punctuation.

   - (A) is correct because no punctuation should be used here.

   - (B), (C), and (D) are wrong because a preposition shouldn't be followed by punctuation.

4. **A** In this Rules question, punctuation is changing in the answer choices. The punctuation appears before the word *and*, but this is a list of only two things, and the sentence doesn't have two independent clauses, so there is no reason to use punctuation with *and* here. Eliminate options with punctuation.

   - (A) is correct because no punctuation is needed.

   - (B), (C), and (D) are wrong because there is no reason to use any punctuation.

5. **C** In this Rules question, punctuation is changing in the answer choices. The first part of the sentence says *According to Sandra Gordon-Salant*, which is an introductory phrase that is not essential to the sentence's meaning. It should therefore be followed by a comma to separate it from the rest of the sentence. Eliminate answers that do not have a comma.

   - (A), (B), and (D) are wrong because they don't use a comma.

   - (C) is correct because it uses a comma after the non-essential phrase.

6. **C** In this Rules question, punctuation is changing in the answer choices. The answers contain commas in several places, so use the process of elimination to eliminate any answers that don't use commas correctly.

   - (A), (B), and (D) are wrong because the phrase *regarding the place of women in science* is not essential to the sentence's meaning and should be surrounded by commas.

   - (C) is correct because there should be commas around the phrase, not within it.

7. **D** In this Rules question, punctuation is changing in the answer choices. Look for independent clauses. The first part of the sentence says *Justin Dart Jr. was an American disability rights activist…who played a significant role in the passage of the Americans with Disabilities Act (ADA)*, which is an independent clause. The second part of the sentence says *a landmark piece of legislation…*, which is a describing phrase that is not essential to the sentence's meaning and should be separated with a comma. Eliminate any option that doesn't use a comma.

   - (A), (B), and (C) are wrong because the non-essential phrase should be separated with a comma.

   - (D) is correct because it uses a comma before the non-essential phrase.

8. **B** In this Rules question, punctuation is changing in the answer choices. The word *ornithologist* is a title for Lincoln, so no punctuation should be used after *ornithologist*. Eliminate answers that use punctuation after *ornithologist*.

   - (A) and (D) are wrong because a comma isn't used after a title.

   - (B) is correct because titles before names have no punctuation.

   - (C) is wrong because it puts a single comma between the subject (*Lincoln*) and its verb (*was*), which isn't correct.

9. **A** In this Rules question, punctuation is changing in the answer choices. The blank comes between the subject (*her 2005 sculpture*) and its verb (*allows*), and there is no other punctuation. A single punctuation mark can't separate a subject and its verb, so eliminate answers with punctuation.

   - (A) is correct because no punctuation should be used here.

   - (B), (C), and (D) are wrong because a single punctuation mark can't come between a subject and its verb.

10. **D** In this Rules question, commas and semicolons are changing in the answer choices. The sentence already contains a semicolon near the end, and the part after it is not an independent clause, which suggests that the sentence contains a list separated by semicolons. In this case, the third item doesn't contain commas, so use the process of elimination to eliminate any answer that isn't properly punctuated.

- (A), (B), and (C) are wrong because they don't have a semicolon after the first item, which ends with *environment*.

- (D) is correct because it puts a semicolon after the first item and puts a comma before the description of *SC/ST*.

Chapter 28
Verbs Drill

Verbs Drill

1 ☐ Mark for Review

Researchers interested in cooperation and how it evolved often use cooperative pulling experiments. In this research, multiple animals _____ exposed to an apparatus that allows them to obtain a reward only if they work together.

Which choice completes the text so that it conforms to the conventions of Standard English?

(A) are

(B) is being

(C) has been

(D) is

2 ☐ Mark for Review

Scientists have recently discovered a new chemical compound named 1938 that may help heal nerve damage. It is hoped that within a decade this new compound _____ patients with a previously unavailable means of reversing the paralysis and loss of function that can stem from nerve injuries.

Which choice completes the text so that it conforms to the conventions of Standard English?

(A) provides

(B) will provide

(C) has provided

(D) is providing

3 ☐ Mark for Review

In 1975, Steven J. Sasson, an electrical engineer, was responsible for inventing the first self-contained digital camera, a portable device that _____ the user to take pictures without the need for film.

Which choice completes the text so that it conforms to the conventions of Standard English?

(A) enable

(B) enables

(C) have enabled

(D) were enabling

4 ☐ Mark for Review

Recent studies show that when pursuing swarms of Mexican free-tailed bats, falcons and hawks steer toward a fixed point within the swarm rather than aim for one individual bat. As the falcon or hawk _____ the target, the nearest bat becomes the intended prey. This process allows falcons and hawks to simplify their hunting and spend less energy determining which bat to target.

Which choice completes the text so that it conforms to the conventions of Standard English?

(A) will approach

(B) approached

(C) approaches

(D) has approached

5 ▢ Mark for Review

The Suffrage Movement in the United States was a significant era of women's activism that aimed to secure the right to vote for women. Among the movement's leaders _____ Alice Paul, co-founder of the National Women's Party.

Which choice completes the text so that it conforms to the conventions of Standard English?

(A) was

(B) were

(C) are

(D) have been

6 ▢ Mark for Review

Ugandan writer and filmmaker Dilman Dila is known for his works of speculative fiction, a category that includes genres containing elements not present in reality, such as science fiction, horror, and fantasy. He often _____ traditional African science and technology in his texts and films. By making people aware of the continent's advancements that predate colonialism, Dila hopes to promote his African readers' and viewers' confidence in their heritage.

Which choice completes the text so that it conforms to the conventions of Standard English?

(A) was highlighting

(B) had highlighted

(C) highlighted

(D) highlights

7 ▢ Mark for Review

The European Union (EU) is the culmination of many efforts to integrate Europe since World War II. Founded in 1993, this political and economic union originally included only Belgium, France, Germany, Italy, Luxembourg, and the Netherlands. Today, the EU _____ to include 27 countries across Europe.

Which choice completes the text so that it conforms to the conventions of Standard English?

(A) had expanded

(B) expands

(C) will expand

(D) has expanded

8 ▢ Mark for Review

French mathematician Claire Voisin has spent her career focusing on algebraic geometry. Throughout her life, she has disproven multiple well-known equations, and the portfolio of her awards _____ diverse, covering a wide range of areas and honors.

Which choice completes the text so that it conforms to the conventions of Standard English?

(A) have been

(B) are

(C) is

(D) were

9 ☐ Mark for Review

In July 2022, astronomers recorded a giant sunspot, named AR3068, emerging from the southeastern side of the sun. Within 24 hours, this already enormous sunspot _____ in size.

Which choice completes the text so that it conforms to the conventions of Standard English?

Ⓐ will triple

Ⓑ has tripled

Ⓒ had tripled

Ⓓ triples

10 ☐ Mark for Review

While there is debate over whether the total amount of the Earth's crust, the layer of rocks that forms the planet's geological continents, _____ static or in flux, the scientific consensus is that the layers are in a constant state of reconfiguration.

Which choice completes the text so that it conforms to the conventions of Standard English?

Ⓐ is

Ⓑ are

Ⓒ have been

Ⓓ were

Chapter 29
Verbs Drill
Explanations

ANSWER KEY

1.	A	6.	D
2.	B	7.	D
3.	B	8.	C
4.	C	9.	C
5.	A	10.	A

VERBS DRILL EXPLANATIONS

1. **A**   In this Rules question, verbs are changing in the answer choices, so it's testing consistency with verbs. Find and highlight the subject, *animals*, which is plural, so a plural verb is needed. Write an annotation saying "plural." Eliminate any answer that is not plural.

    - (A) is correct because it's plural.

    - (B), (C), and (D) are wrong because they are singular.

2. **B**   In this Rules question, verbs are changing in the answer choices, so it's testing consistency with verbs. Find and highlight the subject, *compound*, which is singular, so a singular verb is needed. All of the answers work with a singular subject, so look for a clue regarding tense. This sentence uses the phrase *within a decade*, so future tense should be used. Highlight that phrase and write an annotation that says "future." Eliminate any answer not in future tense.

    - (A) and (D) are wrong because they're in present tense.

    - (B) is correct because it's in future tense.

    - (C) is wrong because it's not in future tense.

3. **B**   In this Rules question, verbs are changing in the answer choices, so it's testing consistency with verbs. Find and highlight the subject, *device*, which is singular, so a singular verb is needed. Write an annotation saying "singular." Eliminate any answer that is not singular.

    - (A), (C), and (D) are wrong because they are plural.

    - (B) is correct because it's singular.

4. **C**   In this Rules question, verbs are changing in the answer choices, so it's testing consistency with verbs. Find and highlight the subject, *falcon or hawk*, which is singular, so a singular verb is needed. All of the answers work with a singular subject, so look for a clue regarding tense. This and the next sentence use present tense verbs: *becomes* and *allows*. Highlight those verbs and write an annotation that says "present." Eliminate any answer not in present tense.

    - (A) is wrong because it's in future tense.

- (B) is wrong because it's in past tense.

- (C) is correct because it's in present tense.

- (D) is wrong because it's not in present tense.

5. **A**   In this Rules question, verbs are changing in the answer choices, so it's testing consistency with verbs. Find and highlight the subject, *Alice Paul*, which is singular, so a singular verb is needed. Write an annotation saying "singular." Eliminate any answer that is not singular.

- (A) is correct because it's singular.

- (B), (C), and (D) are wrong because they are plural.

6. **D**   In this Rules question, verbs are changing in the answer choices, so it's testing consistency with verbs. Find and highlight the subject, *He*, which is singular, so a singular verb is needed. All of the answers work with a singular subject, so look for a clue regarding tense. The previous sentence uses present tense verbs: *is* and *includes*. Highlight those verbs and write an annotation that says "present." Eliminate any answer not in present tense.

- (A), (B), and (C) are wrong because they're in past tense.

- (D) is correct because it's in present tense.

7. **D**   In this Rules question, verbs are changing in the answer choices, so it's testing consistency with verbs. Find and highlight the subject, *the EU*, which is singular, so a singular verb is needed. All of the answers work with a singular subject, so look for a clue regarding tense. This sentence uses the word *Today*. Highlight that word and write an annotation that says "present." Eliminate any answer not in present tense.

- (A) is wrong because it's in past tense.

- (B) is wrong because the intended meaning is not that *the EU* currently expands but that it has increased in size going up to today.

- (C) is wrong because it's in future tense.

- (D) is correct because it's in a form of present tense and indicates that the EU has grown to include additional countries over time, going up to today.

8. **C**   In this Rules question, verbs are changing in the answer choices, so it's testing consistency with verbs. Find and highlight the subject, *portfolio*, which is singular, so a singular verb is needed. Write an annotation saying "singular." Eliminate any answer that is not singular.

- (A), (B), and (D) are wrong because they are plural.

- (C) is correct because it's singular.

9. **C** In this Rules question, verbs are changing in the answer choices, so it's testing consistency with verbs. Find and highlight the subject, *sunspot*, which is singular, so a singular verb is needed. All of the answers work with a singular subject, so look for a clue regarding tense. The previous sentence says *In July 2022*. Highlight that phrase and write an annotation that says "past." Eliminate any answer not in past tense.

- (A) is wrong because it's in future tense.

- (B) is wrong because *has tripled* suggests an event that continues to the present, but this occurred in 2022.

- (C) is correct because it's in past tense.

- (D) is wrong because it's in present tense.

10. **A** In this Rules question, verbs are changing in the answer choices, so it's testing consistency with verbs. Find and highlight the subject, *crust*, which is singular, so a singular verb is needed. Write an annotation saying "singular." Eliminate any answer that is not singular.

- (A) is correct because it's singular.

- (B), (C), and (D) are wrong because they are plural.

Chapter 30
Pronouns and
Nouns Drill

Pronouns and Nouns Drill

1 ⬗ Mark for Review

Archaeoacoustics is a field of anthropology that studies the significance of sound in different locations and time periods. One example of an archaeoacoustic phenomenon occurs at a pyramid in Mexico. When people clap _____ hands near the pyramid, the sound echoes off the structure and mimics the call of a local bird.

Which choice completes the text so that it conforms to the conventions of Standard English?

Ⓐ it's

Ⓑ its

Ⓒ their

Ⓓ they're

2 ⬗ Mark for Review

In her Pulitzer-Prize winning book *The Warmth of Other Suns*, Isabel Wilkerson tells the _____ who left the South in search of a better life in northern cities.

Which choice completes the text so that it conforms to the conventions of Standard English?

Ⓐ story's of some of the millions of African Americans

Ⓑ story's of some of the millions of African Americans'

Ⓒ stories of some of the millions of African Americans

Ⓓ stories of some of the millions of African American's

3 ☐ Mark for Review

The 1968 Kentucky Derby experienced a five-year controversy over whether the winner, Dancer's Image, had an advantage due to the use of an illegal substance. Peter Fuller, the owner of the horse, believed he may have been sabotaged; _____ of support for Martin Luther King Jr.'s widow had drawn negative attention during a time of division over King's role in social justice issues.

Which choice completes the text so that it conforms to the conventions of Standard English?

- (A) Fuller's proclamations
- (B) Fuller's proclamation's
- (C) Fullers proclamations
- (D) Fullers proclamation's

4 ☐ Mark for Review

US Route 66, one of the original highways in the US Numbered Highway System, was established on November 11, 1926. One of the most famous highways, _____ originally ran from Chicago, Illinois, to Santa Monica, California. Although the highway was officially decommissioned in 1985, several states have kept the "66" designation, and different sections of the road have been listed in the National Register of Historic Places.

Which choice completes the text so that it conforms to the conventions of Standard English?

- (A) it
- (B) they
- (C) one
- (D) this

5 ☐ Mark for Review

According to research, parents who rely on digital resources to relax are less likely to utilize positive parenting techniques with their children. The study was completed at the University of Waterloo, and _____ findings could help create guidelines for parents who wish to develop healthy stress-management and relaxation techniques that will benefit their entire families.

Which choice completes the text so that it conforms to the conventions of Standard English?

- (A) its
- (B) their
- (C) they're
- (D) it's

Chapter 31
Pronouns and Nouns Drill Explanations

ANSWER KEY

1. C
2. C
3. A

4. A
5. A

PRONOUNS AND NOUNS DRILL EXPLANATIONS

1. **C**   In this Rules question, pronouns and apostrophes are changing in the answer choices, so it's testing consistency with pronouns. Find and highlight the word that the pronoun refers back to: *people*. This word is plural, so in order to be consistent, a plural pronoun is needed. Eliminate any answer that isn't consistent with *people* or is incorrectly punctuated.

    *   (A) and (B) are wrong because they are singular.

    *   (C) is correct because it is plural and possessive.

    *   (D) is wrong because it means "they are."

2. **C**   In this Rules question, apostrophes with nouns are changing in the answer choices. Determine whether each word possesses anything. The stories and African Americans don't possess anything. Eliminate any answer that doesn't match this.

    *   (A) and (B) are wrong because *stories* shouldn't be possessive.

    *   (C) is correct because neither *stories* nor *African Americans* is possessive.

    *   (D) is wrong because *African Americans* shouldn't be possessive.

3. **A**   In this Rules question, apostrophes with nouns are changing in the answer choices. Determine whether each word possesses anything. Fuller possesses the proclamations, but the proclamations don't possess anything. Eliminate any answer that doesn't match this.

    *   (A) is correct because *Fuller* is possessive and *proclamations* is not.

    *   (B) is wrong because *proclamations* shouldn't be possessive.

    *   (C) and (D) are wrong because *Fuller* should have an apostrophe + *s* to show possession.

4. **A** In this Rules question, pronouns are changing in the answer choices, so it's testing consistency with pronouns. Find and highlight the word the pronoun refers back to, *One*, which is singular, so a singular pronoun is needed. Write an annotation saying "singular." Eliminate any answer that isn't singular or doesn't clearly refer back to *One of the most famous highways*.

    - (A) is correct because *it* is singular and is consistent with *One of the most famous highways*.

    - (B) is wrong because it is plural.

    - (C) and (D) are wrong because *one* and *this* don't refer back to a specific thing.

5. **A** In this Rules question, pronouns and apostrophes are changing in the answer choices, so it's testing consistency with pronouns. Find and highlight the word that the pronoun refers back to: *study*. This word is singular, so in order to be consistent, a singular pronoun is needed. Eliminate any answer that isn't consistent with *the study* or is incorrectly punctuated.

    - (A) is correct because it is singular and possessive.

    - (B) and (C) are wrong because they are plural.

    - (D) is wrong because it means "it is."

Chapter 32
Modifiers Drill

Modifiers Drill

Unlike other animals that hibernate, _____ however, they are considered true hibernators because of changes in their metabolism and heart rate that allow them to remain inactive for months at a time.

Which choice completes the text so that it conforms to the conventions of Standard English?

(A) brown bears do not exhibit a steep decrease in body temperature during their long winter sleep;

(B) brown bears' body temperature does not decrease steeply during their long winter sleep;

(C) the long winter sleep of brown bears is not accompanied by a steep decrease in body temperature;

(D) the decrease in brown bears' body temperature is not steep during their long winter sleep;

The builders of Chetro Ketl, located in modern-day New Mexico, abandoned the site after an extended period of drought in the 12th century, and the building's purpose is disputed today. Scholars have generally explained it as a seasonally occupied ceremonial site. Writing that Chetro Ketl was a permanent royal palace, _____

Which choice completes the text so that it conforms to the conventions of Standard English?

(A) this previously established consensus is not supported by archaeologist Stephen Lekson.

(B) archaeologist Stephen Lekson disagrees with this previously established consensus.

(C) the disagreement of archaeologist Stephen Lekson with this previously established consensus is notable.

(D) the establishment of this consensus is not supported by archaeologist Stephen Lekson.

3 ☐ Mark for Review

In the 1780s, English philosopher and social theorist Jeremy Bentham proposed a design for a prison that would enable a single guard to observe the totality of the population of prisoners, though the guard would not be able to observe everyone at once. Derived from the Greek word for "all seeing," _____ to act as though they were being watched at all times, since they could never be sure whether the guard was observing them at a given moment.

Which choice completes the text so that it conforms to the conventions of Standard English?

Ⓐ the term "panopticon" was selected for the prison, which was intended to compel the prisoners

Ⓑ the panopticon was intended to compel the prisoners

Ⓒ there was the panopticon, which was said to theoretically compel all prisoners

Ⓓ the single guard would have a view of all prisoners, who would be compelled

4 ☐ Mark for Review

The *Panchatantra* is an ancient Indian book of fables with animal characters such as the scheming jackal minister Damanaka and his virtuous friend Karataka. Composed as a complex structure of interconnected tales set within an overarching narrative, _____ medieval literature across the Eurasian continent.

Which choice completes the text so that it conforms to the conventions of Standard English?

Ⓐ over 50 languages were used to translate the *Panchatantra*, which influenced

Ⓑ the influence of the *Panchatantra*, which was translated into over 50 languages, was important in

Ⓒ storytellers translated the *Panchatantra* into over 50 languages, and these translations influenced

Ⓓ the *Panchatantra* was translated into over 50 languages and influenced

5 ☐ Mark for Review

In February of 1851, at the Paris Observatory, French physicist Léon Foucault debuted what was to become his most famous contribution to science—the Foucault pendulum. Conceived as a method for demonstrating the rotation of the Earth, _____ above a circular area and observed over a long period of time, thus revealing that the plane of the pendulum's oscillation rotated.

Which choice completes the text so that it conforms to the conventions of Standard English?

(A) Foucault designed the pendulum to be suspended from the ceiling

(B) the pendulum was designed to be suspended from the ceiling

(C) Foucault's premise was that the pendulum could be suspended from the ceiling

(D) the ceiling was where a pendulum would be suspended

Chapter 33
Modifiers Drill
Explanations

ANSWER KEY

1. A
2. B
3. A

4. D
5. B

MODIFIERS DRILL EXPLANATIONS

1. **A**   In this Rules question, the subjects of the answers are changing, which suggests it may be testing modifiers. Look for and highlight a modifying phrase: *Unlike other animals that hibernate*. Whoever is *Unlike other animals that hibernate* needs to come immediately after the comma. Eliminate any answer that doesn't start with an animal.

    *   (A) is correct because *brown bears* are a type of animal.

    *   (B), (C), and (D) are wrong because *brown bears' body temperature, the long winter sleep of brown bears,* and *the decrease in brown bears' body temperature* are not a type of animal.

2. **B**   In this Rules question, the subjects of the answers are changing, which suggests it may be testing modifiers. Look for and highlight a modifying phrase: *Writing that Chetro Ketl was a permanent royal palace.* Whoever is *Writing* needs to come immediately after the comma. Eliminate any answer that doesn't start with someone who can write.

    *   (A), (C), and (D) are wrong because *this previously established consensus, the disagreement of archaeologist Stephen Lekson,* and *the establishment of this consensus* can't write.

    *   (B) is correct because *archaeologist Stephen Lekson* can write.

3. **A**   In this Rules question, the subjects of the answers are changing, which suggests it may be testing modifiers. Look for and highlight a modifying phrase: *Derived from the Greek word for "all seeing."* Whatever was *Derived from the Greek word for "all seeing"* needs to come immediately after the comma. Eliminate any answer that doesn't start with something that can be derived from a word.

    *   (A) is correct because *the term "panopticon"* could have been derived from a Greek word.

    *   (B), (C), and (D) are wrong because *the panopticon, there was,* and *the single guard* can't be derived from a Greek word.

4.   **D**   In this Rules question, the subjects of the answers are changing, which suggests it may be testing modifiers. Look for and highlight a modifying phrase: *Composed as a complex structure of interconnected tales set within an overarching narrative*. Whatever was *Composed as a complex structure of interconnected tales set within an overarching narrative* needs to come immediately after the comma. Eliminate any answer that doesn't start with something that can be composed.

- (A), (B), and (C) are wrong because *over 50 languages, the influence of the Panchatantra,* and *storytellers* can't be composed.

- (D) is correct because *the Panchatantra* is described as a book, so it could have been composed.

5.   **B**   In this Rules question, the subjects of the answers are changing, which suggests it may be testing modifiers. Look for and highlight a modifying phrase: *Conceived as a method for demonstrating the rotation of the Earth*. Whatever was *Conceived as a method for demonstrating the rotation of the Earth* needs to come immediately after the comma. Eliminate any answer that doesn't start with something that can be conceived.

- (A) and (D) are wrong because *Foucault* and *the ceiling* can't be conceived.

- (B) is correct because *the pendulum* was an invention, so it was conceived.

- (C) is wrong because Foucault's *premise* wasn't conceived *as a method* for demonstrating something—it's the pendulum itself that would demonstrate something.

Chapter 34
Transitions Drill

Transitions Drill

1 ☐ Mark for Review

Globular clusters, groups of stars held together in a spherical shape by gravity, appeared as fuzzy blobs when telescopes were first invented. _____ Omega Centauri was originally listed as a non-stellar object in 1677 until astronomer James Dunlop was able to identify it as a globular cluster in 1826.

Which choice completes the text with the most logical transition?

(A) Nevertheless,

(B) For instance,

(C) Still,

(D) Furthermore,

2 ☐ Mark for Review

Discovered by a Polish archaeological team during the 1960s, *Saint Anne* is a Makurian wall painting believed to be painted between the 8th and 9th centuries. The painting was found in present-day Sudan at the Faras Cathedral. _____ the painting is in the collection of Poland's National Museum in Warsaw.

Which choice completes the text with the most logical transition?

(A) At any rate,

(B) Likewise,

(C) Consequently,

(D) Currently,

3 ☐ Mark for Review

Paleontologists from the United Kingdom and Morocco state that the remains of mid-Cretaceous marine reptiles known as plesiosaurs have been found primarily in marine deposits from oceans; _____ some appear in low-salinity or freshwater environments.

Which choice completes the text with the most logical transition?

- Ⓐ accordingly,
- Ⓑ in addition,
- Ⓒ however,
- Ⓓ therefore,

4 ☐ Mark for Review

Quiriguá is an ancient Mayan archaeological site located in Guatemala. When the forces of King K'ak' Tiliw Chan Yopaat defeated those of the nearby city of Copán in 738 CE, Quiriguá experienced a period of dramatic expansion. _____ the region relied on the trade of jade and cacao to further develop.

Which choice completes the text with the most logical transition?

- Ⓐ Thus,
- Ⓑ Otherwise,
- Ⓒ Then,
- Ⓓ Instead,

5 ☐ Mark for Review

American inventor John Loud attempted to develop the first ballpoint pen in order to write on leather, but as this version was too rough to use for letter-writing, it did not gain any popularity. _____ László Bíró, a Hungarian-Argentine inventor, developed a ballpoint pen that could use the same ink used in newspaper printing and found great success.

Which choice completes the text with the most logical transition?

- Ⓐ By the same token,
- Ⓑ Hence,
- Ⓒ Indeed,
- Ⓓ On the other hand,

6 ☐ Mark for Review

American historian and philosopher of science Thomas Kuhn introduced the term "paradigm shift" in his 1962 book *The Structure of Scientific Revolutions*. In the book, Kuhn stated that scientific fields do not progress only in a linear and continuous way; occasionally they experience a fundamental change, called a paradigm shift. _____ new ideas and theories are explored.

Which choice completes the text with the most logical transition?

- Ⓐ Similarly,
- Ⓑ For instance,
- Ⓒ As a result,
- Ⓓ Regardless,

7 🔖 Mark for Review

The hippopotamus (*Hippopotamus amphibius*) is considered one of the most dangerous animals due to its hostile and erratic behavior as well as its jaw that is capable of producing 1,800 pounds per square inch of force, giving it the ability to bite a crocodile in half. _____ hippopotamuses are predominantly herbivores, with the vast majority of their diet coming from plants.

Which choice completes the text with the most logical transition?

Ⓐ However,

Ⓑ As a result,

Ⓒ After all,

Ⓓ By contrast,

8 🔖 Mark for Review

In 1952, Chemist Edith M. Flanigen was hired by the Union Carbide Corporation, a chemical company, where she would invent over 200 synthetic substances over the course of her 42-year career. She is credited with inventing a certain molecular sieve, a crystal compound with microscopic pores designed to filter complex substances. _____ she was one of the inventors of a synthetic emerald that was used in early laser technology as well as in jewelry.

Which choice completes the text with the most logical transition?

Ⓐ Still,

Ⓑ However,

Ⓒ For instance,

Ⓓ Moreover,

9 🔖 Mark for Review

For many years, scientists believed that phytoplankton, microorganisms that form the basis of most aquatic ecosystems, would not receive enough sunlight under the Antarctic ice to grow in large numbers, or bloom. Researcher Christopher Hovat and his team, however, recently used specialized autonomous buoys to measure different variables under the ice and determined that it is possible for phytoplankton to bloom under the ice. _____ the Southern Ocean potentially contains up to five million square kilometers with the right conditions for phytoplankton to bloom.

Which choice completes the text with the most logical transition?

Ⓐ Moreover,

Ⓑ In fact,

Ⓒ Therefore,

Ⓓ Though,

10 🔖 Mark for Review

Abdulkadir Hersi Siyad, better known by his nickname Yamyam, was one of the first Somali poets to become well-known for his written works, as the Somali alphabet was formally introduced in 1972. _____ Somali poetry is typically presented within the language's oral literary tradition.

Which choice completes the text with the most logical transition?

Ⓐ Now,

Ⓑ Even today,

Ⓒ Still,

Ⓓ As a result,

Chapter 35
Transitions Drill
Explanations

ANSWER KEY

1.	B	6.	C
2.	D	7.	A
3.	C	8.	D
4.	C	9.	B
5.	D	10.	B

TRANSITIONS DRILL EXPLANATIONS

1. **B** This is a transition question, so highlight ideas that relate to each other. The preceding sentence states that *Globular clusters…appeared as fuzzy blobs when telescopes were first invented*, and this sentence describes an example of a *globular cluster*. These ideas agree, so a same-direction transition is needed. Make an annotation that says "agree." Eliminate any answer that doesn't match.

    - (A) and (C) are wrong because *Nevertheless* and *Still* are opposite-direction transitions.

    - (B) is correct because *For instance* is used for examples.

    - (D) is wrong because this sentence isn't an additional point based on the previous sentence.

2. **D** This is a transition question, so highlight ideas that relate to each other. The preceding sentence states that *The painting was found in present-day Sudan at the Faras Cathedral*, and this sentence describes where the painting is located today. These ideas agree, so a same-direction transition is needed. Make an annotation that says "agree." Eliminate any answer that doesn't match.

    - (A) is wrong because *At any rate* is an opposite-direction transition.

    - (B) is wrong because this sentence isn't a similar point to the previous sentence.

    - (C) is wrong because this sentence isn't a consequence of the previous sentence.

    - (D) is correct because *Currently* implies that this sentence is about the painting's location today, which is supported by the shift from past tense to present tense.

3. **C** This is a transition question, so highlight ideas that relate to each other. The first part of the sentence says *Paleontologists from the United Kingdom and Morocco state that the remains of mid-Cretaceous marine reptiles…have been found primarily in marine deposits from oceans*, and the second part of the sentence says *some appear in low-salinity or freshwater environments*. These ideas disagree because oceans consist of saltwater and there is a contrast between where they have *primarily* been found and where *some* have also been found, so an opposite-direction transition is needed. Make an annotation that says "disagree." Eliminate any answer that doesn't match.

    - (A), (B), and (D) are wrong because they are same-direction transitions.

    - (C) is correct because *however* is an opposite-direction transition.

4. **C** This is a transition question, so highlight ideas that relate to each other. The preceding sentence references a time when *Quiriguá experienced a period of dramatic expansion*, and this sentence states what occurred after this event. These ideas involve a time change, so write an annotation that says "time change." Eliminate any answer that doesn't match.

- (A) is wrong because this sentence isn't an effect of the previous sentence.

- (B) and (D) are wrong because *Otherwise* and *Instead* are opposite-direction transitions.

- (C) is correct because *Then* is used to describe events that occur after other events.

5. **D** This is a transition question, so highlight ideas that relate to each other. The preceding sentence states that *John Loud attempted to develop the first ballpoint pen…but…it did not gain any popularity*, and this sentence describes why Bíró's pen was different. These ideas disagree, so an opposite-direction transition is needed. Make an annotation that says "disagree." Eliminate any answer that doesn't match.

- (A), (B), and (C) are wrong because *By the same token, Hence,* and *Indeed* are same-direction transitions.

- (D) is correct because *On the other hand* is an opposite-direction transition.

6. **C** This is a transition question, so highlight ideas that relate to each other. The preceding sentence states that *Kuhn stated that scientific fields do not progress only in a linear and continuous way; occasionally they experience a fundamental change*, and this sentence describes what this *paradigm shift* causes. These ideas agree, so a same-direction transition is needed. Make an annotation that says "agree." Eliminate any answer that doesn't match.

- (A) is wrong because this sentence isn't a similar point to the previous sentence.

- (B) is wrong because this sentence isn't an example based on the previous sentence.

- (C) is correct because *As a result* supports that the things in this sentence were caused by the shift in the previous sentence.

- (D) is wrong because *Regardless* is an opposite-direction transition.

7. **A** This is a transition question, so highlight ideas that relate to each other. The preceding sentence describes how *dangerous* hippopotamuses are thought to be, and this sentence states that they are *primarily herbivores*, suggesting they aren't that dangerous. These ideas disagree, so an opposite-direction transition is needed. Make an annotation that says "disagree." Eliminate any answer that doesn't match.

- (A) is correct because *However* is an opposite-direction transition.

- (B) and (C) are wrong because *As a result* and *After all* are same-direction transitions.

- (D) is wrong because the sentences don't contrast two things.

8.   **D**   This is a transition question, so highlight ideas that relate to each other. The preceding sentence states that *She is credited with inventing a certain molecular sieve,* and this sentence describes an additional achievement of Flanigen. These ideas agree, so a same-direction transition is needed. Make an annotation that says "agree." Eliminate any answer that doesn't match.

- (A) and (B) are wrong because *Still* and *However* are opposite-direction transitions.

- (C) is wrong because this sentence is not an example of the previous sentence.

- (D) is correct because *Moreover* adds an additional point building upon the previous idea.

9.   **B**   This is a transition question, so highlight ideas that relate to each other. The preceding sentence states that *Researcher Christopher Hovat…recently used specialized autonomous buoys to measure different variables under the ice and determined that it is possible for phytoplankton to bloom under the ice*, and this sentence describes further detail related to this idea. These ideas agree, so a same-direction transition is needed. Make an annotation that says "agree." Eliminate any answer that doesn't match.

- (A) is wrong because this sentence isn't an elaboration based on the previous sentence.

- (B) is correct because *In fact* supports and reinforces the previous idea.

- (C) is wrong because this sentence isn't an effect of the previous sentence.

- (D) is wrong because *Though* is an opposite-direction transition.

10.   **B**   This is a transition question, so highlight ideas that relate to each other. The preceding sentence states that *Abdulkadir Hersi Siyad…was one of the first Somali poets to become well-known for his written works, as the Somali alphabet was formally introduced in 1972*, and this sentence describes the current presentation of *Somali poetry*, which is that it still is primarily *oral*, rather than written. These ideas agree, so a same-direction transition is needed. Make an annotation that says "agree." Eliminate any answer that doesn't match.

- (A) is wrong because this sentence isn't a change from the initial way *Somali poetry* was presented.

- (B) is correct because *Even today* emphasizes that Siyad's works are unusual, given that the poetry is typically oral even now.

- (C) is wrong because *Still* is an opposite-direction transition.

- (D) is wrong because this sentence is not caused by the previous sentence.

Chapter 36
Rhetorical Synthesis Drill

Rhetorical Synthesis Drill

1 ▢ Mark for Review

While researching a topic, a student has taken the following notes:

- The Stikine River is a river in North America.
- It runs through northern British Columbia, Canada, and southeastern Alaska, US.
- The river flows west and south for 610 km.
- The Garonne River is a river in Europe.
- It runs through southwestern France and northern Spain.
- The river flows north and west for 602 km.

The student wants to compare the lengths of the two rivers. Which choice most effectively uses relevant information from the notes to accomplish this goal?

(A) The Garonne River flows for 602 km, while the slightly longer Stikine River flows for 610 km.

(B) Some of the rivers in the world, including one in Europe, are around 600 km long.

(C) Both the Stikine River in North America and the Garonne River in Europe flow through two countries.

(D) The Stikine River flows for 610 km through northern British Columbia and southeastern Alaska.

2 ▢ Mark for Review

While researching a topic, a student has taken the following notes:

- Mireille Dosso is an Ivorian microbiologist and virologist.
- She was appointed director of the Pasteur Institute in Abidjan, Ivory Coast, in 2004.
- She led successful efforts against the H1N1 swine fever pandemic in 2019.
- She led successful efforts against dengue fever in 2019.

The student wants to highlight a similarity among Dosso's achievements. Which choice most effectively uses relevant information from the notes to accomplish this goal?

(A) Mireille Dosso is an Ivorian microbiologist and virologist who was appointed director of the Pasteur Institute in Abidjan, Ivory Coast, in 2004.

(B) Dosso was appointed director of the Pasteur Institute in Abidjan, Ivory Coast, in 2004 and led successful efforts against the H1N1 swine fever pandemic in 2019.

(C) In 2019, Ivorian microbiologist and virologist Mireille Dosso led successful efforts against both the H1N1 swine fever pandemic and dengue fever.

(D) Director of the Pasteur Institute in Abidjan, Ivory Coast, Mireille Dosso led successful efforts against dengue fever in 2019.

3 ☐ Mark for Review

While researching a topic, a student has taken the following notes:

- The Republic of Benin existed for one day.
- It was established on September 19, 1967.
- It was a puppet state of Biafra.
- Albert Nwazu Okonkwo was its head of government.
- It ceased to exist after the Nigerian federal forces occupied Benin City.

The student wants to emphasize the beginning and end of the Republic of Benin. Which choice most effectively uses relevant information from the notes to accomplish this goal?

(A) The Republic of Benin was established on September 19, 1967, and ceased to exist after one day, once the Nigerian federal forces occupied Benin City.

(B) A puppet state of Biafra, the Republic of Benin ceased to exist after the Nigerian federal forces occupied Benin City.

(C) Albert Nwazu Okonkwo was the head of government of the Republic of Benin.

(D) The Republic of Benin was established as a puppet state of Biafra on September 19, 1967.

4 ☐ Mark for Review

While researching a topic, a student has taken the following notes:

- Marlon James is a Jamaican novelist.
- His first novel, *John Crow's Devil*, tells the story of the fictional town of Gibbeah, Jamaica.
- In *John Crow's Devil*, two men fight to be the town's spiritual leader.
- His second novel, *The Book of Night Women*, tells the story of an enslaved woman named Lilith.
- In *The Book of Night Women*, Lilith is asked to join a slave revolt.

The student wants to introduce plot elements of two novels. Which choice most effectively uses relevant information from the notes to accomplish this goal?

(A) Jamaican novelist Marlon James's first novel, *John Crow's Devil*, tells the story of the fictional town of Gibbeah, Jamaica.

(B) In Marlon James's second novel, *The Book of Night Women*, the character Lilith is asked to join a slave revolt.

(C) The fictional town of Gibbeah, Jamaica, is the setting for *John Crow's Devil* by Marlon James, a Jamaican novelist.

(D) In Marlon James's first novel, *John Crow's Devil*, two men fight to be the town's spiritual leader; in his second novel, *The Book of Night Women*, an enslaved woman named Lilith is asked to join a slave revolt.

5 🔖 Mark for Review

While researching a topic, a student has taken the following notes:

- Inō Tadataka, a Japanese cartographer, was the first person to survey Japan using modern techniques.
- He was in his 50s when he started the survey.
- It's estimated that he spent 3,736 days taking measurements.
- He walked over 34,000 kilometers.
- He spent 17 years total on the project.
- Although he completed several smaller maps, the map of the entire coastline of Japan was completed by his team 3 years after his death.

The student wants to emphasize the amount of effort Inō Tadataka put into surveying Japan. Which choice most effectively uses relevant information from the notes to accomplish this goal?

(A) Inō Tadataka was in his 50s when he started surveying Japan.

(B) Inō Tadataka walked over 34,000 kilometers and spent over 3,700 days taking measurements to complete his survey of Japan.

(C) Inō Tadataka's team completed his map of the coastline of Japan.

(D) Inō Tadataka completed small maps of Japan based on his 17 years of surveying.

6 🔖 Mark for Review

While researching a topic, a student has taken the following notes:

- Olga Tokarczuk is a Polish writer, activist, and clinical psychologist.
- She was born in Sulechów, Poland, and studied at the University of Warsaw.
- Her 2007 novel *Flights* won the Man Booker International Prize in 2018.
- *Flights* is a novel composed of 116 short pieces that explore the idea of modern-day travel.

The student wants to introduce *Flights* to an audience unfamiliar with the novel and its author. Which choice most effectively uses relevant information from the notes to accomplish this goal?

(A) *Flights*, written by Olga Tokarczuk, is a novel composed of 116 short pieces that explore the idea of modern-day travel.

(B) An award-winning novel composed of 116 short pieces, *Flights* (2007) was written by Polish writer, activist, and clinical psychologist Olga Tokarczuk.

(C) Olga Tokarczuk's 2007 novel *Flights* won the Man Booker International Prize in 2018.

(D) Olga Tokarczuk, who wrote *Flights* and later won the Man Booker International Prize, was born in Sulechów, Poland, and studied at the University of Warsaw.

7 ☐ Mark for Review

While researching a topic, a student has taken the following notes:

- *Organ²/As Slow as Possible* is a musical piece for organ written by John Cage.
- *Organ²/As Slow as Possible* is an adaptation by John Cage of his piano piece *ASLSP*.
- One performance is currently happening at St. Burchardi Church in Halberstadt, Germany.
- This performance began on September 5, 2001.
- This performance is scheduled to end on September 5, 2640.

The student wants to introduce *Organ²/As Slow as Possible* to an audience familiar with *ASLSP*. Which choice most effectively uses relevant information from the notes to accomplish this goal?

(A) An adaptation of *ASLSP*, John Cage's *Organ²/As Slow as Possible* is a musical piece for organ.

(B) The performance of John Cage's *Organ²/As Slow as Possible* at St. Burchardi Church began on September 5, 2001, and is scheduled to end on September 5, 2640.

(C) John Cage adapted his piano piece *ASLSP* to create the organ piece *Organ²/As Slow as Possible*.

(D) A performance of *Organ²/As Slow as Possible*, a musical piece for organ written by John Cage, started on September 5, 2001.

8 ☐ Mark for Review

While researching a topic, a student has taken the following notes:

- Bisa Butler is an American fiber artist who creates quilts that resemble paintings.
- Her works portray well-known historical figures as well as ordinary people and celebrate African American life.
- The primary materials she uses are kente cloth and African wax printed fabrics.
- Her pieces are large because they are made to life scale, allowing viewers to look into the eyes of her subjects.
- Her portraits sometimes use clothing or materials worn by their subjects.

The student wants to emphasize the authenticity of the quilted portraits. Which choice most effectively uses relevant information from the notes to accomplish this goal?

(A) Butler's portraits celebrate African American life and resemble paintings.

(B) Kente cloth, African wax printed fabrics, and materials worn by the subjects may all be used in Butler's quilts.

(C) Viewers can look into the eyes of Butler's subjects, some of whom are historical figures and some of whom are ordinary people.

(D) Butler makes her quilts life-size and sometimes uses clothing worn by her subjects.

9 ☐ Mark for Review

While researching a topic, a student has taken the following notes:

- Many consumers are interested in being able to purchase healthier food.

- Moosa Alsubhi and his colleagues wanted to find out whether people would be willing to pay more for healthier foods and what factors influence willingness to pay.

- Alsubhi and his team conducted a review of fifteen studies that reported the results of twenty-six experiments.

- Twenty-three of the twenty-six experiments found that consumers would pay more money for healthier foods.

- The review also showed that certain demographic factors, such as age and gender, influenced the willingness to pay more.

The student wants to emphasize the study's methodology. Which choice most effectively uses relevant information from the notes to accomplish this goal?

(A) Moosa Alsubhi and his team wanted to know whether consumers would be willing to pay more for healthier foods.

(B) Out of twenty-six experiments, twenty-three showed that consumers are willing to pay more for healthier foods.

(C) To find out whether people would be willing to pay more for healthier food, Moosa Alsubhi and his team conducted a review of twenty-six experiments.

(D) Moosa Alsubhi and his team found that certain demographic factors influenced people's willingness to pay more for healthier foods.

10 ☐ Mark for Review

While researching a topic, a student has taken the following notes:

- In a recent study, Nour Makarem and colleagues at Columbia University Mailman School of Public Health examined whether sleep quality should be added to a list of measures of cardiovascular health.

- They had 2,000 adults from an ongoing US study of cardiovascular health and risk factors participate in a sleep exam and record their sleep data.

- They found that sleep duration could predict future cardiovascular disease.

- They found that other aspects of sleep health, such as efficiency and regularity, were also predictive of future cardiovascular disease.

- The findings suggest that healthcare providers interested in their patients' cardiovascular health should ask about sleep patterns.

The student wants to summarize the study. Which choice most effectively uses relevant information from the notes to accomplish this goal?

(A) A recent study by Nour Makarem and colleagues found that sleep data, such as duration, efficiency, and regularity, can be used to predict future cardiovascular disease.

(B) The participants in Nour Makarem's study were asked to record data about their sleep, such as duration and regularity.

(C) Nour Makarem and colleagues wanted to know whether sleep could be a measure of cardiovascular health.

(D) Patients' sleep patterns can be used by healthcare providers to predict potential cardiovascular disease.

Chapter 37
Rhetorical Synthesis
Drill Explanations

ANSWER KEY

1.	A	6.	B
2.	C	7.	A
3.	A	8.	D
4.	D	9.	C
5.	B	10.	A

RHETORICAL SYNTHESIS DRILL EXPLANATIONS

1. **A**   This is a Rhetorical Synthesis question, so highlight the goal(s) stated in the question: *compare the lengths of the two rivers*. Eliminate any answer that doesn't fulfill this purpose.

    - (A) is correct because it includes specific lengths for both rivers.

    - (B) and (D) are wrong because they only include one length.

    - (C) is wrong because it doesn't include any information about *lengths*.

2. **C**   This is a Rhetorical Synthesis question, so highlight the goal(s) stated in the question: *highlight a similarity among Dosso's achievements*. Eliminate any answer that doesn't fulfill this purpose.

    - (A), (B), and (D) are wrong because they don't describe a *similarity*.

    - (C) is correct because the word *both* shows a similarity in what Dosso did.

3. **A**   This is a Rhetorical Synthesis question, so highlight the goal(s) stated in the question: *emphasize the beginning and end of the Republic of Benin*. Eliminate any answer that doesn't fulfill this purpose.

    - (A) is correct because it describes both *the beginning and end of the Republic of Benin*.

    - (B) is wrong because it only describes the *end* of the Republic of Benin.

    - (C) is wrong because it doesn't describe the *beginning* or the *end* of the Republic of Benin.

    - (D) is wrong because it only describes the *beginning* of the Republic of Benin.

4. **D**   This is a Rhetorical Synthesis question, so highlight the goal(s) stated in the question: *introduce plot elements of two novels*. Eliminate any answer that doesn't fulfill this purpose.

    - (A), (B), and (C) are wrong because they each only mention one novel.

    - (D) is correct because it discusses *plot elements* of *John Crow's Devil* and *The Book of Night Women*.

5. **B** This is a Rhetorical Synthesis question, so highlight the goal(s) stated in the question: *emphasize the amount of effort Inō Tadataka put into surveying Japan*. Eliminate any answer that doesn't fulfill this purpose.

    - (A), (C), and (D) are wrong because they don't mention anything about the *amount of effort*.

    - (B) is correct because the high numbers of kilometers and days represent the *amount of effort* it took to complete the survey.

6. **B** This is a Rhetorical Synthesis question, so highlight the goal(s) stated in the question: *introduce Flights to an audience unfamiliar with the novel and its author*. Eliminate any answer that doesn't *introduce Flights* in a way that assumes the audience is *unfamiliar with the novel and its author*.

    - (A) is wrong because it doesn't introduce the author, but the audience is unfamiliar with her.

    - (B) is correct because it introduces the novel and the author since the audience is unfamiliar with both.

    - (C) is wrong because it doesn't introduce the novel or the author, but the audience is unfamiliar with them.

    - (D) is wrong because it doesn't introduce the novel, but the audience is unfamiliar with it.

7. **A** This is a Rhetorical Synthesis question, so highlight the goal(s) stated in the question: *introduce Organ²/As Slow as Possible to an audience familiar with ASLSP*. Eliminate any answer that doesn't *introduce Organ²/As Slow as Possible* in a way that assumes the audience is *familiar with ASLSP*.

    - (A) is correct because it introduces *Organ²/As Slow as Possible* and doesn't explain *ASLSP* since the audience is familiar with it.

    - (B) is wrong because they don't introduce *Organ²/As Slow as Possible*.

    - (C) is wrong because it states what *ASLSP* is, but the audience is already familiar with this piece.

    - (D) is wrong because it doesn't relate *Organ²/As Slow as Possible* back to *ASLSP*.

8. **D** This is a Rhetorical Synthesis question, so highlight the goal(s) stated in the question: *emphasize the authenticity of the quilted portraits*. Eliminate any answer that doesn't fulfill this purpose.

    - (A) and (C) are wrong because they don't mention anything related to *authenticity*.

    - (B) is wrong because it isn't clear how some of these items relate to *authenticity*.

    - (D) is correct because if the portraits are *life-size* and use *clothing worn by her subjects*, they are authentic to the people they represent.

9. **C** This is a Rhetorical Synthesis question, so highlight the goal(s) stated in the question: *emphasize the study's methodology*. Eliminate any answer that doesn't fulfill this purpose.

    - (A), (B), and (D) are wrong because they don't describe *the study's methodology*.

    - (C) is correct because it describes how the study was performed.

10. **A** This is a Rhetorical Synthesis question, so highlight the goal(s) stated in the question: *summarize the study*. Eliminate any answer that doesn't fulfill this purpose.

    - (A) is correct because it describes the study and its findings.

    - (B), (C), and (D) are wrong because they don't describe the main findings of the study, so they don't *summarize* it as well as (A) does.

Chapter 38
Math Diagnostic Drill

Math Diagnostic Drill

1 ⚑ Mark for Review

What is the sum of $6z^2 - 3z$ and $5z^2 - 2z$?

Ⓐ $11z^2 - 5z$

Ⓑ $11z^2 + 5z$

Ⓒ $11z^4 - 5z^2$

Ⓓ $11z^4 + 5z^2$

2 ⚑ Mark for Review

$$f(x) = 3x - 4$$

The function f is defined by the given equation. What is the value of $f(x)$ when $x = -3$?

Ⓐ -13

Ⓑ -5

Ⓒ -4

Ⓓ 1

3 ⚑ Mark for Review

If the number n is at least 6 more than two-thirds of 12, what is the least possible value of n?

4 ⚑ Mark for Review

Data set A	67	71	75	81	82	90	99
Data set B	68	74	75	82	89	94	98

The table gives the values in data set A and data set B. Which of the following statements correctly compares the mean of data set A and the mean of data set B?

Ⓐ The means of data set A and data set B are equal.

Ⓑ The mean of data set A is greater than the mean of data set B.

Ⓒ The mean of data set A is less than the mean of data set B.

Ⓓ There is not enough information to compare the means.

5 | Mark for Review

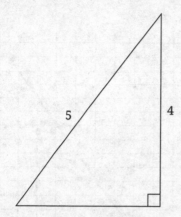

Note: Figure not drawn to scale

The triangle shown has an area of 6 square centimeters. What is the perimeter of the triangle, in centimeters?

(A) 11

(B) 12

(C) 15

(D) 16

6 | Mark for Review

If $37 = \frac{x}{20} - 3$, what is the value of x?

7 | Mark for Review

On a balancing scale, 40 gumballs weigh 12 ounces. At this rate, what is the number of gumballs that would weigh 36 ounces on the balancing scale?

8 ☐ Mark for Review

$$a = 100 + bc$$

The given equation relates the positive numbers a, b, and c. Which equation correctly expresses b in terms of a and c?

(A) $b = \frac{a}{100} - c$

(B) $b = \frac{a}{c} - 100$

(C) $b = \frac{a - 100}{c}$

(D) $b = a - 100 - c$

9 ☐ Mark for Review

The graph of $f(x) = -x^2 + 4x + 32$ reaches its maximum at (a, b). What is the value of a?

(A) -10

(B) -2

(C) 2

(D) 10

10 ☐ Mark for Review

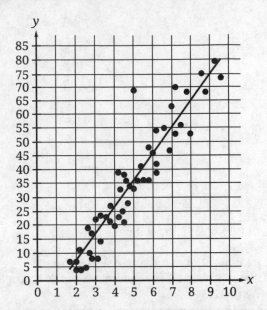

The scatterplot shows the relationship between two variables, x and y. A line of best fit is also shown. Which of the following equations best represents the line of best fit shown?

(A) $y = 5x + 15$

(B) $y = 10x - 15$

(C) $y = 15 - 10x$

(D) $y = x^2 + 10$

11 ☐ Mark for Review

At a certain gym, a membership costs $50 per month, and there is a one-time registration fee of r dollars. An individual wants to sign up for a membership but can spend no more than $555. Which of the following inequalities represents this situation, where m is the number of months in the membership?

(A) $50m + r \le 555$

(B) $50m + r \ge 555$

(C) $50r + m \le 555$

(D) $50r + m \ge 555$

12 ☐ Mark for Review

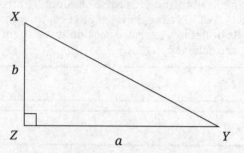

Note: Figure not drawn to scale

Right triangle XYZ is shown. Which of the following is equivalent to $\dfrac{b}{a}$?

(A) $\tan(X)$

(B) $\tan(Y)$

(C) $\cos(X)$

(D) $\cos(Y)$

13 ☐ Mark for Review

During his 12-minute exercise session, Brian spent 35% of his time doing crunches. How many <u>seconds</u> of Brian's exercise session were spent doing crunches?

Ⓐ 4.2

Ⓑ 35

Ⓒ 252

Ⓓ 720

14 ☐ Mark for Review

$$y > \frac{1}{7}(2y + 10)$$

Which of the following is a possible solution to the given inequality?

Ⓐ 0

Ⓑ 1

Ⓒ 2

Ⓓ 3

15 ☐ Mark for Review

Time (days)	Number of bacteria
0	50
3	100
6	150
9	200

The table shows the number of bacteria in a colony over the course of 9 days. Which type of function best models how the number of bacteria changes over time?

Ⓐ Decreasing exponential

Ⓑ Decreasing linear

Ⓒ Increasing exponential

Ⓓ Increasing linear

16 ☐ Mark for Review

The expression $4x^2 - 12$ is equivalent to $4(x + c)(x - c)$. If c is a positive constant, what is the value of c?

Ⓐ $\sqrt{3}$

Ⓑ 3

Ⓒ $\sqrt{12}$

Ⓓ 12

17 ☐ Mark for Review

$$f(x) = 2x^2 + 3x - 6$$

The function f is defined by the given equation. In the xy-plane, the graph of $y = g(x)$ is the result of translating the graph of $y = f(x)$ left 2 units. Which equation defines function g?

Ⓐ $g(x) = 2x^2 + 3x - 4$

Ⓑ $g(x) = 2x^2 + 3x + 8$

Ⓒ $g(x) = 2x^2 + 7x + 4$

Ⓓ $g(x) = 2x^2 + 11x + 8$

Chapter 39
Math Diagnostic
Drill Explanations

WHAT'S NEXT

Now that you have warmed up with many different types of Digital PSAT Math questions, review the explanations (especially for questions that you got wrong), and choose where to go next. The list below will tell you which drill to go to for more questions from that topic. You decide if that's based on the questions you missed or if it's for more practice in a topic for which you are close to achieving proficiency. Use the list below to pick your next drills.

Answer Key

Q #	Ans.	✔	Drill	Q #	Ans.	✔	Drill
1	A		Algebra Basics	10	B		Data and Statistics
2	A		Functions and Graphs Basics	11	A		Word Problems
3	14		Word Problems	12	B		Geometry and Trigonometry
4	C		Data and Statistics	13	C		Percents and Proportions
5	B		Geometry and Trigonometry	14	D		Algebra Intermediate
6	800		Algebra Basics	15	D		Functions and Graphs Intermediate
7	120		Percents and Proportions	16	A		Algebra Advanced
8	C		Algebra Intermediate	17	D		Functions and Graphs Advanced
9	C		Functions and Graphs Intermediate				

Diagnostic Math Drill

MATH DIAGNOSTIC DRILL EXPLANATIONS

1. **A** The question asks for an equivalent form of an expression. Work the question one piece at a time, and eliminate answers after each piece. Start by combining the terms that have z^2. Add $6z^2$ to $5z^2$ to get $6z^2 + 5z^2 = 11z^2$. Eliminate (C) and (D) because they do not include $11z^2$. Next, combine the terms that have z. Add $-3z$ to $-2z$ to get $-3z + (-2z) = -5z$. Eliminate (B) because it adds $5z$ instead of subtracting it. The correct answer is (A).

2. **A** The question asks for the value of a function. In function notation, the number inside the parentheses is the x-value that goes into the function, or the input, and the value that comes out of the function is the y-value, or the output. The question provides an input value of -3, so plug $x = -3$ into the function to get $f(-3) = 3(-3) - 4$, which becomes $f(-3) = -9 - 4$. This simplifies to $f(-3) = -13$. The correct answer is (A).

3. **14** The question asks for a value given a specific situation. Translate the English into math one piece at a time. *At least* means $\geq$, so translate *the number n is at least* as $n \geq$. Translate *more than* as addition and *of* as multiplication. Thus, *6 more than two-thirds of 12* becomes $6 + \frac{2}{3}(12)$. The full inequality becomes $n \geq 6 + \frac{2}{3}(12)$. Simplify on the right side of the inequality to get $n \geq 6 + 8$, and then $n \geq 14$. Since n can be greater than or equal to 14, the least possible value of n is 14. The correct answer is 14.

4. **C** The question asks for a comparison of the means, or averages, of two data sets. For averages, use the formula $T = AN$, in which T is the *Total*, A is the *Average*, and N is the *Number of things*. For both lists, the number of things and the total can be determined, so there is enough information to compare the means; eliminate (D). Since the *Number of things* is the same, the data set with the larger total will have the greater average. Try ballparking: most values in data set B are greater than or equal to the corresponding values in data set A, so data set B will have the larger total and the greater average, making (C) correct.

    To solve, use the average formula to calculate the averages. First, apply the formula to data set A, in which there are 7 values that add up to $67 + 71 + 75 + 81 + 82 + 90 + 99 = 565$. The average formula becomes $565 = A(7)$. Divide both sides of the equation by 7 to get $80.71 \approx A$. Now do the same for data set B, in which there are 7 values that add up to $68 + 74 + 75 + 82 + 89 + 94 + 98 = 580$. The average formula becomes $580 = A(7)$. Divide both sides of the equation by 7 to get $82.86 \approx A$. The mean of data set A, 80.71, is less than that of data set B, 82.86, which is (C).

    Using either method, the correct answer is (C).

5. **B** The question asks for the perimeter of a geometric figure. Start by redrawing the figure and labels on the scratch paper. The question gives the area of the triangle, so write down the formula for the area of a triangle, either from memory or after looking it up on the reference sheet: $Area = \frac{1}{2} \times base \times height$, or

$A = \dfrac{1}{2}bh$. Plug in the area and the height to get $6 = \dfrac{1}{2}(b)(4)$, which becomes $6 = 2b$. Divide both sides of the equation by 2 to get $3 = b$. Label the base of the triangle as 3. The perimeter of a geometric figure is the sum of all of its sides. Add the lengths of the three sides to get $P = 3 + 4 + 5$, or $P = 12$. The correct answer is (B).

6. **800** The question asks for the solution to an equation. To solve for x, add 3 to both sides of the equation to get $40 = \dfrac{x}{20}$. Next, multiply both sides of the equation by 20 to get $800 = x$. The correct answer is 800.

7. **120** The question asks for a value given a rate. Begin by reading the question to find information about the rate. The question states that *40 gumballs weigh 12 ounces* and asks for *the number of gumballs that would weigh 36 ounces*. Set up a proportion, being sure to match up the units. The proportion is $\dfrac{40 \text{ gumballs}}{12 \text{ ounces}} = \dfrac{x \text{ gumballs}}{36 \text{ ounces}}$. Cross-multiply to get $(40)(36) = (12)(x)$, which becomes $1{,}440 = 12x$. Divide both sides of the equation by 12 to get $120 = x$. The correct answer is 120.

8. **C** The question asks for an equation in terms of specific variables. The question asks about the relationship among variables and there are variables in the answer choices, so one option is to make up numbers for the variables. However, that might get messy with three variables, and all of the answer choices have b on the left side of the equation, so the other option is to solve for b. To begin to isolate b, subtract 100 from both sides of the equation to get $a - 100 = bc$. Divide both sides of the equation by c to get $\dfrac{a - 100}{c} = b$. Flip the two sides of the equation to get $b = \dfrac{a - 100}{c}$. The correct answer is (C).

9. **C** The question asks for the x-coordinate of the point at which a quadratic function reaches its maximum. A parabola reaches its minimum or maximum value at its vertex, so find the x-coordinate of the vertex. One method is to enter the equation into the built-in graphing calculator, then scroll and zoom as needed to find the vertex. The vertex is at $(2, 36)$, so the value of the x-coordinate is 2.

To solve algebraically, find the value of h, which is the x-coordinate of the vertex (h, k). When a quadratic is in standard form, which is $ax^2 + bx + c$, the x-coordinate of the vertex can be found using the formula $h = -\dfrac{b}{2a}$. In this quadratic, $a = -1$ and $b = 4$, so the formula becomes $h = -\dfrac{4}{2(-1)}$, then $h = -\dfrac{4}{-2}$ or $h = 2$.

Using either method, the correct answer is (C).

10.　**B**　The question asks for an equation that represents a line of best fit on a scatterplot. Compare features of the graph to the answer choices. Choice (D) has an x^2 term, meaning that the graph of (D) will be a parabola and not a line. Eliminate (D). The remaining equations in the answer choices are all close to the form $y = mx + b$, in which m is the slope and b is the y-intercept, except the mx and b terms are reversed in (C). The line of best fit ascends from left to right, so the slope is positive. Eliminate (C) because it has a slope of –10. Compare the remaining answer choices. One difference between (A) and (B) is the sign of the y-intercept. The y-intercept is the y-coordinate of the point where $x = 0$, which is not shown on the graph. Use the mouse pointer or edge of the scratch paper to visually extend the line of best fit on the left side of the graph to see that the value will be negative. Eliminate (A) because it has a positive y-intercept. The correct answer is (B).

11.　**A**　The question asks for an inequality that represents a specific situation. Translate the information one piece at a time, and eliminate answers after each piece. One piece of information says that the individual *can spend no more than $555*. Translate *no more than* as less than or equal to, or ≤. Thus, the correct inequality must contain ≤ 555. Eliminate (B) and (D) because the inequality sign is going in the wrong direction. The question also states that *a membership costs $50 per month* and that *m is the number of months*. Multiply the cost per month by the number of months to get $50m$. Eliminate (C) because it has $50r$ instead of $50m$. The correct answer is (A).

12.　**B**　The question asks for an equivalent trigonometric function. Start by redrawing the figure and labels on the scratch paper. Next, write out SOHCAHTOA to remember the trig functions. The CAH part defines the cosine as $\frac{adjacent}{hypotenuse}$. Neither a nor b is the hypotenuse of the triangle, so $\frac{b}{a}$ cannot be a cosine. Eliminate (C) and (D). The TOA part defines the tangent as $\frac{opposite}{adjacent}$. Side b is opposite angle Y, and side a is adjacent to angle Y, so $\frac{b}{a}$ is equivalent to $\frac{opposite}{adjacent}$ for angle Y. Thus, $\frac{b}{a} = \tan(Y)$. The correct answer is (B).

13.　**C**　The question asks for a measurement and gives conflicting units. To convert minutes to seconds, set up a proportion. Be sure to match up units. There are 60 seconds in 1 minute, so the proportion is $\frac{60 \text{ seconds}}{1 \text{ minute}} = \frac{x \text{ seconds}}{12 \text{ minutes}}$. Cross-multiply to get $(60)(12) = (1)(x)$, which becomes $720 = x$. The question states that *Brian spent 35% of his time doing crunches*. *Percent* means out of 100, so translate 35% as $\frac{35}{100}$. Take 35% of 720 seconds to get $\frac{35}{100}(720) = 252$ seconds. The correct answer is (C).

14.　**D**　The question asks for a possible solution to an inequality. To start solving for y, multiply both sides of the inequality by 7 to get rid of the fraction. The inequality becomes $7y > 2y + 10$. Subtract $2y$ from both sides of the inequality to get $5y > 10$. Divide both sides of the inequality by 5 to get $y > 2$. Eliminate (A), (B), and (C) because they are not greater than 2. The correct answer is (D).

15. **D** The question asks for a description of a function that models a specific situation. Compare the answer choices. Two choices say the function is decreasing, and two say it is increasing. Look at the *Number of bacteria* column in the table to see that the number of bacteria increases as the time increases, so this function is increasing. Eliminate (A) and (B) because they describe a decreasing function. The difference between (C) and (D) is whether the function is linear or exponential. From day 0 to day 3, the number of bacteria increases by $100 - 50 = 50$. From day 3 to day 6, the number of bacteria increases by $150 - 100 = 50$. From day 6 to day 9, the number of bacteria increases by $200 - 150 = 50$. The number of bacteria increases by the same amount over each three-day period, so the function is linear. The correct answer is (D).

16. **A** The question asks for the value of a constant based on two equivalent expressions. The question provides a quadratic in both standard form, which is $ax^2 + bx + c$, and factored form, which is $a(x - m)(x - n)$. Use FOIL to expand the factored form quadratic into standard form: $4(x + c)(x - c) = 4(x^2 - cx + cx - c^2)$. Combine the middle terms to get $4(x^2 - c^2)$. Distribute the 4 to get $4x^2 - 4c^2$. Now set this equal to the standard form expression, $4x^2 - 12$, and match up terms. It might make things clearer to write the two expressions above each other:

$$4x^2 - 4c^2$$

$$4x^2 - 12$$

Therefore, $4c^2 = 12$. Divide both sides of this equation by 4 to get $c^2 = 3$. Take the square root of both sides of the equation to get $c = \pm\sqrt{3}$. Only $\sqrt{3}$ is an answer choice, so it is correct. The correct answer is (A).

17. **D** The question asks for the equation of a function that has been translated from the graph of another function. The equation of function f is a quadratic, meaning the graph will be a parabola. One approach is to find the vertex of function f and then apply the shift. Enter the $f(x)$ equation into the built-in graphing calculator, then scroll and zoom as needed to find the vertex, which is indicated by a gray dot. Click on the dot to see that the coordinates of the vertex are $(-0.75, -7.125)$. The vertex of a graph shifted 2 units to the left would be at $(-2.75, -7.125)$. Graph each of the equations in the answer choices, and see which one has a vertex at $(-2.75, -7.125)$. Only (D) does, so it is correct.

To solve algebraically, recall that, when graphs are translated, adding inside the parentheses shifts the graph to the left. To shift $f(x)$ by 2 units to the left, add 2 inside the parentheses to get $f(x + 2) = 2(x + 2)^2 + 3(x + 2) - 6$. Use FOIL to expand the first term to get $f(x + 2) = 2(x^2 + 4x + 4) + 3(x + 2) - 6$. Distribute the 2 on the terms in the first set of parentheses and the 3 on the terms in the second set to get $f(x + 2) = 2x^2 + 8x + 8 + 3x + 6 - 6$. Combine like terms to get $f(x + 2) = 2x^2 + 11x + 8$. Since $g(x)$ is translated 2 units to the left of $f(x)$, it is equivalent to $f(x + 2)$, so $g(x) = 2x^2 + 11x + 8$.

Using either method, the correct answer is (D).

Chapter 40
Algebra Basics Drill

Algebra Basics Drill

1 ☐ Mark for Review

What is the value of $x - 3$ when $x = 26$?

(A) 23

(B) 26

(C) 29

(D) 36

2 ☐ Mark for Review

If $7(x - y) = 4$, what is the value of $x - y$?

(A) $\frac{4}{7}$

(B) $\frac{7}{4}$

(C) 4

(D) 7

3 ☐ Mark for Review

Which of the following expressions is a factor of $12x^2 + 30x$?

(A) 4

(B) $2.5x$

(C) $6x$

(D) $42x$

4 ☐ Mark for Review

If $x = 14 - y$, what is the value of $3x$ when $y = 11$?

(A) −9

(B) −3

(C) 3

(D) 9

5 ⬛ 🔖 Mark for Review

$$x^2 - x = 12$$

What is the positive solution to the given equation?

6 ⬛ 🔖 Mark for Review

If $|2x + 10| = 14$, what is the negative value of $x + 5$?

7 ⬛ 🔖 Mark for Review

If $\frac{3x + 2}{7} = \frac{2x + 5}{7}$, what is the value of x?

8 ⬛ 🔖 Mark for Review

The density of an object is calculated using the equation $d = \frac{m}{v}$, where m is the mass and v is the volume. According to the formula, what is the mass, m, in terms of d and v?

Ⓐ $m = d + v$

Ⓑ $m = dv$

Ⓒ $m = \frac{d}{v}$

Ⓓ $m = \frac{v}{d}$

Chapter 41
Algebra Basics Drill
Explanations

ANSWER KEY

1. A
2. A
3. C
4. D

5. 4
6. −7
7. 3
8. B

ALGEBRA BASICS DRILL EXPLANATIONS

1. **A** The question asks for the value of an expression. Substitute 26 for x in the expression $x - 3$ to get $26 - 3$, which becomes $26 - 3 = 23$. The correct answer is (A).

2. **A** The question asks for the value of an expression based on an equation. When a Digital PSAT question asks for the value of an expression, there is usually a straightforward way to solve for the expression without needing to completely isolate the variable. Divide both sides of the equation by 7 to get $x - y = \dfrac{4}{7}$. The question asks for the value of $x - y$, so stop here. The correct answer is (A).

3. **C** The question asks for a factor of an expression. The correct answer must be a value that both terms of the expression can be divided by without leaving a remainder. Look at the answer choices and the process of elimination. The second term, $30x$, cannot be divided by 4. Eliminate (A). The first term, $12x^2$, cannot be divided by $2.5x$. Eliminate (B). Both terms are divisible by $6x$: $\dfrac{12x^2}{6x} = 2x$, and $\dfrac{30x}{6x} = 5$. Keep (C). Neither term is divisible by $42x$. Eliminate (D). The correct answer is (C).

4. **D** The question asks for the value of an expression. Substitute 11 for y in the equation $x = 14 - y$ to get $x = 14 - 11$, which becomes $x = 3$. Next, substitute 3 for x in the expression $3x$ to get $3(3) = 9$. The correct answer is (D).

5. **4** The question asks for the positive solution to a quadratic equation. Rewrite the equation as a quadratic in standard form, which is $ax^2 + bx + c = 0$. Subtract 12 from both sides of the equation to get $x^2 - x - 12 = 0$. Now factor the quadratic part of the equation. Find two numbers that multiply to −12 and add to −1. These are −4 and 3. Thus, the quadratic factors into $(x - 4)(x + 3) = 0$. Now set each factor equal to 0 to get two equations: $x - 4 = 0$ and $x + 3 = 0$. Add 4 to both sides of the first equation to get $x = 4$. Subtract 3 from both sides of the second equation to get $x = -3$. The question asks for the positive solution, which is 4. The correct answer is 4.

6. **−7** The question asks for a solution to an equation with an absolute value. With an absolute value, the value inside the absolute value bars can be either positive or negative, so this equation has two possible solutions. The value in the absolute values bars could equal 14 or −14, so set $2x + 10$ equal to each. The question asks for the value of the expression $x + 5$, so it is not necessary to completely isolate the variable. When $2x + 10 = 14$, divide both sides of the equation by 2 to get $x + 5 = 7$. This is not a negative value, so set $2x + 10$ equal to −14. When $2x + 10 = −14$, divide both sides of the equation by 2 to get $x + 5 = −7$. The question asks for the negative value of $x + 5$, so stop here. The correct answer is −7.

7. **3** The question asks for the solution to an equation. To solve for x, multiply both sides of the equation by 7 to get $3x + 2 = 2x + 5$. Subtract $2x$ from both sides of the equation to get $x + 2 = 5$. Subtract 2 from both sides of the equation to get $x = 3$. The correct answer is 3.

8. **B** The question asks for an equation in terms of specific variables. The question asks about the relationship among variables and there are variables in the answer choices, so one option is to make up numbers for the variables. However, that might get messy with three variables, and all of the answer choices have m on the left side of the equation, so the other option is to solve for m. To begin to isolate m, multiply both sides of the equation by v to get $dv = m$. Flip the two sides of the equation to get $m = dv$. The correct answer is (B).

Chapter 42
Algebra Intermediate Drill

Algebra Intermediate Drill

1 ☐ Mark for Review

If $2x^2 - 3y = 23$, $y = 3$, and $x < 0$, what is the value of x?

2 ☐ Mark for Review

$$3x + 2y = -21$$
$$5x + 6y = -35$$

If (x, y) is a solution to the given system of equations, what is the value of $x + y$?

Ⓐ -14

Ⓑ -7

Ⓒ 14

Ⓓ 56

3 ☐ Mark for Review

$$y = 0.5x + 11.5$$

For which of the following tables are all of the values of x and their corresponding values of y solutions to the given equation?

Ⓐ
x	y
0	0
1	0.5
2	1.0
3	1.5

Ⓑ
x	y
0	11.5
1	11.0
2	10.5
3	10.0

Ⓒ
x	y
0	11.5
1	12.0
2	12.5
3	13.0

Ⓓ
x	y
0	11.5
1	12.5
2	13.5
3	14.5

4 🔖 Mark for Review

$$\frac{2p+q}{5} = 3r$$

The given equation relates the variables p, q, and r. Which equation correctly expresses q in terms of p and r?

Ⓐ $q = 15r - 2p$

Ⓑ $q = \dfrac{3r - 2p}{5}$

Ⓒ $q = \dfrac{2p - 3r}{5}$

Ⓓ $q = 2p - 15r$

5 🔖 Mark for Review

For all positive values of x and y, which of the following is equivalent to $\sqrt[5]{x^{15}y^{5}}$?

Ⓐ $x^{\frac{1}{3}}y$

Ⓑ x^{3}

Ⓒ $x^{3}y$

Ⓓ $x^{20}y^{10}$

6 🔖 Mark for Review

$$x - 7 = \sqrt{x - 1}$$

Which of the following are solutions to the given equation?

  I. 5
 II. 10

Ⓐ Neither I nor II

Ⓑ I only

Ⓒ II only

Ⓓ I and II

7 🔖 Mark for Review

$$15x^{2} - 4x - 32 = 0$$

What is the negative solution to the given equation?

Ⓐ -8

Ⓑ -4

Ⓒ $-\dfrac{8}{5}$

Ⓓ $-\dfrac{4}{3}$

8 Mark for Review

$$\frac{3x - 3}{2} = \frac{9}{x - 2}$$

Which of the following is a solution to the given equation?

(A) −4

(B) −2

(C) 1

(D) 4

9 Mark for Review

$$c(2x - 5) = 14x - 35$$

In the given equation, c is a constant. If the equation has infinitely many solutions, what is the value of c?

10 Mark for Review

If $2x + 5 \leq 9$, what is the greatest possible value of $2x - 5$?

(A) −3

(B) −1

(C) 0

(D) 2

11 Mark for Review

What is the sum of the solutions to the equation $3x^2 + 24x - 6 = 0$?

(A) $-6\sqrt{2}$

(B) −8

(C) 8

(D) $6\sqrt{2}$

12 ⬚ Mark for Review

The population P of a town can be modeled by the equation $P = 7,500(1.1)^d$, where d is the number of decades after the year 2000. Based on this model, what will be the approximate population of the town in the year 2040?

Ⓐ 10,980

Ⓑ 33,000

Ⓒ 330,000

Ⓓ 339,444

13 ⬚ Mark for Review

$$5\left|x + 6\right| - 3\left|x + 6\right| = 36$$

What is the negative solution to the given equation?

⬚

14 ⬚ Mark for Review

$$\frac{3}{2}x - 3y = -9$$

The given equation is one of two in a system of equations that has no real solutions. Which of the following could be the second equation in the system?

Ⓐ $-\frac{1}{2}x - y = -3$

Ⓑ $-\frac{1}{2}x - y = 3$

Ⓒ $\frac{1}{2}x - y = -3$

Ⓓ $\frac{1}{2}x - y = 3$

Chapter 43
Algebra Intermediate
Drill Explanations

ANSWER KEY

1.	−4	8.	D
2.	B	9.	7
3.	C	10.	B
4.	A	11.	B
5.	C	12.	A
6.	C	13.	−24
7.	D	14.	D

ALGEBRA INTERMEDIATE DRILL EXPLANATIONS

1. **−4** The question asks for a value in a system of equations. One method is to enter both equations into the built-in graphing calculator, then scroll and zoom as needed to find the points of intersection. The graphs intersect at (−4, 3) and (4, 3). The question states that $x < 0$, so $x = −4$.

    To solve the system for the x-coordinate algebraically, substitute 3 for y in the first equation. The equation becomes $2x^2 − 3(3) = 23$, and then $2x^2 − 9 = 23$. Add 9 to both sides of the equation to get $2x^2 = 32$. Divide both sides of the equation by 2 to get $x^2 = 16$. Take the square root of both sides of the equation to get $x = ±4$. The question states that $x < 0$, so $x = −4$.

    Using either method, the correct answer is −4.

2. **B** The question asks for the value of an expression given a system of equations. When a Digital PSAT question asks for the value of an expression, there is usually a straightforward way to solve for the expression without needing to completely isolate either variable. Try stacking and adding the two equations.

$$3x + 2y = −21$$
$$+ \ \underline{5x + 6y = −35}$$
$$8x + 8y = −56$$

    The question asks for the value of $x + y$, so divide both sides of the resulting equation by 8 to get $x + y = −7$. The correct answer is (B).

3. **C** The question asks for the table that contains values that are solutions to an equation. When given an equation and asked for a table of values, plug values from the table into the equation to see which ones work. Three of the tables have the same y-value when $x = 0$, but all four tables have different y-values when $x = 1$. Plug $x = 1$ into the equation to get $y = 0.5(1) + 11.5$, which becomes $y = 0.5 + 11.5$, and then $y = 12$. Eliminate (A), (B), and (D) because they have a value other than 12 when $x = 1$. The correct answer is (C).

4. **A** The question asks for an equation in terms of a specific variable. The question asks about the relationship among variables and there are variables in the answer choices, so one option is to make up numbers for the variables. However, that might get messy with three variables, and all of the answer choices have q on the left side of the equation, so the other option is to solve for q. To begin to isolate q, multiply both sides of the equation by 5 to get $2p + q = 15r$. Subtract $2p$ from both sides of the equation to get $q = 15r - 2p$. The correct answer is (A).

5. **C** The question asks for an equivalent form of an expression. Figure out one piece at a time and use the process of elimination. Start by rewriting the expression with fractional exponents. In a fractional exponent, the numerator is the power, and the denominator is the root. Taking the 5th root of a value raised to the 15th power can be written using the fractional exponent $\frac{15}{5}$, or 3. Thus, $\sqrt[5]{x^{15}} = x^3$. Eliminate (A) and (D) because they do not contain this term. Taking the 5th root of a value raised to the 5th power can be written using the fractional exponent $\frac{5}{5}$, or 1. Thus, $\sqrt[5]{y^5} = y^1$, or simply y. Eliminate (B) because it does not contain this term. The correct answer is (C).

6. **C** The question asks for the solution(s) to an equation. One approach is to enter the equation into the built-in graphing calculator, then scroll and zoom to find the solutions. The graph shows a single vertical line indicating a solution at 10. Since the question asks for all the possible solutions, the answer is (C).

    Another option is to test the numbers in the statements. Plug $x = 5$ into the equation to get $5 - 7 = \sqrt{5 - 1}$, which becomes $-2 = \sqrt{4}$, and then $-2 = 2$. This is not true, so 5 is not a solution to the equation. Eliminate (B) and (D) because they include statement (I). Next, plug $x = 10$ into the equation to get $10 - 7 = \sqrt{10 - 1}$, which becomes $3 = \sqrt{9}$, and then $3 = 3$. This is true, so 10 is a solution to the equation. Eliminate (A) because it does not include statement (II). Only (C) includes statement (II) but not statement (I), so it is correct.

    Using either method, the correct answer is (C).

7. **D** The question asks for the negative solution to a quadratic equation. The equation is a quadratic in standard form, which is $ax^2 + bx + c$. However, this quadratic is difficult to factor, so look for a different approach. One approach is to use the built-in calculator. Enter the expression into the built-in calculator, then scroll and zoom as needed to see the negative x-intercept, which is indicated by a gray dot at $(-1.333, 0)$. The fraction $-\frac{4}{3}$ equals $-1.\overline{33}$, making (D) correct.

It is also possible to find the solutions using the quadratic formula or to test the answer choices one at a time until one of them makes the equation true.

Using any of these methods, the correct answer is (D).

8. **D** The question asks for the solution to an equation. One method is to enter the equation into the built-in calculator, then scroll and zoom as needed to see the x-intercepts. These are indicated by vertical lines at -1 and 4. Only 4 is in the answer choices, so (D) is correct.

Another approach is to test the answers one at a time until one of them makes the equation true. Rewrite the answers on the scratch paper, and label them "x." Start with the easier number in the middle and try (C), 1. Plug 1 into the equation for x to get $\frac{3(1) - 3}{2} = \frac{9}{1 - 2}$. Simplify both sides of the equation to get $\frac{3 - 3}{2} = \frac{9}{-1}$, and then $0 = -9$. This is not true, so eliminate (C).

A larger value will make both sides of the equation positive, so try (D), 4. Plug 4 into the equation for x to get $\frac{3(4) - 3}{2} = \frac{9}{4 - 2}$. Simplify both sides of the equation to get $\frac{12 - 3}{2} = \frac{9}{2}$, and then $\frac{9}{2} = \frac{9}{2}$. This is true, so (D) is correct.

Using either method, the correct answer is (D).

9. **7** The question asks for the value of a constant in an equation. A linear equation has infinitely many solutions when the variable terms are the same and the constants are the same. Make the two sides of the equation look the same by distributing the c on the left side. The equation becomes $2cx - 5c = 14x - 35$. Set either pair of terms equal to each other, and solve for c. Set the constants equal to each other to get $-5c = -35$, and then divide both sides of the equation by -5 to get $c = 7$. To check, set the x-terms equal to each other to get $2cx = 14x$, and then divide both sides of the equation by $2x$ to get $c = 7$. The correct answer is 7.

10. **B** The question asks for the greatest possible value of an expression given an inequality. When a PSAT question asks for the value of an expression, there is usually a straightforward way to solve for the expression without needing to completely isolate the variable. First, subtract 5 from both sides of the inequality to get $2x \leq 4$. Next, subtract 5 again from both sides of the inequality to get $2x - 5 \leq -1$. The question asks for the greatest possible value of $2x - 5$, so stop here. The expression can be -1 or less. The correct answer is (B).

11. **B** The question asks for the sum of the solutions to a quadratic equation. This quadratic is difficult to factor without using the quadratic formula, but a shortcut is to recall that when a quadratic is in standard form, $ax^2 + bx + c = 0$, the sum of the solutions is $-\frac{b}{a}$. In this case, $a = 3$, $b = 24$, and $c = -6$. Plug in the values for a and b to get $-\frac{24}{3} = -8$, which is (B).

Another option is to enter the equation into the built-in graphing calculator, then scroll and zoom as needed to find the solutions. The solutions are indicated by gray dots at (−8.243, 0) and (0.243, 0). Add the two x-values to get −8.243 + 0.243 = −8, which is (B).

Using either method, the correct answer is (B).

12. **A**   The question asks for a value given a specific situation. The population is increasing by a percentage over time, so this question is about exponential growth. Write down the growth and decay formula. When the change is a percentage, the formula is *final amount = original amount*$(1 \pm rate)^{number\ of\ changes}$. In this case, the *final amount* is P, the *original amount* is 7,500, the *rate* is 0.1, and the *number of changes* is d. The question asks for the value of the population, P, in 2040, which is 2040 − 2000 = 40 years after 2000. The question states that *d is the number of decades after the year 2000*. Since there are 10 years in a decade, there are $\dfrac{40}{10}$ = 4 decades from 2000 to 2040. Plug 4 into the equation for d to get $P = 7,500(1.1)^4 \approx 10,981$. This is closest to 10,980. The correct answer is (A).

13. **−24**   The question asks for the negative solution to an equation with absolute values. One method is to enter the equation into the built-in graphing calculator. The values of x are shown by vertical lines; scroll and zoom as needed to see that these cross the x-axis at −24 and 12. The question asks for the negative solution, which is −24.

To solve algebraically, recall that, with an absolute value, the value inside the absolute value bars can be either positive or negative, so this equation has two possible solutions. To start solving for x, treat the absolute value symbols the same as parentheses and combine the absolute value terms on the left side of the equation to get $2|x + 6| = 36$. Next, divide both sides of the equation by 2 to get $|x + 6| = 18$. The value in the absolute value bars could equal 18 or −18, so set $x + 6$ equal to each. Setting it equal to −18 is likely to lead to the negative solution, so start there. When $x + 6 = −18$, subtract 6 from both sides of the equation to get $x = −24$. This is the negative solution, so stop here.

Using either method, the correct answer is −24.

14. **D**   The question asks for the equation that makes a system of equations have no real solutions. A system of linear equations in two variables has no real solutions when the slopes are the same but the y-intercepts are different, making the lines parallel. One way to find the equation of a parallel line is to compare the slopes and y-intercepts. All of the equations are linear equations in standard form, $Ax + By = C$. In this form, the slope is $-\dfrac{A}{B}$, and the y-intercept is $\dfrac{C}{B}$. Both would need to be calculated for all of the equations, which is time-consuming.

A more efficient method is to use the built-in calculator to graph the first equation and the equations in the answer choices and find the answer choice that graphs a parallel line. Be careful: the graphs of (A) and (B) are parallel to each other, but they are not parallel to the first line; eliminate (A) and (B). The graph of (C) is the same line as the graph of the equation in the question stem, which would make the system have infinitely many solutions; eliminate (C). Click on the circular symbols next to the equations in (A), (B), and (C) to show only the line graphed by the equation in (D) and the line graphed by the first equation. The line for (D) is parallel to the first line, so it is the equation that gives the system no real solutions. The correct answer is (D).

Chapter 44
Algebra Advanced
Drill

Algebra Advanced Drill

1 ☐ Mark for Review

$$2x + 7y = 5$$
$$-3x - 3y = 15$$

What value of y satisfies the given system of equations?

(A) -3

(B) 3

(C) 5

(D) 8

2 ☐ Mark for Review

$$(-4x^2 + 3x - 7) - 3(x^2 - 5x - 2)$$

If the given expression is rewritten in the form $ax^2 + bx + c$, what is the value of $a + b + c$?

3 ☐ Mark for Review

$$\frac{1}{3}x^2 + 4x + c = 0$$

In the given equation, c is a constant. If the equation has at least one real solution, what is the greatest possible value of c?

4 ☐ Mark for Review

For what integer value of k is $5x - k$ a factor of the expression $10x^2 - x - 3$?

(A) -3

(B) -1

(C) 1

(D) 3

5 Mark for Review

$$(3x + my)(5x - ny) = ax^2 + 14xy - 8y^2$$

In the given equation, a, m, and n are non-zero constants. What is the value of $5m - 3n$?

6 ☐ Mark for Review

$$y = \frac{ax - 16}{2a}$$

$$y + 2 = \frac{1}{8}ax$$

In the given system of equations, a is a constant. If the system has infinitely many solutions, what is the value of a?

Chapter 45
Algebra Advanced
Drill Explanations

ANSWER KEY

1.	B	4.	D	
2.	10	5.	14	
3.	12	6.	4	

ALGEBRA ADVANCED DRILL EXPLANATIONS

1. **B** The question asks for the y-value of the solution to a system of equations. One method is to enter both equations into the built-in graphing calculator, then scroll and zoom as needed to find the solution. The lines intersect at the point $(-8, 3)$. The question asks for the y-value, which is 3, so (B) is correct.

   To solve for y algebraically, look for a way to make the x-terms disappear. Multiply both sides of the first equation by 3 to get $6x + 21y = 15$. Multiply both sides of the second equation by 2 to get $-6x - 6y = 30$. Now that the equations contain the term $6x$ with opposite signs, stack and add the two equations.

$$
\begin{array}{r}
6x + 21y = 15 \\
+ \underline{(-6x - 6y = 30)} \\
15y = 45
\end{array}
$$

   Divide both sides of the resulting equation by 15 to get $y = 3$.

   Using either method, the correct answer is (B).

2. **10** The question asks for the value of an expression based on the coefficients in another expression. Distribute the -3 in the initial expression to get $-4x^2 + 3x - 7 - 3x^2 + 15x + 6$. Combine like terms to get $-7x^2 + 18x - 1$. This expression is now in the form $ax^2 + bx + c$, so $a = -7$, $b = 18$, and $c = -1$. Plug these values into the second expression to get $a + b + c = -7 + 18 - 1$, or $a + b + c = 10$. The correct answer is 10.

3. **12** The question asks for the value of a constant in a quadratic. To determine when a quadratic equation has at least one real solution, use the discriminant. The discriminant is the part of the quadratic formula under the square root sign and is written as $D = b^2 - 4ac$. When the discriminant is positive, the quadratic has exactly two real solutions; when the discriminant is 0, the quadratic has exactly one real solution; and when the discriminant is negative, the quadratic has no real solutions. Thus, the discriminant of this quadratic must be greater than or equal to 0. The quadratic is given in standard form, $ax^2 + bx + c = 0$, so $a = \dfrac{1}{3}$, $b = 4$, and $c = c$. Plug these values into the discriminant formula to get

$D = 4^2 - 4\left(\dfrac{1}{3}\right)c$. Since there is at least one real solution, $4^2 - 4\left(\dfrac{1}{3}\right)c \geq 0$. Simplify the left side of the inequality to get $16 - \dfrac{4}{3}c \geq 0$, then add $\dfrac{4}{3}c$ to both sides of the inequality to get $16 \geq \dfrac{4}{3}c$. Multiply both sides of the inequality by 3 to get $48 \geq 4c$, and then divide both sides of the inequality by 4 to get $12 \geq c$. The largest number that is less than or equal to 12 is 12, so this is the greatest possible value of c. The correct answer is 12.

4. **D** The question asks for the value of a constant in the factor of an expression. When working with factors of a quadratic, think about FOIL: First, Outer, Inner, Last. The first two terms must multiply to $10x^2$, so if the first term of one factor is $5x$, the first term of the other factor must be $\dfrac{10x^2}{5x} = 2x$. The last two terms must multiply to -3, and the question states that k is an integer, so the options are -3 and 1 or -1 and 3. Test which combination will add up to $-x$ when multiplied by $5x$ and $2x$. The factors $(5x - 3)$ and $(2x + 1)$ meet this requirement. To check, use FOIL to expand $(5x - 3)(2x + 1)$ to get $10x^2 + 5x - 6x - 3$. Combine the x-terms to get $10x^2 - x - 3$, which is the original expression. If $5x - k = 5x - 3$, then $k = 3$. The correct answer is (D).

5. **14** The question asks for the value of an expression based on an equation with three constants. The question provides a quadratic in both standard form, which is $ax^2 + bx + c$, and factored form, which is $a(x - m)(x - n)$. Use FOIL (First, Outer, Inner, Last) to expand the factored quadratic on the left into standard form: $(3x + my)(5x - ny) = 15x^2 - 3nxy + 5mxy - mny^2$. Combine the middle terms to get $15x^2 + (-3n + 5m)xy - mny^2$. Now set this equal to the standard form expression, $ax^2 + 14xy - 8y^2$, and match up terms. It might make things clearer to write the two expressions above each other:

$$15x^2 + (-3n + 5m)xy - mny^2$$
$$ax^2 + 14xy - 8y^2$$

Therefore, $a = 15$, $-3n + 5m = 14$, and $mn = -8$. The question asks for the value of $5m - 3n$, so switch the order of the terms on the left side of the second equation to get $5m - 3n = 14$. The correct answer is 14.

6. 4 The question asks for the value of a constant in a system of linear equations with infinitely many solutions. A linear equation has infinitely many solutions when the x-terms are the same and the constants are the same. Make the two equations look similar in order to compare the terms. Clear the fractions first. Multiply both sides of the first equation by $2a$ to get $2ay = ax - 16$. Multiply both sides of the second equation by 8 to get $8(y + 2) = (1)ax$, and then $8y + 16 = ax$. Subtract 16 from both sides of the second equation to get $8y = ax - 16$. Write the two equations above each other to see how they match up:

$$2ay = ax - 16$$
$$8y = ax - 16$$

Both equations have $ax - 16$ on the right side, so the left sides must be equal to each other. Set $2ay$ equal to $8y$ and solve for a: $2ay = 8y$. Divide both sides of this equation by $2y$ to get $a = 4$. The correct answer is 4.

Chapter 46
Word Problems Drill

Word Problems Drill

1 ☐ Mark for Review

At a juice bar, s servings of banana smoothie are made by adding b bananas to a blender. If $s = b - 4$ and $b \geq 5$, how many additional servings of banana smoothie can be made with each additional banana?

(A) One

(B) Two

(C) Three

(D) Four

2 ☐ Mark for Review

When 6 is subtracted from $10p$, the result is t. Which equation represents the relationship between p and t?

(A) $6p - 10 = t$

(B) $6(p - 10) = t$

(C) $10(p - 6) = t$

(D) $10p - 6 = t$

3 ☐ Mark for Review

A shopper spent an average of x dollars on each of 5 shirts and an average of y dollars on each of 3 hats. The shopper spent a total of \$225. Which of the following equations represents this situation?

(A) $x + y = 225$

(B) $3x + 5y = 225$

(C) $5x + 3y = 225$

(D) $15x + 15y = 225$

4 ☐ Mark for Review

The number of logs remaining in a firewood supply after logs have been burned for d days can be modeled by the equation $F = -23d + 1{,}235$. What is the best interpretation of the number 23 in this context?

(A) The number of logs burned each day

(B) The initial number of logs before any were burned

(C) The number of days it takes to burn 1,235 logs

(D) The total number of logs burned after d days

5 Mark for Review

A certain species of freshwater crayfish can grow to a length of 11.5 centimeters. Approximately how long can the species of freshwater crayfish grow in inches?
(1 inch ≈ 2.54 centimeters)

(A) 1.45

(B) 4.53

(C) 8.96

(D) 29.21

6 Mark for Review

The amount of solvent, in milliliters, remaining in a beaker that is being emptied at a constant rate can be modeled by the equation $s = 500 - 0.4t$, where t is the time in seconds. If the beaker starts with 500 milliliters of solvent, at what value of t will the beaker be empty?

7 Mark for Review

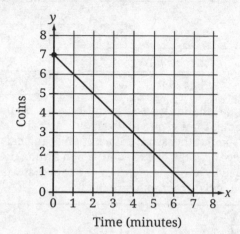

In a certain game, players start with a certain number of coins and then spend their coins until they run out. The graph shows the number of coins, y, possessed by one player x minutes after the start of the game. What is the best interpretation of the y-intercept of the graph?

(A) The player spends 1 coin per minute.

(B) The player spends 7 coins per minute.

(C) After 7 minutes, the player had 0 coins remaining.

(D) The player started with 7 coins.

8 ☐ Mark for Review

		Species	
		Dogs	Cats
Color	Brown	13	9
	Black	21	7

An animal shelter held an adoption event to find new homes for a group of dogs and cats. The table shows the numbers and colors of dogs and cats that were adopted at the event. Each animal was classified as only one color. Of the cats that were adopted, what fraction were black?

Ⓐ $\frac{7}{50}$

Ⓑ $\frac{16}{50}$

Ⓒ $\frac{7}{16}$

Ⓓ $\frac{9}{16}$

9 ☐ Mark for Review

Time (seconds)	Height (feet)
0	10
1	13
2	14
3	13
4	10
5	5

The table shows the height of a projectile that is launched from a 10-foot-tall platform. If $H(t)$ represents the height of the projectile, in feet, and t represents the time since launch, in seconds, which of the following functions represents the relationship between height and time since launch?

Ⓐ $H(t) = -t^2 - 4t + 10$

Ⓑ $H(t) = -t^2 + 4t + 10$

Ⓒ $H(t) = t^2 - 4t + 10$

Ⓓ $H(t) = t^2 + 4t - 10$

10 ☐ Mark for Review

The total weight of a carton of oranges is 27.3 pounds, of which 9.6 pounds is the weight of the carton itself. If a fruit vendor pays $46.25 for a carton of oranges, which of the following is closest to the cost of the oranges, in dollars per pound?

Ⓐ $1.70

Ⓑ $2.60

Ⓒ $4.80

Ⓓ $6.50

11 ☐ Mark for Review

The speed, in miles per hour, of a particular experimental spacecraft t minutes after it is launched is modeled by the function M, which is defined as $M(t) = 200(3)^{\frac{t}{3}}$. According to this model, what is the speed, in miles per hour, 9 minutes after the spacecraft is launched?

12 ☐ Mark for Review

Carla received some money for her birthday and decided to use it to start saving up to buy a video game console. The amount of money she has saved is given by the equation $y = 45x + 100$, where y is the amount of money she has saved and x is the number of weeks since she started saving for the console. Which statement is the best interpretation of $(x, y) = (3, 235)$ in this context?

Ⓐ Carla saved $3 each week for 235 weeks.

Ⓑ Carla had $3 saved after 235 weeks.

Ⓒ Carla saved $235 each week for 3 weeks.

Ⓓ Carla had $235 saved after 3 weeks.

13 ☐ Mark for Review

Sarah and Lizzie each plant one bamboo stalk. After one week, Sarah's bamboo stalk is three times as tall as Lizzie's bamboo stalk. If the sum of the heights of the two stalks of bamboo is 52 inches, how tall, in inches, is Sarah's bamboo stalk?

Ⓐ 13

Ⓑ 39

Ⓒ 52

Ⓓ 156

14 ☐ Mark for Review

A theater sells tickets for matinee and nighttime showings. The matinee tickets cost $8 each, and the nighttime tickets cost $14 each. The theater needs to sell at least 200 tickets for a total of at least $3,000. If m represents the number of matinee tickets sold and n represents the number of nighttime tickets sold, which of the following systems of inequalities represents this situation?

Ⓐ $8m + 14n \le 3,000$
$m + n \le 200$

Ⓑ $8m + 14n \le 3,000$
$m + n \ge 200$

Ⓒ $8m + 14n \ge 3,000$
$m + n \le 200$

Ⓓ $8m + 14n \ge 3,000$
$m + n \ge 200$

15 ☐ Mark for Review

The combined weight of a refrigerator, a dishwasher, and a food processor is 360 pounds. The refrigerator weighs 40% less than the dishwasher and the food processor combined. What is the weight, in pounds, of the refrigerator?

- (A) 82
- (B) 90
- (C) 135
- (D) 257

Chapter 47
Word Problems Drill
Explanations

ANSWER KEY

1. A
2. D
3. C
4. A
5. B
6. 1250
7. D
8. C

9. B
10. B
11. 5400
12. D
13. B
14. D
15. C

WORD PROBLEMS DRILL EXPLANATIONS

1. **A** The question asks for the value of one variable in terms of another. The question asks about the relationship among variables, so try out some numbers. The question states that $b \geq 5$, so start by plugging $b = 5$ into the equation $s = b - 4$ to get $s = 5 - 4 = 1$. The question asks how many additional servings can be made with each additional banana, so increase the number of bananas by 1 and plug in $b = 6$. The equation becomes $s = 6 - 4 = 2$. There is 1 serving with 5 bananas and 2 servings with 6 bananas, so $2 - 1 = 1$ additional servings can be made with each additional banana. The correct answer is (A).

2. **D** The question asks for an equation based on the relationship between two variables. Translate the English to math in bite-sized pieces. Translate *6 is subtracted from 10p* as $10p - 6$. Translate *the result is t* as $= t$. Therefore, the entire equation is $10p - 6 = t$. The correct answer is (D).

3. **C** The question asks for an equation that represents a given situation. Translate the English to math in bite-sized pieces. One piece of information says that x represents the average cost of a shirt, and another piece says that y represents the average cost of a hat. All of the answer choices have 225 on the right side of the equation, which correctly translates the total amount spent on shirts and hats. The left side of the equation must also represent the total amount. If x and y represent the average cost per shirt and the average cost per hat, respectively, the coefficients of x and y must represent the numbers of shirts and hats. Therefore, the coefficient of x must be 5 and the coefficient of y must be 3. Eliminate (A), (B), and (D) because they have different values for the coefficients of x and y. The correct answer is (C).

4. **A** The question asks for the interpretation of a term in context. Start by reading the final question, which asks for the meaning of the number 23. Rewrite the equation on the scratch paper. Then label the parts of the equation with the information given, and eliminate answers that do not match the labels. The question states that the equation models the number of logs remaining after d days, so label F as the number of logs remaining and d as the number of days. The number 23 is multiplied by the number of days, so it must be an amount per day. Eliminate (B), (C), and (D) because they are not an amount per day. Since 23 is negative, it makes sense that it is the number of logs being subtracted from the initial number of logs, or the number of logs burned, each day.

It is also possible to recognize that the equation is in slope-intercept form, $y = mx + b$, in which m represents the slope, or rate of change, and b represents the y-intercept, or the initial value. The question asks about the number 23, which is the value for m, or the rate of change. Therefore, 23 represents the number of logs burned per day.

Using either method, the correct answer is (A).

5.   **B**   The question asks for a measurement and gives conflicting units. To convert centimeters to inches, set up

a proportion. Be sure to match up units. The question states that *1 inch ≈ 2.54 centimeters*, so the propor-

tion is $\dfrac{1 \text{ inch}}{2.54 \text{ centimeters}} = \dfrac{x \text{ inches}}{11.5 \text{ centimeters}}$. Cross-multiply to get $(2.54)(x) = (1)(11.5)$, which becomes

$2.54x = 11.5$. Divide both sides of the equation by 2.54 to get $x ≈ 4.528$. This is closest to 4.53. The cor-

rect answer is (B).

6.   **1250**   The question asks for the value of a variable in an equation that models a specific situation. The equation $s = 500 - 0.4t$ represents the amount of solvent, s, remaining in a beaker that is being emptied at a constant rate. Since s represents the amount of solvent remaining, the beaker will be empty when $s = 0$. Plug 0 into the equation for s and solve for t. The equation becomes $0 = 500 - 0.4t$. Add $0.4t$ to both sides of the equation to get $0.4t = 500$. Divide both sides of the equation by 0.4 to get $t = 1,250$. Leave out the comma when entering the answer in the fill-in box. The correct answer is 1250.

7.   **D**   The question asks for the interpretation of a feature of a graph that represents a specific situation. Start by reading the final question, which asks for the best interpretation of the y-intercept. The y-intercept is the y-value when $x = 0$. The question states that the graph represents *the number of coins, y, possessed by one player x minutes after the start of the game*. The y-intercept is thus the number of coins when 0 minutes have gone by. Find $x = 0$ on the x-axis of the graph, and then move up—using the mouse pointer or the edge of the scratch paper as a ruler—to see that the line intercepts the y-axis at the point $(0, 7)$. Thus, when $x = 0$, $y = 7$, which means that the player had 7 coins at the start of the game. The correct answer is (D).

8.   **C**   The question asks for a fraction based on a table. Read carefully to find the numbers that make up the

fraction. The question asks about the *cats that were adopted*, so start there. According to the table, 9

brown cats and 7 black cats were adopted, for a total of $9 + 7 = 16$ adopted cats. The question then asks

about those adopted cats that *were black*, so that value is 7. Therefore, the fraction of adopted cats that

were black is $\dfrac{7}{16}$. The correct answer is (C).

9.   **B**   The question asks for a function that represents values given in a table for a specific situation. In function notation, the number inside the parentheses is the x-value that goes into the function, or the input, and the value that comes out of the function is the y-value, or the output. In this case, t is the input and $H(t)$ is the output. The table includes 5 input and output values, and the correct equation must work

for every pair of values. Plug in values from the table and eliminate functions that don't work. Because 0 and 1 are likely to make more than one answer work, try the third row of the table and plug in $t = 2$ and $H(t) = 14$. Choice (A) becomes $14 = -(2)^2 - 4(2) + 10$, or $14 = -4 - 8 + 10$, and then $14 = -2$. This is not true, so eliminate (A). Choice (B) becomes $14 = -(2)^2 + 4(2) + 10$, or $14 = -4 + 8 + 10$, and then $14 = 14$. This is true, so keep (B) but check the remaining answers just in case. Choice (C) becomes $14 = (2)^2 - 4(2) + 10$, or $14 = 4 - 8 + 10$, and then $14 = 6$; eliminate (C). Choice (D) becomes $14 = (2)^2 + 4(2) - 10$, or $14 = 4 + 8 - 10$, and then $14 = 2$; eliminate (D). The correct answer is (B).

10. **B** The question asks for a value given a specific situation. Translate the information in bite-sized pieces. The question states that *the total weight of a carton of oranges is 27.3 pounds, of which 9.6 pounds is the weight of the carton itself*. Find the weight of the oranges by subtracting the weight of the carton from the total weight. The weight of the oranges is $27.3 - 9.6 = 17.7$ pounds. To find the cost per pound, divide the total cost by the weight of the oranges to get $\dfrac{\$46.25}{17.7 \text{ pounds}} \approx \$2.61$ per pound of oranges. The closest value is \$2.60. The correct answer is (B).

11. **5400** The question asks for the value of a function. In function notation, the number inside the parentheses is the x-value that goes into the function, or the input, and the value that comes out of the function is the y-value, or the output. The question provides an input value of 9, so plug $t = 9$ into the function to get $M(9) = 200(3)^{\frac{9}{3}}$, which becomes $M(9) = 200(3)^3$. Continue simplifying the right side of the equation to get $M(9) = 200(27)$, and then $M(9) = 5,400$. Leave out the comma when entering the answer in the fill-in box. The correct answer is 5400.

12. **D** The question asks for the interpretation of coordinates in a function. Start by reading the final question, which asks for the best interpretation of the coordinates (3, 235). The question states that *x is the number of weeks since she started saving for the console*, so $x = 3$ means that Carla has been saving for 3 weeks. Eliminate (A) and (B) because they state that she has been saving for 235 weeks. The question also states that *y is the amount of money she has saved*, so $y = 235$ means that Carla has saved a total of \$235. Eliminate (C) since it states that she saved \$235 each week. The correct answer is (D).

13. **B** The question asks for a value given a specific situation. Since the question asks for a specific value and the answers contain numbers in increasing order, try using the answers. Rewrite the answer choices on the scratch paper and label them "height of Sarah's bamboo stalk." Next, start with a number in the middle and try (B), 39. If Sarah's bamboo stalk is 39 inches tall and the sum of the heights is 52 inches, Lizzie's bamboo stalk is $52 - 39 = 13$ inches tall. The question also states that *Sarah's bamboo stalk is three times as tall as Lizzie's bamboo stalk*. If Lizzie's bamboo stalk is 13 inches tall, Sarah's bamboo stalk is $(3)(13) = 39$ inches tall. In both cases, the height of Lizzie's bamboo stalk is 13 inches and the height of Sarah's bamboo stalk is 39 inches, so stop here. The correct answer is (B).

14. **D** The question asks for a system of inequalities that represents a specific situation. Translate the information in bite-sized pieces, and eliminate after each piece. One piece of information says that *the theater needs to sell at least 200 tickets*. Translate *at least 200* as greater than or equal to 200, or ≥ 200. Eliminate (A) and (C) because the inequality sign in the second inequality is facing the wrong direction. Compare the remaining answer choices. Choices (B) and (D) have the same second inequality, so focus on the first inequality. The question states that the total from selling tickets is *at least $3,000*. Translate this as greater than or equal to 3,000, or ≥ 3,000. Eliminate (B) because the inequality sign in the first inequality is facing the wrong direction. The correct answer is (D).

15. **C** The question asks for a value given a specific situation. Since the question asks for a specific value and the answers contain numbers in increasing order, try using the answers. Rewrite the answer choices on the scratch paper and label them "weight of the refrigerator." Next, start with a number in the middle and try (B), 90. If the refrigerator weighs 90 pounds and the combined weight of all three appliances is 360 pounds, the combined weight of the dishwasher and food processor is $360 - 90 = 270$ pounds. The questions states that *the refrigerator weighs 40% less than the dishwasher and the food processor combined*, so find 40% of 270 pounds. *Percent* means out of 100, so translate 40% as $\dfrac{40}{100}$ to get $\left(\dfrac{40}{100}\right)(270) =$ 108 pounds. The refrigerator weighs 40% less, so subtract this result from the combined weight of the dishwasher and the food processor to get $270 - 108 = 162$ pounds. The two weights of the refrigerator, 90 pounds and 162 pounds, are not equal, so eliminate (B).

It may be difficult to tell whether a larger or smaller number is needed, so pick a direction and try (C), 135. If the refrigerator weighs 135 pounds, the dishwasher and food processor together weigh $360 - 135 = 225$ pounds. Find 40% of 225 pounds and subtract it from 225 pounds: $225 - \left(\dfrac{40}{100}\right)(225) =$ $225 - 90 = 135$ pounds. The two weights of the refrigerator are the same, 135 pounds, so this answer works. The correct answer is (C).

Chapter 48
Functions and
Graphs Basics Drill

Functions and Graphs Basics Drill

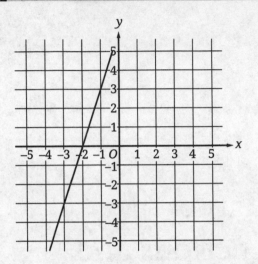

The (x, y) coordinates of the x-intercept of the graph shown are $(x, 0)$. What is the value of x?

(A) -5

(B) -2

(C) 0

(D) 6

Linear function f is defined by $f(x) = ax - 6$. The graph of $y = f(x)$ in the xy-plane passes through the point $(3, 0)$. What is the slope of the line?

(A) -3

(B) -2

(C) 2

(D) 18

$$f(x) = 5x^2 + 12$$

The function f is defined by the given equation. What is the value of $f(x)$ when $x = -5$?

4 ☐ Mark for Review

The function f is defined by $f(x) = 2x + 1$. If $f(a) = 2$, what is the value of a?

(A) $-\frac{1}{2}$

(B) $\frac{1}{2}$

(C) 2

(D) 5

5. ☐ Mark for Review

$$y = x^2 + 5x - 8$$
$$y = x - 3$$

Which of the following ordered pairs (x, y) is a solution to the given system of equations?

(A) $(-5, -8)$

(B) $(-1, -12)$

(C) $(4, 1)$

(D) $(6, 3)$

6 ☐ Mark for Review

x	$f(x)$
-1	0
0	-2
1	0
2	6

The table gives four values of x and their corresponding values of $f(x)$. Which of the following equations could define function f?

(A) $f(x) = x^2 - 2$

(B) $f(x) = x^2 + 2$

(C) $f(x) = 2x^2 - 2$

(D) $f(x) = 2x^2 + 2$

7 ☐ Mark for Review

Line l is defined by the equation $y = 2x + 7$. When graphed in the xy-plane, which of the following lines is perpendicular to line l?

(A) $y = -\frac{1}{2}x + 3$

(B) $y = \frac{1}{2}x + 3$

(C) $y = 2x - \frac{1}{7}$

(D) $y = 2x + \frac{1}{7}$

Chapter 49
Functions and
Graphs Basics Drill
Explanations

ANSWER KEY

1. B
2. C
3. 137
4. B

5. A
6. C
7. A

FUNCTIONS AND GRAPHS BASICS DRILL EXPLANATIONS

1. **B** The question asks for a value based on a graph. Specifically, the question asks for the value of the x-intercept on the graph of a line. This is the point at which $y = 0$ and the graph intersects the x-axis. Look on the graph for the point on the line at which the y-coordinate equals 0 and the graph passes through the x-axis. This point is $(-2, 0)$, making the x-coordinate equal to -2. The correct answer is (B).

2. **C** The question asks for the slope of a line. In function notation, the number inside the parentheses is the x-value that goes into the function, or the input, and the value that comes out of the function is the y-value, or the output. The question gives a point on the line, which means the input value is 3 and the output value is 0. Plug 3 for x and 0 for $f(x)$ into the function to get $0 = 3a - 6$. The equation is in slope-intercept form, $y = mx + b$, in which m is the slope and b is the y-intercept. Since x is 3, a is m, so solve for a to find the slope. Add 6 to both sides of the equation to get $6 = 3a$, then divide both sides of the equation by 3 to get $2 = a$. The correct answer is (C).

3. **137** The question asks for the value of a function. In function notation, the number inside the parentheses is the x-value that goes into the function, or the input, and the value that comes out of the function is the y-value, or the output. The question provides an input value of -5, so plug $x = -5$ into the function to get $f(-5) = 5(-5)^2 + 12$, which becomes $f(-5) = 125 + 12$, and then $f(-5) = 137$. The correct answer is 137.

4. **B** The question asks for a value given a function. In function notation, the number inside the parentheses is the x-value that goes into the function, or the input, and the value that comes out of the function is the y-value, or the output. The question provides an output value of 2, and the answers have numbers that could represent the input value, so test the answers until one of them works. Rewrite the answers on the scratch paper and label them "a." Start with the easier of the two middle numbers and try (C), 2. Plug in 2 for a and the function becomes $f(2) = 2(2) + 1$. Simplify to get $f(2) = 4 + 1$, and then $f(2) = 5$. This does not match the output value of 2 given in the question, so eliminate (C). The result

was too large, so also eliminate (D) and try (B), $\frac{1}{2}$. Plug in $\frac{1}{2}$ for a and the function becomes $f\left(\frac{1}{2}\right) = 2\left(\frac{1}{2}\right) + 1$. Simplify to get $f\left(\frac{1}{2}\right) = 1 + 1$, and then $f\left(\frac{1}{2}\right) = 2$. This matches the output value given in the question, so stop here. The correct answer is (B).

5. **A**   The question asks for the solution to a system of equations. One approach is to enter both equations into the built-in graphing calculator, then scroll and zoom as needed to find the points of intersection. There are two points of intersection. Click on the gray dots to see that the points are at (–5, –8) and (1, –2). Only (–5, –8) is an answer choice, so (A) is correct.

Another option is to test the answers to find one that makes both equations true. Rewrite the answer choices on the scratch paper and label them "(x, y)." Start with (A) and plug $x = -5$ and $y = -8$ into the easier second equation to get $-8 = -5 - 3$, which becomes $-8 = -8$. This is true, so try the same point in the first equation. When $x = -5$ and $y = -8$, the first equation becomes $-8 = (-5)^2 + 5(-5) - 8$. Simplify to get $-8 = 25 - 25 - 8$, and then $-8 = -8$. This is also true, so the point in (A) works in both equations, and it is the correct answer.

Using either method, the correct answer is (A).

6. **C**   The question asks for the function that represents values given in a table. In function notation, the number inside the parentheses is the x-value that goes into the function, or the input, and the value that comes out of the function is the y-value, or the output. The table includes 4 pairs of input and output values, and the correct equation must work for every pair of values. Test values from the table in the answer choices, and eliminate functions that don't work. Because 0 and 1 are likely to make more than one answer work, try the first row of the table and plug $x = -1$ and $f(x) = 0$ into the answer choices. Choice (A) becomes $0 = (-1)^2 - 2$, then $0 = 1 - 2$, and finally $0 = -1$. This is not true, so eliminate (A). Choice (B) becomes $0 = (-1)^2 + 2$, then $0 = 1 + 2$, and finally $0 = 3$; eliminate (B). Choice (C) becomes $0 = 2(-1)^2 - 2$, then $0 = 2(1) - 2$. Continue simplifying to get $0 = 2 - 2$, and finally $0 = 0$. This is true, so keep (C), but check (D) just in case. Choice (D) becomes $0 = 2(-1)^2 + 2$, then $0 = 2(1) + 2$. Continue simplifying to get $0 = 2 + 2$, and then $0 = 4$; eliminate (D). The correct answer is (C).

7. **A**   The question asks for the equation that represents a line. Specifically, the question asks for the equation of a line that is *perpendicular to line l*, which means that the two lines have slopes that are negative reciprocals of each other. The question gives the equation of line l, so find the slope of that line. The equation is in slope-intercept form, $y = mx + b$, where m is the slope and b is the y-intercept. In the equation, $m = 2$, so the slope of line l is 2. The slope of a line perpendicular to line l is thus $-\frac{1}{2}$. Eliminate (B), (C), and (D) because they have slopes other than $-\frac{1}{2}$. The correct answer is (A).

Chapter 50
Functions and Graphs Intermediate Drill

Functions and Graphs Intermediate Drill

1 ☐ Mark for Review

$$f(x) = 2x^2 + 3$$

The function f is defined by the given equation. For which of the following values does $f(x) = 21$?

- (A) -9
- (B) -3
- (C) 0
- (D) 1

2 ☐ Mark for Review

The graph of $y = f(x)$ in the xy-plane has a y-intercept of -6. Which of the following equations could define linear function f?

- (A) $x - 2y = -6$
- (B) $x - 2y = 6$
- (C) $2x - y = -6$
- (D) $2x - y = 6$

3 ☐ Mark for Review

A scientist uses the function s to measure the level of sulfur dioxide in the atmosphere, where $s(y)$ is the sulfur dioxide level, in parts per billion, and y is the number of years since the scientist began the study. The sulfur dioxide level was 75 parts per billion when the study began, and it has increased by 5% each year since the study began. Which of the following equations defines function s?

- (A) $s(y) = 5(1.05)^y$
- (B) $s(y) = 75(0.95)^y$
- (C) $s(y) = 75(1.05)^y$
- (D) $s(y) = 75(5)^y$

4 ⬜ Mark for Review

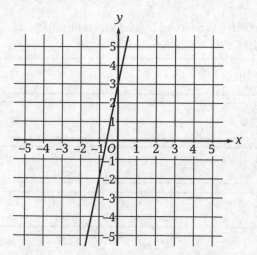

The graph of linear function f is shown in the xy-plane. If $y = f(x)$, what is the equation of the graph?

(A) $f(x) = \frac{1}{5}x + \frac{1}{3}$

(B) $f(x) = \frac{1}{5}x + 3$

(C) $f(x) = 5x + 3$

(D) $f(x) = 5x + 5$

5 ⬜ Mark for Review

$$f(x) = \sqrt[3]{3x}$$

Function f is defined by the given equation. For what value of x does $f(x) = 3$?

(A) 1

(B) 3

(C) 9

(D) 27

6 ⬜ Mark for Review

Every night for 10 nights after a magic show opens, the audience is 10% less than the night before. What type of function best models the relationship between the size of the audience and time?

(A) Decreasing exponential

(B) Decreasing linear

(C) Increasing exponential

(D) Increasing linear

7 ⬜ Mark for Review

$$cx - 5y = 6$$
$$2x - 3y = 8$$

When graphed in the xy-plane, the given system of equations has no real solutions. What is the value of the constant c?

(A) $-\frac{10}{3}$

(B) $-\frac{13}{11}$

(C) $\frac{13}{11}$

(D) $\frac{10}{3}$

8 ☐ Mark for Review

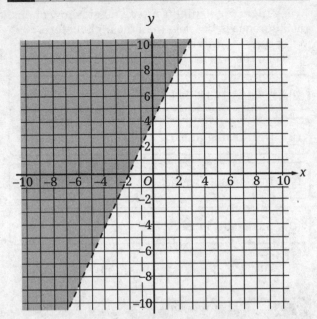

The graph of $y = f(x)$ is shown, where function f is defined by an inequality. Which of the following ordered pairs (x, y) is a solution to this inequality?

(A) $(-3, 0)$

(B) $(0, -3)$

(C) $(0, 3)$

(D) $(3, 0)$

9 ☐ Mark for Review

$$g(x) = 2 + |x - 2|$$

Function g is defined by the given equation. If $g(-2) = g(a)$, what is the value of a?

(A) 0

(B) 2

(C) 4

(D) 6

10 ☐ Mark for Review

Function g is defined by the equation $g(x) = cx^2 + 18$. If c is a constant and $g(2) = 10$, what is the value of $g(-2)$?

(A) -10

(B) 10

(C) 18

(D) 26

11 ⬚ Mark for Review

In function f, $f(0) = 1{,}250$. If the value of $f(x)$ decreases by 4% for every increase in the value of x by 1, which equation defines f?

Ⓐ $f(x) = 0.96(1{,}250)^x$

Ⓑ $f(x) = 1.04(1{,}250)^x$

Ⓒ $f(x) = 1{,}250(0.96)^x$

Ⓓ $f(x) = 1{,}250(1.04)^x$

12 ⬚ Mark for Review

$$y = (x - 5)(x + 6)$$
$$y = x + 6$$

When graphed in the xy-plane, the given equations intersect at two points. Which of the following is the x-coordinate of one of those points?

Ⓐ 0

Ⓑ 5

Ⓒ 6

Ⓓ 12

13 ⬚ Mark for Review

Time (seconds)	Population (thousands)
1	2
2	6
3	18
4	54

The table shows the population growth of a certain bacteria over a period of four seconds. Which function models the relationship between population $P(t)$, in thousands, and time t, in seconds?

Ⓐ $P(t) = 3t$

Ⓑ $P(t) = 2t^2$

Ⓒ $P(t) = 2(3t)$

Ⓓ $P(t) = 2(3)^{(t-1)}$

14 ⬚ Mark for Review

In the xy-plane, the graph of function g has x-intercepts at -4, 2, and 4. Which of the following equations could define function g?

Ⓐ $g(x) = (x - 4)(x - 2)(x + 4)$

Ⓑ $g(x) = (x - 4)(x + 2)(x + 4)$

Ⓒ $g(x) = (x - 4)^2(x - 2)$

Ⓓ $g(x) = (x + 2)(x + 4)^2$

Chapter 51
Functions and
Graphs Intermediate
Drill Explanations

ANSWER KEY

1.	B		8.	A
2.	D		9.	D
3.	C		10.	B
4.	C		11.	C
5.	C		12.	C
6.	A		13.	D
7.	D		14.	A

FUNCTIONS AND GRAPHS INTERMEDIATE DRILL EXPLANATIONS

1. **B** The question asks for a value given a function. In function notation, the number inside the parentheses is the x-value that goes into the function, or the input, and the value that comes out of the function is the y-value, or the output. The question provides an output value of 21, and the answers have numbers that could represent the input value, so try out the numbers in the answer choices until one of them results in the correct output. Rewrite the answer choices on the scratch paper and label them "x." Next, start with a middle value and try (B), –3. Plug –3 into the function to get $f(-3) = 2(-3)^2 + 3$. Simplify to get $f(-3) = 2(9) + 3$, then $f(-3) = 18 + 3$, and finally $f(-3) = 21$. This matches the output value given in the question, so stop here. The correct answer is (B).

2. **D** The question asks for the equation of a line with a given y-intercept. The equations in the answer choices are all in standard form, $Ax + By = C$. When a linear equation is in standard form, the y-intercept is $\dfrac{C}{B}$. Determine the y-intercept of each answer choice to see which has a y-intercept of –6. For (A), the y-intercept is $\dfrac{-6}{-2}$, or 3. This is not equal to the target y-intercept of –6, so eliminate (A). For (B), the y-intercept is $\dfrac{6}{-2}$, or –3; eliminate (B). For (C), the y-intercept is $\dfrac{-6}{-1}$, or 6; eliminate (C). For (D), the y-intercept is $\dfrac{6}{-1}$ or –6, which matches the target y-intercept.

   It is also possible to convert each answer choice into slope-intercept form, $y = mx + b$, and find the equation in which $b = -6$. Another option is enter the equation from each answer choice into the built-in graphing calculator to determine the y-intercept of each one.

   Using any method, the correct answer is (D).

3. **C** The question asks for a function that represents a specific situation. The sulfur dioxide level is increasing by a certain percentage over time, so this question is about exponential growth. Write down the growth and decay formula, which is *final amount* = (*original amount*)$(1 \pm rate)^{number\ of\ changes}$. In this case, $s(y)$ is the *final amount*, and the question states that the *original amount* is 75. Eliminate (A) because it does not have 75 as the original amount in front of the parentheses. Since this situation involves an increase,

the original amount must be multiplied by (1 + *rate*). The rate given in the question is 5% or 0.05, so the value in parentheses should be 1 + 0.05, or 1.05. Eliminate (B) and (D) because they do not have the value of 1.05 inside the parentheses. The only remaining answer is (C), and it matches the growth formula. The correct answer is (C).

4. **C**   The question asks for an equation that represents a graph. One approach is to enter the equation from each answer choice into the built-in graphing calculator and see which graph looks most like the graph shown in the question.

Another approach is to compare features of the graph to the answer choices. The equations in the answer choices are all in the form $y = mx + b$, in which m is the slope and b is the y-intercept. The y-intercept is the y-coordinate of the point where $x = 0$, which is at 3 on this graph. Eliminate (A) and (D) because they have different y-intercepts. Compare the remaining answer choices. The difference between (B) and (C) is the slope. Find the slope by using the formula $slope = \frac{y_2 - y_1}{x_2 - x_1}$. The graph has points at (0, 3) and (–1, –2), so plug those values into the slope formula to get $slope = \frac{3 - (-2)}{0 - (-1)}$, which becomes $slope = \frac{5}{1}$, or $slope = 5$. Eliminate (B) because it has a slope of $\frac{1}{5}$ instead of 5, which leaves (C) as the correct answer.

Using either method, the correct answer is (C).

5. **C**   The question asks for a value given a function. In function notation, the number inside the parentheses is the x-value that goes into the function, or the input, and the value that comes out of the function is the y-value, or the output. The question provides an output value of 3, and the answers have numbers that could represent the x-value, so try out the numbers in the answer choices until one of them results in the correct output. Rewrite the answer choices on the scratch paper and label them "x." Next, start with a middle value and try (B), 3. Plug 3 into the function to get $f(3) = \sqrt[3]{3(3)}$, or $f(3) = \sqrt[3]{9}$. Use a calculator to get $f(3) \approx 2.08$. This is not 3, so eliminate (B).

The result was close but too small, so also eliminate (A) and try (C), 9, next. Plug 9 into the function to get $f(3) = \sqrt[3]{3(9)}$, or $f(3) = \sqrt[3]{27}$. The cube root of 27 is 3, which matches the output value given in the question. The correct answer is (C).

6. **A**   The question asks for description of a function that models a specific situation. Compare the answer choices. Two choices say that the function is increasing, and two say it is decreasing. The question states that *the audience is 10% less than the night before*, so the audience size is decreasing. Eliminate (C) and (D) because they describe an increasing function. The difference between (A) and (B) is whether the function is exponential or linear. Try some numbers to see how the function changes. Make the

attendance on the first night 100. On the second night, the attendance is 10% less. *Percent* means out of 100, so translate 10% as $\frac{10}{100}$. Thus, 10% of 100 is $\frac{10}{100}$ (100) = 10. The audience was 10% *less*, so subtract 10 from 100 to get 90. The attendance the next night was 10% less again, so take 10% of 90 and subtract it from 90 to get $90 - \frac{10}{100}$ (90) = 90 – 9 = 81. The audience decreased by 10 the first time and by 9 the second time. This is not the same amount, so the function is not linear; eliminate (B). The correct answer is (A).

7. **D** The question asks for the value of a constant in a system of equations. A system of linear equations in two variables has no real solution when the lines are parallel. Parallel lines have the same slope. The equations are in standard form, $Ax + By = C$. When a linear equation is in standard form, the slope is $-\frac{A}{B}$. In the first equation, $A = c$ and $B = -5$. Therefore, the slope of the first equation is $-\frac{c}{-5}$, which simplifies to $\frac{c}{5}$. In the second equation, $A = 2$ and $B = -3$, so the slope of the second equation is $-\frac{2}{-3}$, which simplifies to $\frac{2}{3}$. Since the lines are parallel, set the slopes equal to each other to get $\frac{c}{5} = \frac{2}{3}$. Cross-multiply to get $(c)(3) = (5)(2)$, and then $3c = 10$. Divide both sides of this equation by 3 to get $c = \frac{10}{3}$. The correct answer is (D).

8. **A** The question asks which point is a solution to an inequality shown by a graph. The shaded region of the graph represents the solutions to the inequality. The answers contain specific points that could be a solution to the inequality, so find each point from the answer choices on the graph, and eliminate any that are not in the shaded area. Only (A), (–3, 0), is within the shaded area of the graph. The correct answer is (A).

9. **D** The question asks for a value given a function. In function notation, the number inside the parentheses is the x-value that goes into the function, or the input, and the value that comes out of the function is the y-value, or the output. The question provides an input value of –2, so plug that into the function for x to get $g(-2) = 2 + |-2 - 2|$, or $g(-2) = 2 + |-4|$. Continue simplifying to get $g(-2) = 2 + 4$, and then $g(-2) = 6$.

To find the other input that gives an output of 6, plug in each answer choice for x and look for one that makes $g(x) = 6$. Rewrite the answer choices on the scratch paper, and label them "x." Start with one of the middle numbers and try (C), 4. Plug $x = 4$ into the function to get $g(4) = 2 + |4 - 2|$, or $g(4) = 2 + |2|$. Continue simplifying to get $g(4) = 2 + 2$, and then $g(4) = 4$. This is not 6, so eliminate (C). The result was too small, so try (D), 6, next. Plug $x = 6$ into the function to get $g(6) = 2 + |6 - 2|$, or $g(6) = 2 + |4|$. Continue simplifying to get $g(6) = 2 + 4$, and then $g(6) = 6$. This is the same output as $g(-2)$, so $a = 6$. The correct answer is (D).

10. **B** The question asks for a value given a function. In function notation, the number inside the parentheses is the x-value that goes into the function, or the input, and the value that comes out of the function is the y-value, or the output. The question provides an input value of 2 and an output value of 10, so set x equal to 2 and $g(x)$ equal to 10, and solve for c. The equation becomes $10 = c(2)^2 + 18$, and then $10 = 4c + 18$. Subtract 18 from both sides of the equation to get $-8 = 4c$. Divide both sides of the equation by 4 to get $-2 = c$.

Next, plug $c = -2$ and $x = -2$ into the function to get $g(-2) = -2(-2)^2 + 18$. Simplify the right side of the equation to get $g(-2) = -2(4) + 18$, which becomes $g(-2) = -8 + 18$, and then $g(-2) = 10$. The correct answer is (B).

11. **C** The question asks for a function that represents a specific situation. The function is decreasing by a certain percentage with each increase of 1, so this question is about exponential decay. Write down the growth and decay formula, which is *final amount* = (*original amount*)$(1 \pm rate)^{number\ of\ changes}$. In this case, $f(x)$ is the *final amount*, and the *original amount* is 1,250. Eliminate (A) and (B) because they do not have 1,250 as the original amount in front of the parentheses. Since this situation involves a decrease, the original amount must be multiplied by $(1 - rate)$. The rate given in the question is 4%, or 0.04, so the value in parentheses should be $1 - 0.04$, or 0.96. Eliminate (D) because it does not have the value of 0.96 inside the parentheses. The only remaining answer is (C), and it matches the growth formula.

Without this formula, it is still possible to answer this question. Plug in two values of x, and eliminate answers that do not work with those values. When $x = 0$, $f(x) = 1,250$, so plug these numbers into the answer choices. Any number raised to the power of zero equals 1, so only (C) and (D) work with these values. When x increases by 1, $f(x)$ decreases by 4%. Thus, $f(1) = 1,250 - \left(\frac{4}{100}\right)(1,250)$, which becomes $f(1) = 1,250 - 50$, and then $f(1) = 1,200$. Plug $x = 1$ and $f(x) = 1,200$ into the remaining answers. Choice (C) becomes $1,200 = 1,250(0.96)^1$, or $1,200 = 1,250(0.96)$, and then $1,200 = 1,200$. Keep (C), but check (D) just in case. Choice (D) becomes $1,200 = 1,250(1.04)^1$, or $1,200 = 1,250(1.04)$, and then $1,200 = 1,300$. This is not true, so eliminate (D), which makes (C) correct.

Using either method, the correct answer is (C).

12. **C** The question asks for the x-coordinate of a point of intersection of a system of equations. One method is to enter both equations into the built-in graphing calculator, then scroll and zoom as needed to find the points of intersection. The graph shows two points of intersection at $(-6, 0)$ and $(6, 12)$. Therefore, the x-coordinate is 6 or -6. Only 6 is an answer choice, so choose (C).

Another approach is to solve algebraically. Since both equations are equal to y, set the right sides of the two equations equal to each other to get $(x - 5)(x + 6) = x + 6$. Divide both sides of the equation by $(x + 6)$ to get $x - 5 = 1$. Add 5 to both sides of the equation to get $x = 6$, which is (C).

Using either method, the correct answer is (C).

13. **D**   The question asks for the function that represents values given in a table. In function notation, the number inside the parentheses is the x-value that goes into the function, or the input, and the value that comes out of the function is the y-value, or the output. The table includes four pairs of input and output values, and the correct equation must work for every pair of values. Plug in values from the table and eliminate functions that don't work. Because 1 is likely to make more than one answer work, try the second row of the table and plug $t = 2$ and $P(t) = 6$ into the answer choices. Choice (A) becomes $6 = 3(2)$, or $6 = 6$. This is true, so keep (A), but check the remaining answers. Choice (B) becomes $6 = 2(2)^2$, or $6 = 2(4)$, and then $6 = 8$. This is not true, so eliminate (B). Choice (C) becomes $6 = 2[3(2)]$, or $6 = 2(6)$, and then $6 = 12$; eliminate (C). Choice (D) becomes $6 = 2(3)^{(2 - 1)}$, or $6 = 2(3)^1$, and then $6 = 6$. Keep (D).

Two answers worked with one pair of values, so try the third row of the table and plug $t = 3$ and $P(t) = 18$ into the remaining answer choices. Choice (A) becomes $18 = 3(3)$, or $18 = 9$; eliminate (A). Choice (D) becomes $18 = 2(3)^{(3 - 1)}$, or $18 = 2(3)^2$. Continue simplifying to get $18 = 2(9)$, and then $18 = 18$; keep (D). The correct answer is (D).

14. **A**   The question asks for a function that represents a specific situation. In function notation, $f(x) = y$. The number inside the parentheses is the x-value that goes into the function, or the input, and the value that comes out of the function is the y-value, or the output. Together, they represent points on the graph of the function. The question provides three x-intercepts, at -4, 2, and 4. These are the points at which the graph crosses the x-axis. One approach is to enter the equation from each answer choice into the built-in graphing calculator and see which graph crosses the x-axis at these three points.

Since the answers are all in factored form, another approach is to use the factors. If a is an x-intercept of a polynomial, $(x - a)$ is a factor of the polynomial. This graph crosses the x-axis at -4, 2, and 4, so the factors must include $(x + 4)$, $(x - 2)$, and $(x - 4)$. Eliminate (B), (C), and (D), which do not contain all of these factors. The correct answer is (A).

Chapter 52
Functions and Graphs Advanced Drill

Functions and Graphs Advanced Drill

Mark for Review

$$y = 5x - 18$$
$$y = x^2 - 5x + 6$$

The graphs of the given equations in the xy-plane intersect at two points. What is the product of the x-coordinates of the two points?

Mark for Review

Line m in the xy-plane has a slope of $-\frac{3}{2}$. Line n is perpendicular to line m and passes through the point $(0, 0)$. Which of the following points lies on line n?

(A) $\left(0, \frac{2}{3}\right)$

(B) $(2, 3)$

(C) $(6, 4)$

(D) $(9, 4)$

---

3 **Mark for Review**

$$g(x) = -(x - 10)(x + 4)$$

Quadratic function g is defined by the given equation. Function h is defined by $h(x) = g(x - 4)$. For what value of x does $h(x)$ reach its maximum?

(A) -1

(B) 3

(C) 4

(D) 7

---

4 **Mark for Review**

In the xy-plane, a parabola with the equation $y = x^2 - 18x + 70$ intersects a line with the equation $y = k$, where k is a constant, at exactly one point. What is the value of k?

---

5 ▢ Mark for Review

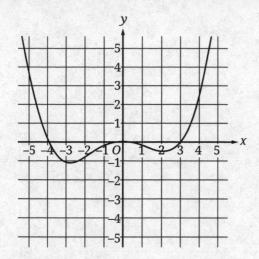

Which of the following could be the equation of the graph shown in the xy-plane?

Ⓐ $f(x) = \frac{1}{50}x(x-4)(x+3)$

Ⓑ $f(x) = \frac{1}{50}x(x-3)(x+4)$

Ⓒ $f(x) = \frac{1}{50}x^2(x-4)(x+3)$

Ⓓ $f(x) = \frac{1}{50}x^2(x-3)(x+4)$

Chapter 53
Functions and
Graphs Advanced
Drill Explanations

ANSWER KEY

1. 24
2. C
3. D

4. −11
5. D

FUNCTIONS AND GRAPHS ADVANCED DRILL EXPLANATIONS

1. **24** The question asks for the value of the product of the x-coordinates of the points of intersection given a system of equations. The quickest method is to enter both equations into the built-in graphing calculator, then scroll and zoom as needed to find the points of intersection. The graph shows the two points of intersection as (4, 2) and (6, 12), so the x-coordinates are 4 and 6. A *product* is the result of multiplication, and $4 \times 6 = 24$, so the answer is 24.

   To solve the system for the x-coordinates algebraically, substitute $5x - 18$ for y in the second equation to get $5x - 18 = x^2 - 5x + 6$. Subtract $5x$ from both sides of the equation to get $-18 = x^2 - 10x + 6$. Add 18 to both sides of the equation to get $0 = x^2 - 10x + 24$. Factor the right side of the equation. Find two numbers that multiply to 24 and add to −10. These are −4 and −6. Thus, the quadratic factors into $0 = (x - 4)(x - 6)$. Now set each factor equal to 0 to get two equations: $x - 4 = 0$ and $x - 6 = 0$. Add 4 to both sides of the first equation to get $x = 4$. Add 6 to both sides of the second equation to get $x = 6$. Multiply the x-values to get $4 \times 6 = 24$.

   Using either method, the correct answer is 24.

2. **C** The question asks for a point on a line. The question states that line n is perpendicular to line m, which means they have slopes that are negative reciprocals of each other. The question gives the slope of line m as $-\dfrac{3}{2}$, so the slope of line n is $\dfrac{2}{3}$. Use this slope and the given point (0, 0) to determine the equation of line n. The equation can be written in $y = mx + b$ form, in which m is the slope, b is the y-intercept, and x and y are the coordinates of a point on the line. The equation becomes $0 = \dfrac{2}{3}(0) + b$, which simplifies to $0 = 0 + b$, or just $0 = b$. Thus, the full equation is $y = \dfrac{2}{3}x + 0$ or $y = \dfrac{2}{3}x$. Now plug the points from the answers into this equation to see which is on the line. In (A), $x = 0$ and $y = \dfrac{2}{3}$, so the equation becomes $\dfrac{2}{3} = \dfrac{2}{3}(0)$ or $\dfrac{2}{3} = 0$. This is not true, so eliminate (A). In (B), $x = 2$ and $y = 3$, so the equation

becomes $3 = \dfrac{2}{3}(2)$ or $3 = \dfrac{4}{3}$. This is not true, so eliminate (B). In (C), $x = 6$ and $y = 4$, so the equation becomes $4 = \dfrac{2}{3}(6)$ or $4 = \dfrac{12}{3}$, which becomes $4 = 4$. This is true, so this point is on the line. If (C) works, (D) cannot also work, so eliminate (D). The correct answer is (C).

3. **D** The question asks for a value of x for which a function reaches its maximum. A parabola reaches its minimum or maximum value at its vertex, so find the x-coordinate of the vertex. The question asks about the graph of a function that has been translated, or shifted, from the graph of the function given in the question. Enter both the $g(x)$ equation and the $h(x)$ equation into the built-in graphing calculator, then scroll and zoom as needed to see the two parabolas. Either use the color-coding or click on the entry field with the $h(x)$ equation to see that the parabola on the right is the graph of $h(x)$. Click on the gray dot at the vertex to see that the vertex is at $(7, 49)$. The question asks for the value of x, which is 7, so (D) is correct.

Another approach is to find the vertex of function g and then apply the shift. Use the built-in graphing calculator to find that the vertex of $g(x)$ is at $(3, 49)$, so the x-coordinate of the vertex is 3. When graphs are translated, subtracting inside the parentheses shifts the graph to the right. Thus, $x - 4$ shifts the graph four units to the right, which shifts the x-coordinate of the vertex from 3 to 7.

Using either method, the correct answer is (D).

4. **−11** The question asks for a value in a system of equations. The equations are both equal to y, so set them equal to each other. The new equation becomes $k = x^2 - 18x + 70$. Put the quadratic in standard form by setting one side equal to 0. Subtract k from both sides of the equation to get $0 = x^2 - 18x + 70 - k$.

The question states that the graphs of the equations in the given system intersect *at exactly one point*, so use the discriminant. The discriminant is the part of the quadratic formula under the square root sign, and it can be written as $D = b^2 - 4ac$. When the discriminant is positive, the quadratic has exactly two real solutions; when the discriminant is 0, the quadratic has exactly one real solution; and when the discriminant is negative, the quadratic has no real solutions. In this case, the quadratic has exactly one real solution, so the discriminant must equal 0.

With the equation in standard form, which is $ax^2 + bx + c = 0$, $a = 1$, $b = -18$, and $c = 70 - k$. Plug these values into the discriminant formula and set it equal to 0 to get $(-18)^2 - 4(1)(70 - k) = 0$. Simplify the left side of the equation to get $324 - 4(70 - k) = 0$. Distribute the -4 to get $324 - 280 + 4k = 0$. Simplify further to get $44 + 4k = 0$, then subtract 44 from both sides of the equation to get $4k = -44$. Finally, divide both sides of the equation by 4 to get $k = -11$. The correct answer is -11.

5. **D** The question asks for an equation that represents a graph. One approach is to enter the equation from each answer choice into the built-in graphing calculator and see which graph looks like the graph in the question. Since the answers are all in factored form, another approach is to use the factors. If $(x - a)$ is a factor of a polynomial, a is a solution. This graph intersects the x-axis at $(-4, 0)$, $(0, 0)$, and $(3, 0)$, so the factors must include $(x + 4)$, x, and $(x - 3)$. Eliminate (A) and (C), which do not contain all of these factors. Next, plug in a point that is on the graph but is not on the x-axis. When $x = 2$, $y \approx -0.5$, so plug those values into the remaining answers. Choice (B) becomes $-0.5 = \frac{1}{50}(2)(2 - 3)(2 + 4)$, or $-0.5 = \frac{1}{50}(2)(-1)(6)$, and then $-0.5 = -0.24$. This is not true, so eliminate (B). Choice (D) becomes $-0.5 = \frac{1}{50}(2)^2(2 - 3)(2 + 4)$, or $-0.5 = \frac{1}{50}(4)(-1)(6)$, and then $-0.5 = -0.48$. This is close, so the equation in (D) could work for the curve in the graph. The correct answer is (D).

Chapter 54
Data and Statistics
Drill

Data and Statistics Drill

1 ☐ Mark for Review

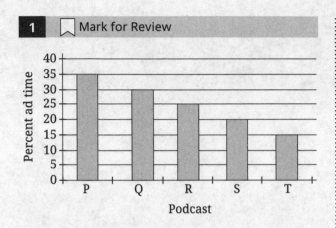

The bar graph shows the percent of time used for ads during 5 different podcasts. What is the percent ad time for the podcast with the lowest percent of time used for ads?

(A) 15

(B) 20

(C) 25

(D) 35

2 ☐ Mark for Review

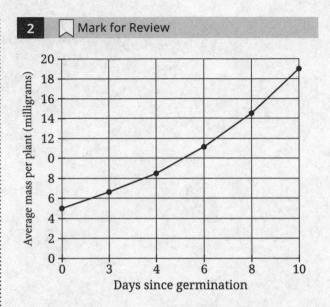

For a group of plants in a greenhouse, the graph shows the average mass per plant from 0 days since germination to 10 days since germination. How many days since germination was the average mass per plant approximately 11 milligrams?

(A) 4

(B) 6

(C) 7

(D) 21

3 🔖 Mark for Review

	Accepted	Rejected
Completed interview	15,700	34,300
Did not complete interview	9,300	40,700

The table shows the results of 100,000 applicants to College C. If an accepted student is selected at random, what is the probability that the student completed an interview?

(A) $\dfrac{93}{1,000}$

(B) $\dfrac{1}{4}$

(C) $\dfrac{93}{250}$

(D) $\dfrac{157}{250}$

4 🔖 Mark for Review

Temperature	Number of days
22	2
25	2
28	3
30	1
34	4
37	0
40	2

The table shows the frequency of daily high temperatures, in degrees Fahrenheit, over a 14-day period. What is the median daily high temperature for the days shown?

(A) 28

(B) 29

(C) 30

(D) 34

5 ☐ Mark for Review

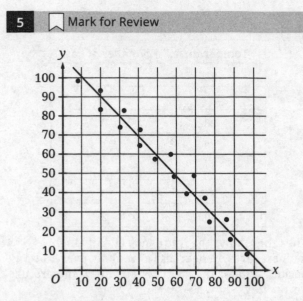

The scatterplot shows the relationship between x and y. Which of the following is closest to the slope of the line of best fit shown?

Ⓐ −10

Ⓑ −1

Ⓒ 1

Ⓓ 10

6 ☐ Mark for Review

10, 2, 3, 5, 7, 1, 5, 2

What is the median of the data shown?

Ⓐ 4

Ⓑ 4.5

Ⓒ 5

Ⓓ 6

7 ☐ Mark for Review

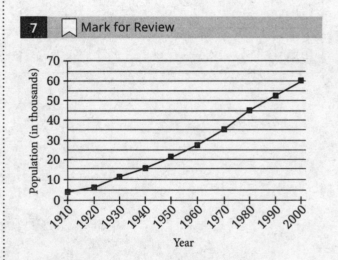

The population of Town A during the 20th century is represented by the given figure. The population of Town A in 1970 was what fraction of the population of Town A in 2000?

8 Mark for Review

The mean of 8 numbers is 65. If one of the numbers, 58, is removed, what is the mean of the remaining 7 numbers?

9 Mark for Review

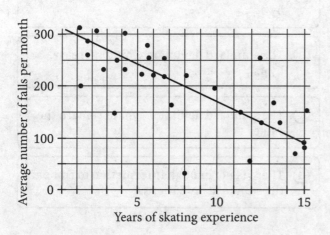

The scatterplot shows the number of years of experience of 30 competitive ice skaters and their mean number of falls on the ice per month. A line of best fit is also shown. For a skater with 10 years of experience, which of the following is closest to the number of falls per month predicted by the line of best fit?

(A) 125

(B) 150

(C) 175

(D) 200

10 Mark for Review

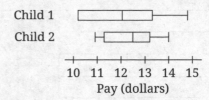

Two children earn money for doing chores each day. The box plots summarize the daily amount earned, in dollars, by each child. Which of the following is a true statement about the mean amounts earned by the two children?

(A) The mean amount earned by child 1 is greater than the mean amount earned by child 2.

(B) The mean amount earned by child 2 is greater than the mean amount earned by child 1.

(C) The mean amount earned by child 1 is equal to the mean amount earned by child 2.

(D) There is not enough information to compare the mean amounts earned by child 1 and child 2.

11 Mark for Review

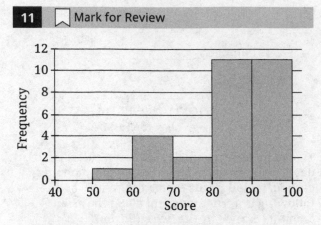

The histogram shows the distribution of the scores of 22 students on a test. Which of the following could be the median score of the 22 students?

(A) 68

(B) 71

(C) 77

(D) 84

12 Mark for Review

Number of Fish Per Tank

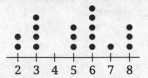

The dot plot represents the number of fish in each of 18 tanks. If 4 fish were added to each tank, how would the standard deviation of the tanks before the addition compare to the standard deviation of the tanks after?

(A) The standard deviation would decrease by 4.

(B) The standard deviation would increase by 4.

(C) The standard deviation would remain the same.

(D) There is not enough information to compare the standard deviations.

Chapter 55
Data and Statistics
Drill Explanations

ANSWER KEY

1. A
2. B
3. D
4. B
5. B
6. A

7. $\dfrac{35}{60}$ or .5833
8. 66
9. C
10. D
11. D
12. C

DATA AND STATISTICS DRILL EXPLANATIONS

1. **A** The question asks for a value based on a graph. First, check the labels on each axis of the bar graph. Podcasts are on the *x*-axis, and the *y*-axis shows the percent ad time. The question asks about the podcast with the lowest percent of ad time, so find the shortest bar, which is for podcast T on the *x*-axis. Look at the top of the bar for podcast T, and then look left to the *y*-axis, using the mouse pointer or the edge of the scratch paper as a ruler if necessary. The top of the bar for podcast T is at 15. Thus, podcast T had a percent ad time of 15. The correct answer is (A).

2. **B** The question asks for a value based on a graph. First, check the labels on each axis of the line graph. Days since germination are on the *x*-axis, and the *y*-axis shows the average mass per plant in milligrams. The question asks about the days since germination when the average mass was about 11 milligrams. Find 11 milligrams on the *y*-axis: it is between the horizontal lines for 10 and 12. Move right from there to the line graph, using the mouse pointer or scratch paper as a ruler if necessary. From there, move down to the *x*-axis to see that the value is 6. Thus, the average mass per plant was 11 milligrams 6 days since germination. The correct answer is (B).

3. **D** The question asks for a probability based on a situation. Probability is defined as $\dfrac{\text{\# of outcomes that fit requirements}}{\text{total \# of possible outcomes}}$. Read carefully to find the numbers that make up the probability. The question says that *an accepted student is selected*, so the total of accepted students is the total number of possible outcomes. Add the accepted students who did and did not complete interviews to find that there were 15,700 + 9,300 = 25,000 accepted students. The question asks about those accepted students who *completed an interview*, so the number of outcomes that fits the requirement is 15,700. Therefore, the probability is $\dfrac{15,700}{25,000}$, which reduces to $\dfrac{157}{250}$. The correct answer is (D).

4. **B** The question asks for the median of a list of numbers presented in a frequency table. A frequency table has two columns: the left-hand column contains the values, and the right-hand column contains the number of times each value occurs, or its frequency. The median of a list of numbers is the middle number when the numbers are arranged in order. In lists with an even number of numbers, the median is the average of the two middle numbers. This list has 14 values, one for each day in the period, so the median will be the average of the seventh and eighth numbers on the list. Start by adding up the first few frequencies to find that there are 2 + 2 + 3 = 7 values represented in the first three rows of the table. Therefore, the seventh value is 28 degrees, and the eighth value is 30 degrees. The median is $\frac{28 + 30}{2} = \frac{58}{2} = 29$. The correct answer is (B).

5. **B** The question asks for the slope of the line of best fit of a scatterplot. The line is descending from left to right, so it has a negative slope. Eliminate (C) and (D) because they have positive slopes. Use two points on the line of best fit to calculate the slope of the line using the formula $slope = \frac{y_2 - y_1}{x_2 - x_1}$. The line of best fit passes through a point close to (0, 100) and through another point close to (100, 0). Plug those values into the slope formula to get $slope = \frac{100 - 0}{0 - 100}$, which becomes $slope = \frac{100}{-100}$, or $slope = -1$. The correct answer is (B).

6. **A** The question asks for the median of the data shown. The median of a list of numbers is the middle number when the numbers are arranged in order. In lists with an even number of numbers, the median is the average of the two middle numbers. Start by putting the numbers of the list in order. The list becomes 1, 2, 2, 3, 5, 5, 7, 10. It has 8 numbers, so the median is the average of the fourth and fifth numbers. These values are 3 and 5, so the median is $\frac{3 + 5}{2} = \frac{8}{2} = 4$. The correct answer is (A).

7. $\frac{35}{60}$ **or .5833**

The question asks for the relationship between two values on a line graph. First, check the labels on each axis of the line graph. Years are on the x-axis, and the y-axis shows the population in thousands. The question asks about the population in 1970 and in 2000, so start by finding 1970 on the x-axis. Move up from there to the line graph, using the mouse pointer or scratch paper as a ruler if necessary. From there, move left to the y-axis to see that the value is halfway between the labeled horizontal lines for 30,000 and 40,000, so the value is 35,000. Next, find 2000 on the x-axis, move up to the line graph, then move left to see that the population then was 60,000. Now make the fraction, with the population from 1970 in the numerator and the population from 2000 in the denominator. This becomes $\frac{35,000}{60,000}$, which must be reduced to fit into the fill-in box. It can be reduced to $\frac{35}{60}$, which fits in the fill-in box, so stop here. The further reduced form, $\frac{7}{12}$, or the decimal form, .5833, would also be accepted as correct. The correct answer is $\frac{35}{60}$ or equivalent forms.

8. **66** The question asks for the mean, or average, of a list of numbers after one value is removed from the list. For averages, use the formula $T = AN$, in which T is the *Total*, A is the *Average*, and N is the *Number of things*. Before 58 is removed from the list, there are 8 numbers with a mean of 65. Use this information to find the total. Plug $N = 8$ and $A = 65$ into the average formula to get $T = (65)(8)$. This becomes $T = 520$. To find the mean of the remaining 7 numbers after 58 is removed, find the new total, which is $520 - 58 = 462$. Now $T = 462$ and $N = 7$. Use the average formula again to get $462 = A(7)$. Divide both sides of the equation by 7 to get $66 = A$. The correct answer is 66.

9. **C** The question asks for a value on a scatterplot. First, check the labels on each axis of the line graph. Years of skating experience are on the *x*-axis, and the *y*-axis shows the average number of falls per month. The question asks about a skater with 10 years of experience, so find 10 on the *x*-axis. Move up from there to the line of best fit, using the mouse pointer or scratch paper as a ruler if necessary. From there, move left to the *y*-axis to see that the value is between the unlabeled horizontal line for 150 and the labeled horizontal line for 200. Eliminate (A), (B), and (D) because those values are not between 150 and 200. The correct answer is (C).

10. **D** The question asks which statement must be true about the means of data given in two box plots. A box plot can be used to determine the median, range, and interquartile range of a data set, but it cannot be used to determine the mean. Eliminate (A), (B), and (C) because it is not possible to compare the means. The correct answer is (D).

11. **D** The question asks for the median of a list of numbers presented in a histogram. A histogram shows data grouped by ranges but does not provide the exact data points. The median of a list of numbers is the middle number when the numbers are arranged in order. In lists with an even number of numbers, the median is the average of the two middle numbers. This list has 22 values, one for each score, so the median will be the average of the eleventh and twelfth numbers on the list. Start by adding up the first few frequencies to find that there are $1 + 4 + 2 = 7$ values represented by the first three bars of the graph. The next 11 scores were between 80 and 90. Therefore, the eleventh value is between 80 and 90, as is the twelfth value. No specific scores are given, but if both middle values from the list are in this range, the median (the average of those two numbers) must also be in this range. Eliminate (A), (B), and (C) because they are not between 80 and 90. The correct answer is (D).

12. **C** The question asks for a comparison of two standard deviations, one before and one after a change to the data. Standard deviation is a measure of the spread of a group of numbers. A group of numbers close together has a small standard deviation, whereas a group of numbers spread out has a large standard deviation. Adding 4 fish to each tank would not change the spread of the data or the shape of the dot plot. Since the distributions are the same, the standard deviations are equal. The correct answer is (C).

Chapter 56
Percents and Proportional Relationships Drill

Percents and Proportional Relationships Drill

1 | Mark for Review

In a recent marathon, 75% of those who entered the race reached the finish line. If 2,400 runners entered the race, how many reached the finish line?

_____

2 | Mark for Review

A student can solve 6 math questions in 12 minutes. Working at the same rate, how many minutes would it take the student to solve 5 math questions?

(A) 6

(B) 9

(C) 10

(D) 11

3 | Mark for Review

What is the area, in acres, of a plot of land that measures 4 square miles?
(1 square mile = 640 acres)

_____

4 | Mark for Review

If 1.2 is $p\%$ of 600, what is the value of p?

(A) 0.2

(B) 5

(C) 20

(D) 500

5 ▢ Mark for Review

On the first test of the semester, Barbara scored a 60. On the last test of the semester, Barbara scored a 75. By what percent did Barbara's score improve?

Ⓐ 15%

Ⓑ 18%

Ⓒ 20%

Ⓓ 25%

6 ▢ Mark for Review

At a bakery, 12 slices of pie cost $30. Which of the following equations models the number of slices of pie, p, that could be purchased for d dollars at this rate?

Ⓐ $p = \frac{2}{5} - d$

Ⓑ $p = \frac{2}{5} + d$

Ⓒ $p = \frac{2}{5}d$

Ⓓ $p = \frac{5}{2}d$

7 ▢ Mark for Review

An office supply vendor that delivers printer ink to companies charges a subscription fee of $230 for its services plus x dollars for each carton of ink. If a company paid $1,364 for 18 cartons of ink, including the subscription fee, what is the value of x?

Ⓐ 46

Ⓑ 52

Ⓒ 63

Ⓓ 78

8 ▢ Mark for Review

A book collector sold 30% of his books to one friend and 60% of his remaining books to another friend. What percent of his original number of books did the book collector have left?

Ⓐ 18%

Ⓑ 28%

Ⓒ 36%

Ⓓ 42%

9 🔖 Mark for Review

An event planning company needs to make 85 batches of cookies for a party. Each batch of cookies takes 20 minutes to prepare. Approximately how long, in hours, will it take the company to bake all 85 batches?

(A) 4

(B) 28

(C) 85

(D) 255

10 🔖 Mark for Review

A certain object has mass of 500 grams and a density of 2,000 grams per cubic meter. What is the volume of the object, in cubic meters?

(A) 0.25

(B) 4

(C) 1,500

(D) 1,000,000

11 🔖 Mark for Review

If the ratio of $\frac{1}{6}$ to $\frac{1}{5}$ is equal to the ratio of 35 to x, what is the value of x?

(A) 24

(B) 30

(C) 36

(D) 42

12 🔖 Mark for Review

During a sale, a clothing store gives customers a discount of 10%. A sales tax of 7% is added after the discount. If a customer's total bill is $103.04, what was the original amount of the bill before the discount and sales tax?

(A) $96.70

(B) $99.20

(C) $107.00

(D) $113.20

Chapter 57
Percents and Proportional Relationships Drill Explanations

ANSWER KEY

1.	1800		7.	C
2.	C		8.	B
3.	2560		9.	B
4.	A		10.	A
5.	D		11.	D
6.	C		12.	C

PERCENTS AND PROPORTIONAL RELATIONSHIPS DRILL EXPLANATIONS

1. **1800** The question asks for a value based on a percentage. Translate the English to math in bite-sized pieces. The question states that *2,400 runners entered the race* and *75% of those...reached the finish line. Percent* means out of 100, so translate 75% as $\frac{75}{100}$. Translate *of* as times. Thus, 75% of 2,400 becomes $\frac{75}{100}(2,400) = 1,800$ runners that reached the finish line. Leave out the comma when entering the answer in the fill-in box. The correct answer is 1800.

2. **C** The question asks for a value given a rate. Begin by reading the question to find information about the rate. The question states that the student *can solve 6 math questions in 12 minutes.* The question asks for the time, in minutes, it would take the student to solve 5 math questions. Set up a proportion, being sure to match up the units. The proportion is $\frac{6 \text{ math questions}}{12 \text{ minutes}} = \frac{5 \text{ math questions}}{x \text{ minutes}}$. Cross-multiply to get $(6)(x) = (12)(5)$, which becomes $6x = 60$. Divide both sides of the equation by 6 to get $x = 10$. The correct answer is (C).

3. **2560** The question asks for a measurement and gives conflicting units. To convert square miles to acres, set up a proportion. Be sure to match up units. The question states that *1 square mile = 640 acres*, so the proportion is $\frac{1 \text{ square mile}}{640 \text{ acres}} = \frac{4 \text{ square miles}}{x \text{ acres}}$. Cross-multiply to get $(1)(x) = (640)(4)$, which becomes $x = 2,560$. Leave out the comma when entering the answer in the fill-in box. The correct answer is 2560.

4. **A** The question asks for a value based on a percentage. Translate the English to math in bite-sized pieces. *Is* translates to "equals," so the first part of the equation is "1.2 =." *Percent* means out of 100, so translate $p\%$ as $\frac{p}{100}$. Translate *of* as times. Thus, $p\%$ of 600 becomes $\frac{p}{100}(600)$, and the full equation is $1.2 = \frac{p}{100}(600)$. Simplify the right side of the equation to get $1.2 = 6p$, then divide both sides of the equation by 6 to get $0.2 = p$ The correct answer is (A).

5. **D** The question asks for a percent based on a certain situation. The question asks for a specific value and the answers contain numbers in increasing order, so try using the answers. Rewrite the answer choices on the scratch paper and label them "% improvement." Next, start with a number in the middle that's easy to work with and try (C), 20%. *Percent* means out of 100, so translate 20% as $\frac{20}{100}$. Take 20% of Barbara's first test score to get $\frac{20}{100}(60) = 12$. Add this to the first test score to get $60 + 12 = 72$. This is not 75, so eliminate (C). A larger percent improvement is needed, so also eliminate (A) and (B). To check (D), take 25% of the first test score to get $\frac{25}{100}(60) = 15$. Add this to the first test score to get $60 + 15 = 75$. This matches the information in the question, so stop here. The correct answer is (D).

6. **C** The question asks for an equation that models a specific situation. There are variables in the answer choices, so try out some numbers. The question states that the number of slices of pie is p and the cost is d. The question also states that *12 slices of pie cost $30*, so when $p = 12$, $d = 30$. Plug these values into the answer choices and eliminate any that don't work. Choice (A) becomes $12 = \frac{2}{5} - 30$. This is not true, so eliminate (A). Choice (B) becomes $12 = \frac{2}{5} + 30$, which is also not true; eliminate (B). Choice (C) becomes $12 = \frac{2}{5}(30)$, or $12 = 12$. This is true, so keep (C), but check (D) just in case. Choice (D) becomes $12 = \frac{5}{2}(30)$, or $12 = 75$; eliminate (D). The correct answer is (C).

7. **C** The question asks for a value given a specific situation. Since the question asks for a specific value and the answers contain numbers in increasing order, try using the answers. Rewrite the answer choices on the scratch paper and label them as "x." Next, start with a number in the middle and try (B), 52. The question states that x is the number of dollars the service charges *for each carton of ink*. If the company purchased 18 cartons of ink, the cost for the ink would be $18(\$52) = \$450$. The question also states that the vendor *charges a subscription fee of $230*, so the total cost for 18 cartons of ink is $\$450 + \$230 = \$680$. This does not match the total cost of *$1,364* that was given in the question, so eliminate (B). The result was too small, so eliminate (A) and try (C), 63. If the cartons cost $63 each, 18 cartons plus the subscription fee would cost $18(\$63) + \$230 = \$1,134 + \$230 = \$1,364$ dollars. This matches the total cost given in the question, so stop here. The correct answer is (C).

8. **B** The question asks for a percentage given a specific situation. The question is about the relationship between unknown numbers, so try using some numbers. Make the *original number of books* = 100 because 100 works well with percents. The questions states that the collector *sold 30% of his books to one friend*, so translate the English to math. *Percent* means out of 100, so translate 30% as $\frac{30}{100}$. Take 30% of 100 to get $\frac{30}{100}$ (100) = 30 books. The collector then sold *60% of his remaining books to another friend*. If the collector started with 100 books and sold 30 to the first friend, he has 100 – 30 = 70 books remaining. Translate 60 percent of 70 as $\frac{60}{100}$ (70) = 42 books. The question asks about the *percent of his original books* the collector had left. He had 70 books remaining after selling to his first friend, so he had 70 – 42 = 28 books remaining after selling to his second friend. These books represent $\frac{28}{100}$ = 28% of his original number of books. The correct answer is (B).

9. **B** The question asks for a measurement and gives conflicting units. The question states that *Each batch of cookies takes 20 minutes to prepare* but asks for the time in <u>hours</u>. There are 60 minutes in 1 hour, so set up a proportion to determine how many batches can be made in one hour. Be sure to match up the units. The proportion is $\frac{1 \text{ batch}}{20 \text{ minutes}} = \frac{x \text{ batches}}{60 \text{ minutes}}$. Cross-multiply to get (1)(60) = (20)(x), which becomes 60 = 20x. Divide both sides of the equation by 20 to get 3 = x. Therefore, 3 batches of cookies can be made in one hour. Set up another proportion to determine how many hours it will take to make 85 batches. The proportion is $\frac{3 \text{ batches}}{1 \text{ hour}} = \frac{85 \text{ batches}}{x \text{ hours}}$. Cross-multiply to get (3)(x) = (1)(85), which becomes 3x = 85. Divide both sides of the equation by 3 to get x = 28.$\overline{3}$ hours. The question asks for the approximate time in hours, and this is closest to 28. The correct answer is (B).

10. **A** The question asks for a measurement of an object. Translate the English to math to determine the volume of the object given the mass and density. Use the units to determine where to start. The question asks for the volume in cubic meters and gives the density in grams per cubic meter and the mass in grams. The mass in grams divided by the volume in cubic meters equals the density in grams per cubic meter. This happens to be the formula for density, which can be written as $D = \frac{m}{V}$. Plug in the known values to get 2,000 = $\frac{500}{V}$. Multiply both sides of the equation by V to get 2,000V = 500. Divide both sides of the equation by 2,000 to get $V = \frac{500}{2,000}$, or V = 0.25. The correct answer is (A).

11. **D** The question asks for the value of x in a ratio given information about another ratio. Translate the English into math in bite-sized pieces. A ratio can be written as a fraction, so translate *the ratio* $\frac{1}{6}$ *to* $\frac{1}{5}$ as $\frac{\frac{1}{6}}{\frac{1}{5}}$. Dividing by a fraction is the same as multiplying by the reciprocal of the fraction, so this can be rewritten as $\frac{1}{6} \cdot \frac{5}{1}$ and then as $\frac{5}{6}$. Now translate *the ratio of 35 to x* as $\frac{35}{x}$. The question states that the two ratios are equal, so set the two fractions equal to each other to get $\frac{5}{6} = \frac{35}{x}$. Cross-multiply to get $(5)(x) = (6)(35)$, or $5x = 210$. Divide both sides of the equation by 5 to get $x = 42$. The correct answer is (D).

12. **C** The question asks for a value given a specific situation. Since the question asks for a specific value and the answers contain numbers in increasing order, try using the answers. Rewrite the answer choices on the scratch paper and label them as "original bill." Next, start with a number in the middle and try (C), $107.00, which is a round number and will be easier to work with. The question states that the *clothing store gives customers a discount of 10%. Percent* means out of 100, so translate 10% as $\frac{10}{100}$. Take 10% of $107 to get $\frac{10}{100}$ ($107) = $10.70. This is a *discount*, so subtract this from the original bill to get $107 − $10.70 = $96.30. The question also states that *A sales tax of 7% is added after the discount.* Translate 7% as $\frac{7}{100}$, and take 7% of $96.30 to get $\frac{7}{100}$ ($96.30) = $6.74. Add this to the discounted cost of $96.30 to get a total bill of $96.30 + $6.74 = $103.04 This matches the *customer's total bill* of $103.04 that was given in the question, so stop here. The correct answer is (C).

Chapter 58
Geometry and
Trigonometry Drill

Geometry and Trigonometry Drill

1 🔖 Mark for Review

A certain triangle has a base that is 7 inches long and an area of 21 square inches. What is the height of the triangle, in inches?

(A) 3

(B) 4

(C) 6

(D) 7

2 🔖 Mark for Review

A triangle has an area of 80 centimeters (cm). If the base of the triangle is $2x$ cm and the height of the triangle is $5x$ cm, what is the value of x?

(A) $\sqrt{8}$

(B) 4

(C) 8

(D) 16

3 🔖 Mark for Review

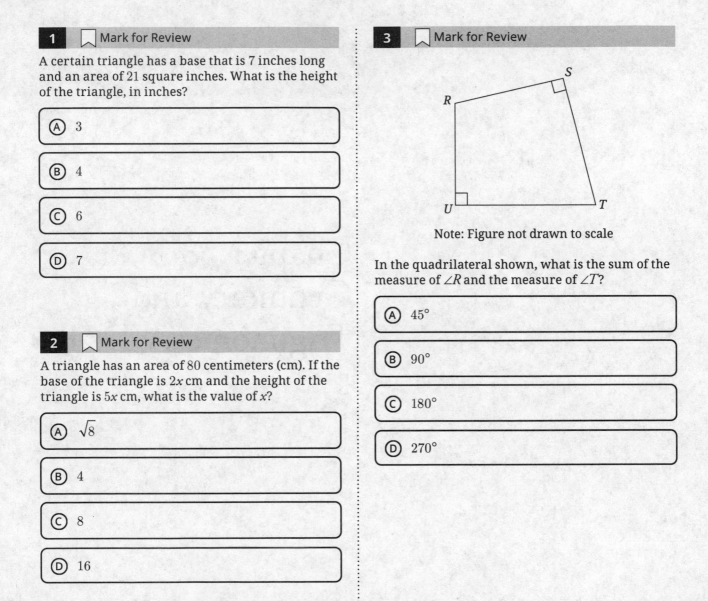

Note: Figure not drawn to scale

In the quadrilateral shown, what is the sum of the measure of $\angle R$ and the measure of $\angle T$?

(A) 45°

(B) 90°

(C) 180°

(D) 270°

4 ☐ Mark for Review

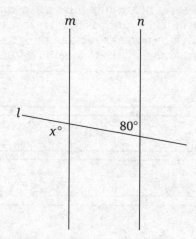

Note: Figure not drawn to scale

In the figure shown, line l intersects parallel lines m and n. If $x = 5a - 15$, what is the value of a?

5 ☐ Mark for Review

The volume of cube X is c times the volume of cube Y, and the side length of cube X is 5 times the side length of cube Y. What is the value of c?

6 ☐ Mark for Review

Note: Figure not drawn to scale

In the given figure, $\cos(90° - a°) = \frac{\sqrt{11}}{6}$. What is the value of $\sin a°$?

Ⓐ $\frac{\sqrt{11}}{6}$

Ⓑ $\frac{\sqrt{11}}{11}$

Ⓒ $\sqrt{6}$

Ⓓ $\frac{6\sqrt{11}}{11}$

7 ☐ Mark for Review

The volume, in square meters, of a certain cylinder is given by the equation $V = \pi \left(\dfrac{1}{2} x \right)^2 (x)$. If the radius of the base of the cylinder is half its height, what is the best interpretation of x in this context?

Ⓐ The radius of the base of the cylinder, in meters

Ⓑ The height of the cylinder, in meters

Ⓒ The volume of the cylinder, in square meters

Ⓓ The ratio of the base of the cylinder to the height of the cylinder

8 ☐ Mark for Review

In triangle ABC, angle A is a right angle and angle B measures $24°$. Triangle XYZ is similar to triangle ABC, where X corresponds to A, Y corresponds to B, and Z corresponds to C. Each side of triangle XYZ is $\dfrac{1}{2}$ the length of the corresponding side of triangle ABC. What is the measure of angle Z?

Ⓐ 24°

Ⓑ 33°

Ⓒ 66°

Ⓓ 132°

9 ☐ Mark for Review

The surface area of a rectangular prism measuring 5 units × 6 units × 8 units is how much greater than the surface area of a rectangular prism measuring 3 units × 6 units × 8 units?

Ⓐ 12

Ⓑ 24

Ⓒ 48

Ⓓ 56

10 ☐ Mark for Review

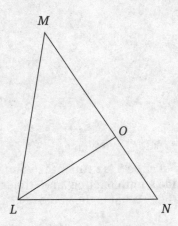

Note: Figure not drawn to scale

In the figure, angle LMO has the same measure as angle OLN. Which of the following is equal to $\dfrac{LN}{LM}$?

Ⓐ $\dfrac{NO}{LO}$

Ⓑ $\dfrac{LO}{NO}$

Ⓒ $\dfrac{LM}{MN}$

Ⓓ $\dfrac{NO}{LN}$

11 ☐ Mark for Review

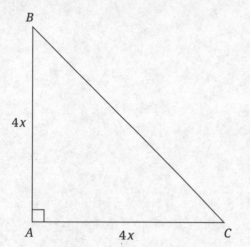

Note: Figure not drawn to scale

Which of the following expressions is equivalent to the length of the hypotenuse of the triangle shown?

Ⓐ $8x$

Ⓑ $\sqrt{16x}$

Ⓒ $\sqrt{16x^2}$

Ⓓ $\sqrt{32x^2}$

12 ☐ Mark for Review

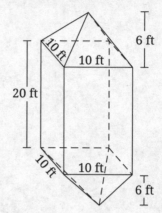

Note: Figure not drawn to scale

An art installation is built from a rectangular solid and two right rectangular pyramids with the dimensions shown in the figure. What is the volume, in square feet, of the art installation?

Ⓐ 200

Ⓑ 400

Ⓒ 2,000

Ⓓ 2,400

Chapter 59
Geometry and Trigonometry Drill Explanations

ANSWER KEY

1.	C	7.	B
2.	B	8.	C
3.	C	9.	D
4.	19	10.	A
5.	125	11.	D
6.	A	12.	D

GEOMETRY AND TRIGONOMETRY DRILL EXPLANATIONS

1. **C** The question asks for a measure on a geometric figure. Start by drawing a triangle on the scratch paper. Next, label the figure with information from the question, which is that the base is 7 inches. Next, write out the formula for the area of a triangle, either from memory or after looking it up on the reference sheet. The formula is *Area* $= \frac{1}{2} \times base \times height$, or $A = \frac{1}{2} bh$. Plug in the values given in the question to get $21 = \frac{1}{2}(7)(h)$. Multiply both sides of the equation by 2 to get $42 = (7)(h)$. Divide both sides of the equation by 7 to get $6 = h$. The correct answer is (C).

2. **B** The question asks for a value based on a geometric figure. Start by drawing a triangle on the scratch paper, then label the figure with the given information. The question gives the area of the triangle, so write out the formula for the area of a triangle, $A = \frac{1}{2} bh$, and plug in the given area to get $80 = \frac{1}{2} bh$. Since the question asks for a specific value and the answers contain numbers in increasing order, test the answer choices one at a time. Write the answers on the scratch paper, label them as "*x*," and start with a middle number. Try (B), 4. If $x = 4$, the base of the triangle is $2(4) = 8$, and the height of the triangle is $5(4) = 20$. Plug these numbers into the area formula to get $80 = \frac{1}{2}(8)(20)$. Simplify the right side of the equation to get $80 = 80$. This is true, so stop here. The correct answer is (B).

3. **C** The question asks for the sum of two angles in a quadrilateral. The sum of the angles in any four-sided figure is 360°, so write an equation to solve for the sum of the measures of $\angle R$ and $\angle T$. The other two angles are labeled with the right angle symbol, meaning they measure 90° each. The equation becomes $360° = 90° + 90° + \angle R + \angle T$. Simplify on the right side of the equation to get $360° = 180° + \angle R + \angle T$. Subtract 180° from both sides of the equation to get $180° = \angle R + \angle T$. The question asks for the sum of the measures of $\angle R$ and $\angle T$, so stop here. The correct answer is (C).

4. **19**   The question asks for a value based on a figure. Start by redrawing the figure and labels on the scratch paper. When a line intersects two parallel lines, two kinds of angles are created: big and small. All of the small angles are equal to each other, all of the big angles are equal to each other, and any small angle plus any big angle = 180°. The angle labeled $x°$ is a small angle, and the angle labeled 80° is a small angle. Thus, $x = 80$. Plug this value for x into the given equation to get $80 = 5a - 15$. Add 15 to both sides of the equation to get $95 = 5a$. Divide both sides of the equation by 5 to get $19 = a$. The correct answer is 19.

5. **125**   The question asks for a value given a proportional relationship between two geometric figures. Start by drawing 2 cubes on the scratch paper as best as possible. Next, label the figures with information from the question. Label one cube as X and the other cube as Y. No specific side lengths are given, so make up a number. Make the side length of cube Y equal 2, and label this on the figure. The question states that *the side length of cube X is 5 times the side length of cube Y*, so the side length of cube X is (5)(2) = 10; label this on the figure.

Next, write down the formula for the volume of a cube, either from memory or after looking it up on the reference sheet. The reference sheet doesn't give the formula for the volume of a cube, but it does give the volume of a rectangular solid: $V = lwh$. All three sides of a cube are the same length, so the formula becomes $V = s^3$. Since cube X has a side length of 10, the volume of cube X is $V = 10^3$, or $V = 1,000$. Since cube Y has a side length of 2, the volume of cube Y is $V = 2^3$, or $V = 8$. Divide the two volumes to find the value of c: $\dfrac{1,000}{8} = 125$. Thus, the volume of cube X is 125 times the volume of cube Y. The correct answer is 125.

6. **A**   The question asks for the value of a trigonometric function. Start by redrawing the figure and labels. There are 180 degrees in a triangle, and two of the angles are labeled as 90° and $a°$, so the third angle must measure $180° - 90° - a°$, or $90° - a°$. Label this on the figure, which now looks like this:

Next, write out SOHCAHTOA to remember the trig functions. The CAH part defines the cosine as $\frac{adjacent}{hypotenuse}$, and the question states that $\cos(90° - a°) = \frac{\sqrt{11}}{6}$. Label the side adjacent to the $(90° - a°)$ angle as $\sqrt{11}$, and label the hypotenuse as 6. The drawing now looks like this:

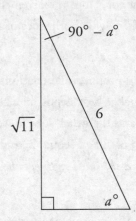

Before using the Pythagorean Theorem to solve for the length of the third side, look to see whether there is already enough information to answer the question. The SOH part of SOHCAHTOA defines the sine as $\frac{opposite}{hypotenuse}$. The side opposite angle a is $\sqrt{11}$, and the hypotenuse is 6. Therefore, $\sin a° = \frac{\sqrt{11}}{6}$. The correct answer is (A).

7. **B** The question asks for the interpretation of a term in context. Start by reading the final question, which asks for the meaning of x. Rewrite the equation on the scratch paper. Then label the parts of the equation with the information given, and eliminate answers that do not match the labels. The equation $V = \pi\left(\frac{1}{2}x\right)^2 (x)$ is in the form of the formula for the volume of a cylinder, which is $V = \pi r^2 h$. Eliminate (C) because the volume of the cylinder is represented by V, not by x. Eliminate (D) because x is either the radius or the height, not the ratio of two parts of the cylinder. The question states that *the radius of the base of the cylinder is half its height*. Translate *is* as equals and *half* as $\frac{1}{2}$ to get *radius* $= \frac{1}{2}h$. Thus, the term $\left(\frac{1}{2}x\right)$ represents the radius; eliminate (A). The remaining term, x, represents the height of the cylinder. The correct answer is (B).

8. **C** The question asks for the value of the measure of an angle on a geometric figure. Start by drawing two triangles that are similar to each other, meaning they have the same angle measures but are different sizes. Be certain to match up the corresponding vertices that are given in the question.

The drawing could look something like this:

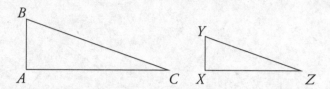

Next, label the figure with the given information. Label angle *A* as 90°, or with the right angle symbol, and label angle *B* as 24°. Because the triangles are similar, corresponding angle measures are the same, so also label angle *X* as 90°, or with the right angle symbol, and angle *Y* as 24°. The drawing now looks like this:

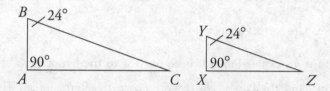

To find the measure of angle *Z*, subtract the sum of the two angles from the total number of degrees in a triangle. There are 180 degrees in a triangle, so 180° − 90° − 24° = *Z*. Simplify to get 66° = *Z*. The correct answer is (C).

9. **D** The question asks for a comparison of the surface areas of two geometric figures. Start by drawing two rectangular prisms as best as possible. Next, label the sides with the information given in the question. The surface area of a geometric figure is the sum of the areas of its sides, or faces. Use the formula for the area of a rectangle, $A = lw$, to find the area of each face. In the first rectangular prism, one 5×6 face has an area of 30 square units, one 5×8 face has an area of 40 square units, and one 6×8 face has an area of 48 square units. There are two of each face, so the surface area is 2(30 + 40 + 48) = 2(118) = 236 square units.

Perform the same calculations to find the surface area of the second rectangular prism. One 3×6 face has an area of 18 square units, one 3×8 face has an area of 24 square units, and one 6×8 face has an area of 48 square units. There are two of each face, so the surface area is 2(18 + 24 + 48) = 2(90) = 180 square units.

The question asks how much greater one surface area is than the other, so subtract the two values to get 236 − 180 = 56. The correct answer is (D).

10. **A** The question asks for a ratio that is equivalent to the ratio of two sides of a triangle. The question states that *angle LMO has the same measure as angle OLN*, so focus on the triangles that contain these angles. Those are triangles *LMN* and *LNO*. These triangles also share angle *N*. If two pairs of corresponding angles have the same measures, the third pair must as well, meaning that these are similar triangles.

Redraw the two triangles next to each other to see more clearly how the angles and vertices match up.

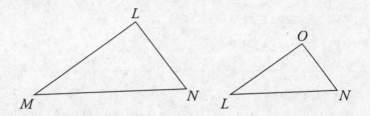

In triangle *LMN*, side *LN* is opposite angle *M* and side *LM* is opposite angle *N*. The sides with the same ratio in triangle *LNO* will be opposite the corresponding angles. Angle *L* corresponds to angle *M*, so side *NO* corresponds to side *LN*. Angle *N* corresponds to angle *N*, so side *LO* corresponds to side *LM*. Thus, $\frac{LN}{LM} = \frac{NO}{LO}$. The correct answer is (A).

11. **D** The question asks for an expression that is equivalent to the hypotenuse of a right triangle. Start by redrawing the figure and the labels. Next, write down the Pythagorean Theorem: $a^2 + b^2 = c^2$. The given side lengths have variables, and so do the answer choices, so make up a number for *x*. Plug in $x = 2$, and the side lengths become $4(2) = 8$. Plug these values into the Pythagorean Theorem to get $8^2 + 8^2 = c^2$. Simplify the left side of the equation to get $64 + 64 = c^2$, and then $128 = c^2$. Take the positive square root of both sides of the equation to get $\sqrt{128} = c$. This is the target value; write it down and circle it.

Now plug $x = 2$ into each answer choice, and eliminate any that do not equal $\sqrt{128}$. Choice (A) becomes $8(2) = 16$. This is not $\sqrt{128}$, so eliminate (A). Choice (B) becomes $\sqrt{16(2)}$, or $\sqrt{32}$; eliminate (B). Choice (C) becomes $\sqrt{16(2)^2}$, or $\sqrt{16(4)}$. Simplify further to get $\sqrt{64}$, which is 8; eliminate (C). Choice (D) becomes $\sqrt{32(2)^2}$, or $\sqrt{32(4)}$. Simplify further to get $\sqrt{128}$. This matches the target value. The correct answer is (D).

12. **D** The question asks for the volume of a geometric figure. Find the volume of each piece of the art installation separately, and then add the volumes together. If possible, redraw the figure on the scratch paper. Next, write down the relevant formulas, either from memory or after looking them up on the reference sheet. The formula for the volume of a rectangular solid is $V = lwh$, and the formula for the volume of a right rectangular prism is $V = \frac{1}{3}lwh$. The dimensions of the rectangular prism are given on the figure as 10, 10, and 20, so the volume becomes $V = (10)(10)(20)$, or $V = 2{,}000$. This is already larger than the values in (A) and (B), so eliminate those answers. Additionally, the volumes of the pyramids still need to be added to the total volume, so the answer must be larger than 2,000; eliminate (C). The correct answer is (D).

Chapter 60
Practice Test 1

PSAT Prep Test 1—Reading and Writing
Module 1

Turn to Section 1 of your answer sheet to answer the questions in this section.

---

1 ☐ Mark for Review

The following text is from Arthur Conan Doyle's 1897 short story "The Adventure of the Abbey Grange." The narrator and his partner are making their way to the scene of a crime.

A drive of a couple of miles through narrow country lanes brought us to a park gate, which was opened for us by an old lodge-keeper, whose <u>haggard</u> face bore the reflection of some great disaster. The avenue ran through a noble park, between lines of ancient elms, and ended in a low, widespread house, pillared in front after the fashion of Palladio.

As used in the text, what does the word "haggard" most nearly mean?

(A) Dull

(B) Exhausted

(C) Friendly

(D) Simple

---

2 ☐ Mark for Review

Born in Uganda in 1977, artist Ronex Ahimbisibwe integrates a variety of elements into his mixed media installations, often _____ aspects of digital art, painting, or photography alongside more traditional sculptures. The diversity of his work reveals previously unseen connections between art and activism, producing compelling expressions of personal themes significant to Ahimbisibwe.

Which choice completes the text with the most logical and precise word or phrase?

(A) utilizing

(B) masking

(C) ignoring

(D) measuring

CONTINUE ➡

3 🔖 Mark for Review

While scholars can rely on journals and letters to deduce what personal inspiration modern playwrights might have drawn upon to compose their plays, few resources of that nature are available for interpreting the motivations behind the works of William Shakespeare. Thus, scholars can only _____ what compelled Shakespeare to create the memorable characters that populate his tragedies, comedies, and history plays.

Which choice completes the text with the most logical and precise word or phrase?

(A) imply

(B) insinuate

(C) speculate

(D) regulate

4 🔖 Mark for Review

Entering the final match, the tennis champion was _____ in her ability to successfully defend her title, but observers noted that her attitude and posture during the match itself gave a contradictory impression, indicating doubt rather than assuredness.

Which choice completes the text with the most logical and precise word or phrase?

(A) ingenious

(B) methodical

(C) hesitant

(D) confident

5 🔖 Mark for Review

The following text is excerpted from Vera Zhelikhovsky's 1901 short story "The General's Will." In the story, a lawyer has been asked to revise the will of a general who is close to dying.

The lawyer was not acquainted with Nazimoff's family; indeed he had never before seen the general, though, like all Russia, he knew of him by repute. But judging from the tone of contempt or of pity with which he spoke of his second wife or her daughter, the lawyer guessed at once that the general's home life was not happy.

Which choice best states the main purpose of the text?

(A) To offer an insight into the lawyer's understanding of his client's circumstances

(B) To contrast the lawyer's interpretation of the will with the general's interpretation

(C) To explain how the lawyer conducts his research on new clients

(D) To demonstrate that the lawyer has great respect for the general

CONTINUE ➡

6 ☐ Mark for Review

Using an assortment of media, including video and sound installations, Australian artist Patricia Piccinini juxtaposes fantastical, hyper-realistic sculptures of animals with dystopian images to voice her environmental and bio-ethical concerns. Though her work has drawn criticism for its perceived brashness, she was recognized in 2016 as one of the most popular artists in the world, with one of her exhibitions attracting over 400,000 visitors.

Which choice best states the main purpose of the text?

(A) To explain why Piccinini's work is more popular with art critics than with environmentalists

(B) To describe Piccinini's work and the differing reactions to it

(C) To draw attention to Piccinini as a true innovator in the art world

(D) To discuss the lengthy process undertaken by Piccinini to create one of her installations

7 ☐ Mark for Review

"How do you memorize all those lines?" Many theater actors are often confronted with this exact query when greeted by admirers after a performance; audience members marvel at actors' abilities to commit such large amounts of text to memory. However, most actors believe that memorizing lines for a play is not the most challenging of the technical and creative demands of performing. Instead, many actors claim that making those memorized lines "come to life" with strong vocal choices and a variety of inflections proves to be a greater challenge.

Which choice best describes the function of the underlined question in the text as a whole?

(A) It shows how actors constantly keep audiences in mind when they create their roles.

(B) It presents a challenge perceived as more difficult by audiences who watch plays than by the actors who perform in those plays.

(C) It indicates the hesitation that many actors feel when approaching a role that involves large amounts of text.

(D) It reveals how technical and creative aspects of acting are often overlooked by audience members.

CONTINUE ➡

8 ☐ Mark for Review

Geochemist Patricia Will and her team have published research stating that samples of rock formations taken from the Moon contain similar chemical signatures to those of Earth. Will and her team claim that these similarities support what is known as the synestia theory, which claims that the Moon was formed when a large object collided with Earth, causing a gaseous explosion, expelling the Moon from the Earth. If verified, these findings would contradict what is known as the accretion theory, which states that the Moon formed independently and attributes the deposit of these gases to comets and meteorites that landed after the Moon's formation.

What does the text most strongly suggest about the chemical signatures reported by Will and her team?

Ⓐ They are stronger evidence for the synestia theory than they are for the accretion theory.

Ⓑ They are the first known evidence of any similarities between the Moon and the Earth.

Ⓒ They were difficult to record given the distance between the Moon and the Earth.

Ⓓ They may have been first recorded by a different group of researchers.

9 ☐ Mark for Review

In hibernation, animals such as bats conserve energy by entering into torpor, a state in which they greatly reduce their body temperature and metabolic rate. A group of scientists at the University of Maryland conducted a study to determine whether the reduction in body function brought on by torpor may yield additional benefits beyond the conservation of energy, such as the slowing of the aging process. The results of the study revealed that periods of hibernation were correlated with DNA methylation activity in the genes of the bats; DNA methylation suppresses a process known as gene transcription, which in turn prevents the production of proteins that lead to aging in bats.

Based on the text, how is DNA methylation believed to be involved in the process of hibernation observed in the scientists' study?

Ⓐ DNA methylation reduces the effectiveness of energy conservation during hibernation.

Ⓑ DNA methylation allows for increased protein production during periods of hibernation.

Ⓒ DNA methylation inhibits an activity that would otherwise cause bats to age more quickly.

Ⓓ DNA methylation improved the bats' ability to enter a state of torpor.

CONTINUE ➡

Number and Species of Dinosaur Fossils
Uncovered at Different Depths Beneath
the Surface at the Argentinian Site

Depth of fossils beneath the surface (feet)	Number of *Aucasaurus* fossils recovered	Number of *Abelisaurus* fossils recovered
0–2	6	7
3–5	13	10
6–8	6	5
9–11	3	2
12 or more	1	0

The area known today as southern Argentina was dominated by several carnivorous dinosaur species during the late Cretaceous Period. A team of paleontologists recently conducted an excavation on an Argentinian site that recovered fossils of two such species—*Aucasaurus* (which lived 84 to 71 million years ago) and *Abelisaurus* (which lived 74 to 70 million years ago). Since the two species occupied the area for several million years each, their fossils were each found at various depths beneath the surface. The highest number of *Abelisaurus* fossils that were recovered from the Argentinian site was found at a depth of _____

Which choice most effectively uses data from the table to complete the text?

Ⓐ 0–2 feet beneath the surface.

Ⓑ 3–5 feet beneath the surface.

Ⓒ 6–8 feet beneath the surface.

Ⓓ 9–11 feet beneath the surface.

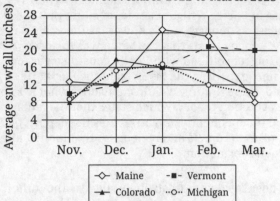

Average Snowfall by Month for Four US States from November 2022 to March 2023

A meteorologist is recording and analyzing average monthly snowfalls (November through March) for four US states. While comparing the data, she notices that in January _____

Which choice most effectively uses data from the graph to complete the statement?

Ⓐ Vermont had a similar average snowfall to Michigan, and Colorado had a similar average snowfall to Maine.

Ⓑ Vermont's average snowfall was greater than that of Michigan, Colorado, and Maine.

Ⓒ Vermont and Colorado had an average snowfall of approximately 16 inches, and Maine and Michigan had an average snowfall of approximately 25 inches.

Ⓓ Vermont, Colorado, and Michigan each had an average snowfall below 20 inches, but Maine's average snowfall that month was above 20 inches.

CONTINUE

12 ⬚ Mark for Review

English painter John William Waterhouse (1849–1917) is renowned for his romanticized paintings of women, many from literature and mythology, who are often depicted in beautiful natural settings. In a recent article for an art journal, a critic has argued that Waterhouse had an exquisite talent for using color to represent the personal characteristics of his subjects.

Which quotation from a scholar discussing Waterhouse's paintings would best support the critic's claim?

(A) "*Boreas* (1904), named by Waterhouse for the Greek god of the north, depicts a beautiful young woman struggling against a powerful wind as she travels through the countryside."

(B) "In his 1915 work *I am Half Sick of Shadows*, Waterhouse masterfully conveys the all-consuming love the Lady of Shallot feels for Lancelot by means of her bright red dress and wistful expression."

(C) "Waterhouse ultimately painted three very different versions of Ophelia, the tragic heroine from Shakespeare's *Hamlet*, with the best-known version depicting her looking sad in an elegant dress sitting beside a lily pond."

(D) "*Circe Invidiosa* (1892) is arguably the greatest of Waterhouse's three depictions of the Greek mythological character Circe from Ovid's *Metamorphoses*, who turns her rival into a sea monster, as her toxic jealousy is palpable."

13 ⬚ Mark for Review

Generic Brand Grocery Sales as a Percentage of Total Sales for a Local Grocery Store, by Food Item, 2020–2022

Grocery Item	2020	2021	2022
white flour	10	12	12
frozen dinners	51	54	55
boxed chocolates	48	48	49
uncooked rice	8	8	9

As economic conditions progressively worsened in a small American town from 2020 through 2022, the town's local grocery store observed that relatively cheap generic grocery brands became popular, but only for foods that were more expensive, such as complete meals or luxury items like chocolates. For relatively inexpensive pantry staples such as flour and rice, name brands remained the products of choice, as the cost difference was often viewed as negligible by consumers. This pattern can be demonstrated by comparing _____

Which choice most effectively uses data from the table to illustrate the claim?

(A) the percentage of 2021 generic white flour sales with the percentage of 2022 generic white flour sales.

(B) the percentage of 2022 generic uncooked rice sales with the percentage of 2022 generic frozen dinner sales.

(C) the percentage of 2020 generic boxed chocolate sales with the percentage of 2022 generic boxed chocolate sales.

(D) the percentage of 2020 generic boxed chocolate sales with the percentage of 2020 generic frozen dinner sales.

CONTINUE ➜

14 ⬚ Mark for Review

Having joined the United States of America in 1845, Florida has a distinctly different culture from those of the other states of the American South. Of particular interest is that the customs, practices, speech patterns, and accents of Floridians more closely resemble those of the Northern states, particularly New York, than anything seen or heard in the rest of the southern states. But why is this the case? In the late 1800s, large numbers of northerners began settling in Florida seeking a subtropical climate and good farmland, and the twentieth century provided a similarly large influx of migrants. While Florida remained geographically southern, it was nonetheless more culturally northern. Thus, the unique position of Florida as the southern-most state that is not truly "southern" demonstrates how _____

Which choice most logically completes the text?

(A) residents of any given US state will understand the cultural practices of the residents of any other US state.

(B) one region can avoid being influenced by the culture of another region.

(C) the customs, practices, speech patterns, and accents of a country can change over time.

(D) migration within a country can affect how an area develops.

15 ⬚ Mark for Review

Writings from the Civil War period display a level of articulateness and eloquence considered superior to that associated with modern American written discourse. Some historians attribute this to class distinctions, as the wealthy and highly educated were more likely to be literate at that time, but literacy rates in modern America are reported as the highest in the country's history. A newer theory suggests that Civil War-era writers of all backgrounds placed a stronger emphasis on clarity of speech than modern Americans do because the technological limitations of the nineteenth century often made it impossible to interact with one's audience and clarify writings in person. This possibility has led some experts to claim that _____

Which choice most logically completes the text?

(A) modern Americans tend to write in the same way that Americans wrote during the Civil War.

(B) Americans' communication skills were probably not considered superior to those of citizens of other countries during the nineteenth century.

(C) the quality of Civil War writings resulted in part from the attitudes about writing that many Americans held at that time.

(D) if modern Americans had access to both extensive wealth and formal education, they would express themselves as well as did Civil War-era Americans.

CONTINUE ➤

16 ☐ Mark for Review

Over 1,300 years old, Dainichido Bugaku is a ritual dance performance that occurs every year on January 2nd in local communities of northern Japan. In some of the nine sacred dances of Dainichido Bugaku, _____ while performing to the instrumental music of the flute and the taiko drum.

Which choice completes the text so that it conforms to the conventions of Standard English?

- (A) dancer's wear mask's
- (B) dancers' wear masks
- (C) dancers wear masks
- (D) dancers' wear masks'

17 ☐ Mark for Review

In 1801, the British defeated the French in Egypt, and under the terms of the Capitulation of Alexandria, a slab known as the Rosetta Stone was taken to London. Over the next 50 years, a team of scholars _____ to decipher the Egyptian hieroglyphic script using the accompanying Greek text on the stone as a guide.

Which choice completes the text so that it conforms to the conventions of Standard English?

- (A) will work
- (B) is working
- (C) works
- (D) worked

18 ☐ Mark for Review

Widely observed in Mexico and celebrated by people of Mexican heritage, Día de los _____ known as the Day of the Dead—includes visiting the graves of the deceased with gifts, candy skulls, and marigold flowers.

Which choice completes the text so that it conforms to the conventions of Standard English?

- (A) Muertos also
- (B) Muertos: also
- (C) Muertos—also
- (D) Muertos, also

19 ☐ Mark for Review

While completing a 1996 mission for the National Aeronautics and Space Administration _____ astronaut Shannon W. Lucid celebrated the Fourth of July holiday as the only American aboard the Russian space station by wearing patriotic socks. Coincidentally, astronaut Susan J. Helms wore identical distinctive socks aboard the space shuttle *Columbia* that same year.

Which choice completes the text so that it conforms to the conventions of Standard English?

- (A) (NASA) and
- (B) (NASA)
- (C) (NASA), and
- (D) (NASA),

CONTINUE ➡

20 ☐ Mark for Review

In the mid-20th century, poliovirus was on the rise, and doctors such as Albert Sabin began researching effective methods to prevent the illness. From 1956 to 1960 Sabin worked with Russian scientists to develop an oral poliovirus vaccine that prevented initial intestinal _____ in 1961 his first oral poliovirus vaccine was licensed and administered in the United States.

Which choice completes the text so that it conforms to the conventions of Standard English?

Ⓐ infection, and

Ⓑ infection

Ⓒ infection and

Ⓓ infection,

21 ☐ Mark for Review

The Triangle Shirtwaist Factory fire of 1911 was one of the deadliest fires in US history. Upon investigating the origin and spread of the fire, _____ before the blaze grew out of control. As a result, legislation was passed to improve factory conditions and protect workers.

Which choice completes the text so that it conforms to the conventions of Standard English?

Ⓐ workers were prevented from escaping as the fire marshal found out that the factory doors were locked

Ⓑ the fire marshal found that the locked factory doors had prevented workers from escaping

Ⓒ escape was prevented for the workers because of the locked factory doors found by the fire marshal

Ⓓ the locked factory doors found by the fire marshal prevented workers from escaping

22 ☐ Mark for Review

As the first Aboriginal and female chancellor of Brock University, Shirley Cheechoo became a voice for individuals of Cree descent. She owns an art gallery and film institute and founded her own film festival. Cheechoo has said that she struggled with a lack of self-assurance as a young person and had to work to find her voice. _____ she provides opportunities for students to build confidence and self-esteem to better prepare them to defend the rights of their people.

Which choice completes the text with the most logical transition?

Ⓐ Similarly,

Ⓑ Thus,

Ⓒ In the end,

Ⓓ As a rule,

CONTINUE ➡

23 ☐ Mark for Review

Written on different materials, including papyrus, animal skin, and copper, the Dead Sea Scrolls are ancient Jewish writings that feature fragments of various religious, legal, and sectarian texts. _____ the Scrolls were thought to have been written by the Essenes, a Jewish sect believed to have lived in the region where the texts were found. Subsequent research and analysis, however, has challenged, complicated, and expanded our understanding of the texts' origins, and there is currently no scholarly consensus surrounding the identity of the scrolls' authors.

Which choice completes the text with the most logical transition?

(A) By contrast,

(B) For example,

(C) Initially,

(D) Eventually,

24 ☐ Mark for Review

The microbiome existing in the human body can benefit and harm a person. _____ the microbes in the gut help digest food and support the immune system. However, the microbiome can also foster growth of harmful bacteria that cause disorders such as inflammatory bowel disease.

Which choice completes the text with the most logical transition?

(A) Ultimately,

(B) Subsequently,

(C) On one hand,

(D) In any case,

CONTINUE →

25 ☐ Mark for Review

While researching a topic, a student has taken the following notes:

- *Anthology of Massachusetts Poets* is a 1922 collection of 90 poems edited by African American writer and poet William Stanley Braithwaite.

- In one of this anthology's poems, "America the Beautiful," Katharine Lee Bates wrote "For amber waves of grain" and "For purple mountain majesties."

- Dorothea Lawrence Mann penned "Blue wonder of the sea and luminous sky" in one of her poems in this collection.

- In a poem in this collection, Charlotte Porter used the line "The vivid sheen of springing green."

The student wants to emphasize a similarity in the imagery of the poems from this collection. Which choice most effectively uses relevant information from the notes to accomplish this goal?

(A) In *Anthology of Massachusetts Poets*, colors are a recurring theme, with one of Dorothea Lawrence Mann's poems including the line "Blue wonder of the sea and luminous sky" and a Katharine Lee Bates' poem describing "amber waves of grain" and "purple mountain majesties."

(B) While Charlotte Porter emphasized the vivid greens of spring, Dorothea Lawrence Mann highlighted the blue wonders of the sea and sky.

(C) Braithwaite's anthology, which contains 90 poems, consists of works by Massachusetts poets.

(D) Charlotte Porter composed the line "The vivid sheen of springing green" in William Stanley Braithwaite's 1922 *Anthology of Massachusetts Poets*.

26 ☐ Mark for Review

While researching a topic, a student has taken the following notes:

- Dental insurance for children normally allows for regular teeth cleanings conducted by medical professionals.

- These cleanings can treat early-stage tooth decay and prevent future decay.

- In a study, 41.7 percent of children with private dental insurance had tooth decay.

- Some children lack dental insurance coverage and may miss teeth cleanings.

- In the same study, 60.7 percent of uninsured children had tooth decay.

The student wants to make and support a generalization about dental insurance. Which choice most effectively uses relevant information from the notes to accomplish this goal?

(A) Children with dental insurance are less likely to suffer from tooth decay because the insurance allows them to receive regular teeth cleanings.

(B) Regular teeth cleanings conducted by medical professionals can treat and prevent tooth decay in children.

(C) In a study, 60.7 percent of uninsured children had tooth decay, while only 41.7 percent of those with private dental insurance had tooth decay.

(D) Children's likelihood of having tooth decay depends on their access to regular teeth cleanings, and those cleanings are more available to those with dental insurance.

CONTINUE →

27 ☐ Mark for Review

While researching a topic, a student has taken the following notes:

- The Milky Way galaxy contains hundreds of billions of stars.
- In the Morgan-Keenan classification system, O-type stars, such as 9 Sagittarii and 10 Lacertae, are rare but bright enough to see from great distances.
- In the same classification system, M-type stars, such as Betelgeuse and Antares, are common but too dim to see with the unaided eye.
- The luminosity, stability, and lifespan of a star affect its capacity to host life.

The student wants to emphasize the different categories in which the Morgan-Keenan system classifies stars. Which choice most effectively uses relevant information from the notes to accomplish this goal?

(A) The luminosity, stability, and lifespan of O-type stars such as 9 Sagittarii and 10 Lacertae affect their capacity to host life.

(B) Rare but bright O-type stars make up one category of the hundreds of billions of stars in the Milky Way galaxy.

(C) Betelgeuse and Antares, classified as M-type stars, are two of the hundreds of billions of stars in the Milky Way galaxy.

(D) Among the hundreds of billions of stars in the Milky Way, 9 Sagittarii and 10 Lacertae are O-type, while Betelgeuse and Antares are M-type.

YIELD

Once you've finished (or run out of time for) this section, use the answer key to determine how many questions you got right. If you got fewer than 15 questions right, move on to Module 2—Easier, otherwise move on to Module 2—Harder.

PSAT Prep Test 1—Reading and Writing
Module 2—Easier

Turn to Section 1 of your answer sheet to answer the questions in this section.

DIRECTIONS

The questions in this section address a number of important reading and writing skills. Each question includes one or more passages, which may include a table or graph. Read each passage and question carefully, and then choose the best answer to the question based on the passage(s).

All questions in the section are multiple-choice with four answer choices. Each question has a single best answer.

---

1 ⬚ Mark for Review

The following text is adapted from John Keats's 1819 poem "To Autumn."

Season of mists and mellow fruitfulness,
　Close bosom-friend of the maturing sun;
Conspiring with him how to load and bless
　With fruit the vines that round the thatch-eves run;
To bend with apples the moss'd cottage-trees,
　And <u>fill</u> all fruit with ripeness to the core.

As used in the text, what does the word "fill" most nearly mean?

Ⓐ Weaken

Ⓑ Steal

Ⓒ Supply

Ⓓ Rot

2 ⬚ Mark for Review

Art historians have dated a newly discovered oil-based painting to the late 1800s. The fact that the painting's canvas was only manufactured from 1862 through 1898 and the oil paints used were available during that same time period _____ the historians' determination.

Which choice completes the text with the most logical and precise word or phrase?

Ⓐ declines

Ⓑ dissolves

Ⓒ supports

Ⓓ analyzes

CONTINUE ➡

3 ☐ Mark for Review

The following text is adapted from Edgar Allan Poe's 1843 short story "The Black Cat."

But to-morrow I die, and to-day I would unburden my soul. My immediate purpose is to place before the world, plainly, succinctly, and without comment, a series of mere household events. In their consequences, these events have terrified—have tortured—have destroyed me.

As used in the text, what does the word "plainly" most nearly mean?

(A) Boringly

(B) Simply

(C) Loudly

(D) Quickly

4 ☐ Mark for Review

The Knickerbocker Crisis, also known as the Panic of 1907, occurred when the New York Stock Exchange fell approximately 50% from its value the prior year due to a loss of confidence in banks. The economic damage done by the crisis was _____ alleviated through J. P. Morgan's pledges of money, which were vital in solidifying the weakened banking system.

Which choice completes the text with the most logical and precise word or phrase?

(A) uncommonly

(B) needlessly

(C) abruptly

(D) largely

5 ☐ Mark for Review

Researchers are seeking ways to replace disintegrated cartilage with a comparable synthetic material, but the process is challenging; the material must be at least as strong as cartilage and securely adhere to the bone surface within a joint. Scientists have reinforced crystallized polyvinyl alcohol with cellulose from bacteria to create a hydrogel that meets both of these conditions. By providing three times the wear resistance of traditional cartilage, this hydrogel could provide a solution for people suffering from arthritis and other joint conditions.

Which choice best describes the function of the underlined sentence in the text as a whole?

(A) It describes traditional treatments for joint conditions requiring cartilage replacement.

(B) It details a potential benefit of utilizing the technology created by the scientists.

(C) It questions the benefits of developing synthetic cartilage to treat joint conditions.

(D) It explains why only a combination of crystallized polyvinyl alcohol and cellulose forms a strong hydrogel.

CONTINUE ➤

6 ☐ Mark for Review

The following text is from Stanley J. Weyman's 1894 novel *Under the Red Robe*. The narrator, Gil de Berault, a man known for his gambling tendencies, has been caught cheating at a card game and is arguing with M. l'Anglais.

"Marked cards, M. l'Anglais?" I said, with a chilling sneer. "They are used, I am told, to trap players—not unbirched schoolboys."

"Yet I say that they are marked!" he replied hotly, in his queer foreign jargon. "In my last hand I had nothing. You doubled the stakes. Bah, sir, you knew! You have swindled me!"

"Monsieur is easy to swindle—when he plays with a mirror behind him," I answered tartly.

And at that there was a great roar of laughter, which might have been heard in the street, and which brought to the table everyone in the eating-house whom his violence had not already attracted.

Which choice best states the main purpose of the text?

(A) To demonstrate a conflict between de Berault and M. l'Anglais

(B) To highlight that M. l'Anglais has a newfound respect for his opponent

(C) To describe a pastime that de Berault and M. l'Anglais both enjoy

(D) To explain de Berault's dismay at having been caught by M. l'Anglais

7 ☐ Mark for Review

An author of experimental horror fiction, Native American writer Stephen Graham Jones, a member of the Blackfeet tribe, is known for his dark and playful style. He has written many novels, including *The Only Good Indians*, which examines the ethics of hunting wild animals. Scholars have drawn connections between Jones and David Foster Wallace because both authors balance elements of morality and humor in their works.

Which choice best describes the function of the underlined sentence in the text as a whole?

(A) It claims that other authors should also incorporate playfulness into their writing styles.

(B) It offers examples of how Native American heritage informed Jones's choice of writing material.

(C) It discusses Jones's works in the context of other famous works that have advocated for animal rights.

(D) It compares Jones's work to that of another author who explores similar themes.

CONTINUE →

8 ☐ Mark for Review

Text 1

According to an article published in the journal *Cognitive Science*, a person's decision-making process in competitions is often driven by both herd mentality and perceived social norms. That is, most people will adjust their behavior to match those of the people around them. For example, if the majority of competitors during a golf tournament are blaming poor play on strong wind conditions, other competitors who had not been blaming the weather previously are more likely to start doing so. According to the authors of the article, the behaviors of others have a greater influence on an individual's behaviors and attitudes than do that individual's specific personality traits.

Text 2

A recent study through the University of Illinois Urbana-Champaign found that in a competitive setting, a person will acknowledge and even give an advantage to behavior that is consistent with the person's baseline personality traits. People who are more generous tend to reward generous behavior, and people who are more selfish tend to reward selfish behavior. People were found to follow this pattern even when doing so negatively impacted their own situations.

Based on the texts, how would the scientists at the University of Illinois Urbana-Champaign (Text 2) most likely respond to the underlined portion of Text 1?

(A) By arguing that herd mentality and perceived social norms have more of an impact on behavior than the authors of the *Cognitive Science* article believe

(B) By conceding that herd mentality and perceived social norms affect behavior during competitions but that baseline personality traits affect behavior during collaborations

(C) By stating that the behaviors of others are not necessarily the dominant factor in determining individual behavior

(D) By asking why the authors of the *Cognitive Science* article assume that people always adapt to social norms

9 ☐ Mark for Review

The chemical composition of the interior of the Moon is not yet fully understood, but scientists are working to identify the elements that exist there. Recent samples taken from the interior of the Moon contain the gases helium (He) and neon (Ne). Other samples from the Moon's interior contain excess argon (Ar) gas. This latter finding is of particular interest to researchers, as it opens up the possibility that the Moon's chemical makeup has been influenced by factors separate from those surrounding its formation, which is not believed to have involved large quantities of argon. By using such discoveries to build an understanding of the Moon's chemical composition over time, researchers hope to be able to state with certainty how the Moon was formed.

According to the text, which gases are present in the interior of the Moon?

(A) Argon only

(B) Helium only

(C) Helium and neon

(D) Helium, neon, and argon

CONTINUE →

10 🔖 Mark for Review

The height above mean sea level is the difference in elevation between a location and a standardized mean sea level location. This value is used to identify the altitudes of towns, buildings, flying objects, and other structures and can be determined using a wide variety of methods. However, climate change affects height above mean sea level, so the measurement of an object at a certain location at any given point in history may not match the object's current height above mean sea level.

Which choice best states the main idea of the text?

- (A) The height above mean sea level measures the relative height of locations and objects based on the height of a specific location at a specific time.

- (B) Despite the possible effects of climate change, the height above mean sea level for a location has not visibly changed over time.

- (C) A universal method for measuring the height of objects and locations above mean sea level has not been decided upon.

- (D) The measurements for height above mean sea level only ever decrease over time.

11 🔖 Mark for Review

Percentages and Sources of Mules and Horses Used by France During World War I

Source	Horses	Mules
France	63%	55%
England	7%	4%
Spain	1%	35%
United States	22%	6%

In World War I, France utilized almost 250,000 horses and mules, which were used to pull weapons and supplies. France supplemented its own populations of these animals by importing them from other countries, such as the United States, England, and Spain. For example, out of all the animals used by France during the war, just 55% of the mules and _____ of the horses actually came from France.

Which choice most effectively uses data from the table to complete the example?

- (A) 7%

- (B) 22%

- (C) 35%

- (D) 63%

CONTINUE

---

12 ☐ Mark for Review

Separation and New Match Rates of Male Albatrosses Based on Personality Traits

Personality trait	Separation Rate	New Match Rate
shyest	81%	52%
moderately shy	53%	61%
moderately bold	37%	75%
boldest	22%	91%

Albatrosses typically mate for life, but occasionally individuals separate from their partners and pair up with others. In an effort to determine to what extent personality influences these separations, a researcher determined the relative shyness and boldness of the males in an albatross population based on play and exhibitions of dominance, then compiled how often each personality type separated from its partner and succeeded in finding a new mate. Looking at the data, a researcher determines that the shyest male albatrosses were _____

Which choice most effectively uses data from the table to complete the statement?

(A) most likely to separate from their mates and most likely to find a new mate.

(B) most likely to separate from their mates and least likely to find a new mate.

(C) least likely to separate from their mates and most likely to find a new mate.

(D) least likely to separate from their mates and least likely to find a new mate.

---

13 ☐ Mark for Review

A student is writing a paper about the 1913 Armory Show, an art show organized by the Association of American Painters and Sculptors. Also known as the International Exhibition of Modern Art, the Armory Show was the first exhibition of art of its magnitude in America and served as a turning point that expanded American art to include the European avant-garde art style in addition to the more realistic American art style of the time. A student claims that American art entered a new era largely due to the influence of the exhibition.

Which quotation from an article about the Armory Show would be the most effective evidence for the student to include in support of this claim?

(A) "The International Exhibition of Modern Art—which came to be known, simply, as the Armory Show—marked the dawn of Modernism in America. It was the first time the phrase 'avant-garde' was used to describe painting and sculpture."

(B) "Two-thirds of the paintings on view were by American artists. But it was the Europeans—Van Gogh, Gauguin, Cezanne, Picasso, Matisse, Duchamp—that caused a sensation."

(C) "Critics reviled the experimental art as "insane" and an affront to their sensibilities. But the media attention drew crowds, and collectors took notice."

(D) "On the evening of the show's opening, 4,000 guests milled around the makeshift galleries in the 69th Regiment Armory on Lexington Avenue."

CONTINUE ➡

14 ☐ Mark for Review

Lithium-ion batteries are able to store large amounts of energy, are known for their high performance, and are used in a wide range of products, from smartphones to electric cars. However, lithium-ion batteries have some notable downsides: they are costly to manufacture, extracting the metal used to create them can harm the environment, and the reserves of those metals are quickly becoming depleted. Akira Kudo of Tohoku University and Yuto Katsuyama of the University of California, Los Angeles, are working to create high-performance, low-cost batteries using relatively inexpensive sodium ions. They have developed electrodes that quickly transport ions across a carbon lattice whose performance increases the finer the lattice structure becomes, suggesting that _____

Which choice most logically completes the text?

Ⓐ sodium-ion batteries may have the potential to replicate the performance of lithium-ion batteries depending on how much their lattice structure can be refined.

Ⓑ the sodium-ion battery's impressive performance derives from its ability to store large amounts of energy.

Ⓒ the sodium-ion battery's overall performance is weaker than that of other batteries, but it has applications in a wider range of products.

Ⓓ sodium ion batteries will prove more effective in the operation of smartphones than they will in the operation of electric cars.

15 ☐ Mark for Review

Initially discovered in 1844, Michigan's banded iron formations are layers of sedimentary rocks that contain the majority of the planet's supply of iron. Because these formations _____ since the Precambrian age, they provide valuable insights into the evolution of Earth's atmosphere as well as ancient oceanic conditions.

Which choice completes the text so that it conforms to the conventions of Standard English?

Ⓐ will exist

Ⓑ have existed

Ⓒ will be existing

Ⓓ exist

16 ☐ Mark for Review

Ibogaine, a substance derived from root bark, has been promoted for its usefulness in the treatment of addiction. In 1993, Deborah Mash, a professor of neurology as well as molecular and cellular pharmacology, wanted _____ ibogaine and obtained clinical trial approval from the FDA.

Which choice completes the text so that it conforms to the conventions of Standard English?

Ⓐ studying

Ⓑ studied

Ⓒ study

Ⓓ to study

CONTINUE

17 🔖 Mark for Review

The acidic precipitation that _____ when sulfur dioxide and nitrogen oxide emissions mix with water in the atmosphere is responsible for killing aquatic life and corroding the structures of buildings.

Which choice completes the text so that it conforms to the conventions of Standard English?

Ⓐ have resulted

Ⓑ results

Ⓒ are resulting

Ⓓ result

18 🔖 Mark for Review

Nineteenth-century Russian novelist Fyodor Dostoevsky was known for exploring psychological, religious, and philosophical ideas in his work. In his final novel, *The Brothers Karamazov*, the character of Ivan wrestled with existential dilemmas, _____ the complexities of faith, doubt, and human existence.

Which choice completes the text so that it conforms to the conventions of Standard English?

Ⓐ navigates

Ⓑ will navigate

Ⓒ navigated

Ⓓ navigating

19 🔖 Mark for Review

Most California redwood (*Sequoia sempervirens*) seedlings don't survive their first three years, but those that do can reach a height of up to 66 feet in just 20 years. How _____ The trees' rapid growth during their early years is a result of their highly efficient mechanisms for absorbing and transporting water and nutrients.

Which choice completes the text so that it conforms to the conventions of Standard English?

Ⓐ can they grow so tall so quickly?

Ⓑ they can grow so tall so quickly!

Ⓒ can they grow so tall so quickly.

Ⓓ they can grow so tall so quickly.

20 🔖 Mark for Review

In 1978, NASA scientist Donald J. Kessler theorized that the presence of too many objects in low Earth orbit could cause more collisions between these objects and create debris that would then increase the probability of additional collisions. This theoretical scenario is called the Kessler syndrome, and _____ may present a serious problem for the satellite missions of future generations.

Which choice completes the text so that it conforms to the conventions of Standard English?

Ⓐ they

Ⓑ we

Ⓒ those

Ⓓ it

CONTINUE ➡

21 ☐ Mark for Review

When European explorers first encountered the penguin, they were reminded of the great auk (*Pinguinus impennis)*, a now-extinct bird, which, like the penguin, was flightless and had black and white plumage. Upon noticing the _____ explorers named the bird "penguin" after the auk's Latin name.

Which choice completes the text so that it conforms to the conventions of Standard English?

(A) resemblance: the

(B) resemblance; the

(C) resemblance, the

(D) resemblance (the

22 ☐ Mark for Review

Formulated by chemist James Lovelock in the 1970s, the Gaia hypothesis postulates that the ecosystems of Earth collectively function as a unified and self-regulating system, analogous to a living organism. Though this has proven to be a controversial idea, there are some observations of the Earth's environment and history that seem to support this analysis. First, the Earth does exhibit various feedback mechanisms that together maintain relatively stable conditions, such as the composition of the atmosphere. _____ although Earth's geological history is riddled with significant external changes, such as fluctuations in solar radiation, the planet has remained within a suitable range for life for 3.8 billion years.

Which choice completes the text with the most logical transition?

(A) Second,

(B) Conversely,

(C) Specifically,

(D) Still,

23 ☐ Mark for Review

Several species of _____ exhibit unique camouflage abilities, enabling them to swiftly alter the colors in their skin via communication between their brains and special pigment-containing skin cells called chromatophores.

Which choice completes the text so that it conforms to the conventions of Standard English?

(A) cuttlefish;

(B) cuttlefish

(C) cuttlefish,

(D) cuttlefish—

24 ☐ Mark for Review

Kreutz sungrazers are comets _____ as first proposed by German astronomer Heinrich Kreutz, are thought to have originated from one large comet that fragmented several hundred years ago.

Which choice completes the text so that it conforms to the conventions of Standard English?

(A) that:

(B) that—

(C) that;

(D) that,

CONTINUE ➤

25 ☐ Mark for Review

Chemist Ada Yonath wanted to study the structure of the infamously unstable ribosomes, the molecules responsible for protein biosynthesis. She believed that by crystallizing the ribosomes, she would be able to overcome the molecules' tendency to disintegrate, though the greater scientific community considered such crystallization an impossible task. To confront this challenge, she first selected ribosomal material isolated from particularly robust bacterial strains. _____ Yonath and her team developed an innovative approach called cryo-crystallography (now a standard in the field of structural biology), whereby ribosome crystals are exposed to cryo-temperature during x-ray measurements.

Which choice completes the text with the most logical transition?

(A) Furthermore,

(B) Moreover,

(C) Similarly,

(D) Next,

26 ☐ Mark for Review

First Nations poet and activist Mihku Paul published her first book of poetry, *20th Century PowWow Playland*, in 2012. In these poems, Paul writes about her experience as a member of an Indigenous tribe. _____ she describes her Maliseet homeland and her dissatisfaction with her education in the Maine public school system.

Which choice completes the text with the most logical transition?

(A) Specifically,

(B) Therefore,

(C) Though,

(D) Besides,

27 ☐ Mark for Review

Russian composer Dmitri Shostakovich was challenged by conductor Nicolai Malko to compose an orchestral piece based on the song "Tea for Two" from the musical *No, No Nanette*. Shostakovich met the challenge, composing *Tahiti Trot* in under an hour. _____ he dedicated the piece to Malko.

Which choice completes the text with the most logical transition?

(A) Still,

(B) Nonetheless,

(C) Moreover,

(D) Similarly,

STOP
If you finish before time is called, you may check your work on this module only.
Do not turn to any other module in the test.

PSAT Prep Test 1—Reading and Writing
Module 2—Harder

Turn to Section 1 of your answer sheet to answer the questions in this section.

---

1 ☐ Mark for Review

Generally, the precise cause of hypertension (high blood pressure) in most patients is unknown, but endocrinologist Morris Brown and epidemiologist Xilin Wu led a study that _____ a gene variant that was shown to produce a hormone that controls levels of salt in the body, which in turn have an impact on blood pressure.

Which choice completes the text with the most logical and precise word or phrase?

(A) published

(B) measured

(C) affected

(D) discovered

---

2 ☐ Mark for Review

The following text is adapted from Amelia B. Edwards's 1873 short story "The Four-Fifteen Express." The narrator is waiting to board a train.

My voyage over, and a few days given up to business in Liverpool and London, I hastened down to Clayborough with all the delight of a schoolboy whose holidays are at hand. My way lay by the Great East Anglian line as far as Clayborough station, where I was to be met by one of the Dumbleton carriages and <u>conveyed</u> across the remaining nine miles of country.

As used in the text, what does the word "conveyed" most nearly mean?

(A) Explained

(B) Transported

(C) Communicated

(D) Questioned

CONTINUE →

3 ☐ Mark for Review

An important part of Costa Rican economic history, oxcarts have been a primary means of transporting goods across the country and helped expand the export of goods. However, the original design of the oxcart wheels utilized spokes that were not suited for the varying and uneven terrain throughout Costa Rica, which led to many of the cart wheels splintering mid-transport. During the 19th century, a new design of oxcart was built using spokeless wheels that could withstand the country's rugged paths and roadways, which in turn _____ a more seamless transportation of goods across the country.

Which choice completes the text with the most logical and precise word or phrase?

- Ⓐ conspired against

- Ⓑ relied on

- Ⓒ contended with

- Ⓓ provided for

4 ☐ Mark for Review

Proponents of the transcendentalist movement of the 1830s believed that people are at their best when self-reliant and independent, and among the movement's membership was journalist Sarah Margaret Fuller, who advocated for women's rights, including education and employment. Educated early in life and considered the best-read person in New England by the time she was in her 30s, Fuller recognized the lack of women's education at the time. She gave private lessons and held discussions with groups of local women, and her influence inspired the likes of Ralph Waldo Emerson and Susan B. Anthony.

Which choice best states the main purpose of the text?

- Ⓐ To provide background on the challenges faced by women seeking careers in journalism in the early 1800s

- Ⓑ To introduce Sarah Margaret Fuller and her influential role in motivating and supporting women to seek education and employment

- Ⓒ To exemplify Sarah Margaret Fuller as a leader in women's employment by discussing her career as a journalist

- Ⓓ To highlight the difficulties faced by women during the transcendentalist movement that differed from the challenges faced by men

CONTINUE ➜

5 ☐ Mark for Review

Debt relief has existed in both ancient and modern times across the world. In Ancient Rome, debtors could have their debts at least partially expunged, but only by performing hard labor or serving a term of imprisonment. Eventually, the Roman government allowed debtors to surrender their property in order to avoid these punishments, and some of the ancient practices of debt relief came to form modern debt relief practices. For example, European and American nations of the twenty-first century will often reduce or even forgive debts by returning most goods to creditors, with the exception of goods deemed necessities for life.

Which choice best states the main purpose of the text?

(A) To compare how modern American practices of debt relief align with modern European practices of debt relief

(B) To provide a comprehensive background on the history of debt relief and predict how debt relief practices may develop in the future

(C) To argue that modern debt relief shouldn't be influenced by Ancient Roman practices of debt relief

(D) To describe the commonalities and differences of debt relief practices from various times and parts of the world

6 ☐ Mark for Review

The following text is from a translation of Georg Ebers's 1880 short story "The Sisters." A servant has just brought meals to a woman named Irene, who comments that the meal is too small for her and her sister Klea.

The reproachful complaint is heard by the messenger outside the door, for the old woman who shoved in the trencher over the threshold answers quickly but not crossly.

"Nothing more to-day, Irene."

"It is disgraceful," cries the girl, her eyes filling with tears, "every day the loaf grows smaller, and if we were sparrows we should not have enough to satisfy us. You know what is due to us and I will never cease to complain and petition."

Which choice best states the main purpose of the text?

(A) To demonstrate Irene's dismay over an aspect of the sisters' living conditions

(B) To imply that Irene has a newfound disgust for the quality of the food at the temple

(C) To explain a disagreement that Irene and Klea frequently discuss

(D) To detail Klea's disdain for Irene's combative attitude

CONTINUE →

7 ☐ Mark for Review

Text 1

In a study of the effects of stress on cognitive performance, developmental scientist Assaf Oshri suggests that exposure to only low-to-moderate stress levels may improve working memory and that higher stress levels will instead have adverse effects on memory. After further research that included MRI brain scans, Oshri concluded that individuals who experienced low-to-moderate stress levels had increased neural activity in the regions of the brain that affect working memory, while individuals who experienced chronically high stress levels had decreased activity in those same regions.

Text 2

While exposure to higher stress levels may impact an individual's working memory temporarily, researcher M. F. Crane argues that systemic self-reflection, a process by which an individual examines the causes of a highly stressful event and how best to prevent the recurrence of such an event, can improve an individual's resilience to stress, reducing the impact of high stress levels on working memory in the future.

Based on the texts, how would Crane (Text 2) most likely respond to the conclusion Oshri (Text 1) reached after his further research?

Ⓐ By suggesting that the research conducted in Text 1 lacked detailed information about the reporting process asked of study participants

Ⓑ By recognizing that repeated exposure to low-to-moderately-stressful events improves brain function

Ⓒ By arguing that there's no quantifiable way to provide an unbiased determination of the level of a stressful event

Ⓓ By emphasizing that exposure to higher stress levels need not be viewed as an entirely negative process

8 ☐ Mark for Review

Dr. Christopher McKay first described the anti-greenhouse effect in 1991, observing that Titan, a moon of Saturn, has a stratosphere with aerosol particles that absorb solar radiation. In the anti-greenhouse effect, the atmosphere prevents solar energy from reaching the surface, which results in surface cooling. In uncontested circumstances, most or all sunlight would be absorbed by Titan's upper atmosphere, and the planet's climate would experience significant cooling. However, Titan's anti-greenhouse effect, which cools Titan by 9 degrees Kelvin (K), is countered by a greenhouse effect, which warms Titan by 21 K.

Which choice best states the main idea of the text?

Ⓐ The study of Saturn's moons gives vital information about how atmospheric conditions operate on other planets.

Ⓑ Titan's anti-greenhouse effect is caused by aerosol particles that absorb solar radiation.

Ⓒ A phenomenon observed in a celestial object coexists with a contradictory phenomenon.

Ⓓ The understanding of the stratospheric particles that block sunlight has undergone considerable development since the 1990s.

CONTINUE

9 ☐ Mark for Review

A maritime technology specialist theorizes that the cause of the 2021 Suez Canal obstruction by the cargo ship *Ever Given* was bank suction, a phenomenon in which the stern of a ship is prone to swing toward and collide with the nearer river bank when navigating a narrow channel. The proximity of the canal's banks resulted in pressure differences on each side of the ship, due to uneven flow around the hull. The narrower bow rotated towards the center of the channel, while the stern moved in towards the closer bank. Possible additional factors that could have contributed to the bank suction caused by *Ever Given* are water depth, bank shape, and ship propeller action.

Based on the text, which choice best describes the 2021 Suez Canal obstruction?

(A) It involved a ship moving through a constricted waterway that led to asymmetric pressure distribution, which resulted in an alteration to the ship's orientation.

(B) It was caused by the pressure of the water through the narrow space around the hull, which forced the ship away from the nearer bank.

(C) It was the result of poor navigation, which brought the ship's hull too close to the near bank, with which the ship collided.

(D) It was exacerbated by the propeller action of the ship, which was too fast for the shape of the canal and the size of the hull.

10 ☐ Mark for Review

The works of the Turkish traveler Evliya Çelebi (1611–1682) are a notable instance of *Seyahâtnâme*, a centuries-old literary tradition founded by Arab travelers and focused on cataloguing the customs of the Ottoman Empire. Çelebi's work went beyond simple commentary, as he interspersed contemporary observations of Ottoman culture with exaggerations or comedic folktales. The result was an engaging cultural narrative which used local Turkish idioms as well as more formal, baroque turns of phrase. Such a hybrid approach would have appealed to a wide audience in the seventeenth century, and Çelebi's focus on the entertainment of his readership rather than strict adherence to historical accuracy helped to spread awareness of Ottoman culture in a more readily digestible fashion.

Which choice best states the main idea of the text?

(A) While the works of Çelebi are not thoroughly historically accurate, they nevertheless are amusing while offering a picture of the traditions and peoples of the Ottoman Empire.

(B) While the practice of *Seyahâtnâme* was traditionally limited to the somber writings of Arab travelers, Çelebi broke with that tradition by incorporating comedy into his works.

(C) While Çelebi's literary approach incorporated comedy to better entertain the reader, he would have been more successful in reaching his audience with a more accurate representation of historical figures.

(D) While the particular *Seyahâtnâme* of Çelebi may include many folktales and some exaggerations, it is nevertheless valuable for its unwavering adherence to historical accuracy.

CONTINUE →

11 ▢ Mark for Review

A longitudinal study explored the effects of nature sounds, specifically those of birdsong, on the mental health of study participants. Participants completed thousands of self-assessments over 30 months, using a phone app to track their moods and report the presence or absence of birdsong. <u>After making sure to account for the influence of other appealing environmental factors, such as the presence of colorful flora or pristine waterways, the team concluded that the presence of birdsong is strongly linked with positive feelings and recommended an initiative to introduce birdsong into more easily accessible public spaces.</u>

Which finding in the study, if true, would most challenge the conclusion in the underlined sentence?

(A) Reports of positive emotions occurred much more often on sunny days than on overcast days, regardless of the presence of birdsong.

(B) Reports on the presence or absence of birdsong varied by participant, as some completed fewer self-assessments than others.

(C) Reports of positive feelings outnumbered reports of negative feelings during instances where birdsong was present.

(D) Reports of negative feelings in the absence of birdsong occurred with equal frequency in both remote bird habitats and easily accessible public spaces.

CONTINUE

12 ☐ Mark for Review

Product Information Presented to Focus Group and Company Executives

Focus Group Data			
	X (company product)	W (competitor product)	Y (decoy product)
retail price (USD)	$400	$500	$550
approximate product lifespan	2 years	3 years	1.5 years
Marketing Plan Presented to Company Executives			
	X (company product)	W (competitor product)	Z (decoy product)
retail price (USD)	$400	$500	$450
approximate product lifespan	2 years	3 years	1.5 years

The marketing team for a battery manufacturer used a focus group to investigate the decoy effect—the introduction of an intentionally unattractive third product to sway consumers' preference between two competing products. When the decoy product is wholly unattractive, meaning its price is higher and its lifespan is shorter than a competitor's product, consumers will be swayed towards the competitor's product. However, when the decoy product is only partially unattractive, that is, only one of its parameters is inferior to a competitor's product, consumers will often be swayed away from the competitor's product. The focus group assembled by the marketing team was swayed by a decoy product, Y, towards preferring the competitor's product, W. Wanting to reverse this trend, the marketing team suggested that the company introduce decoy product Z instead.

Which choice best describes data from the table that support the marketing team's plan?

(A) Product Y is wholly unattractive compared to Product W but is more attractive than Product X in both respects.

(B) Product Z is wholly unattractive compared to Product X but is more attractive than Product W in one respect.

(C) Product W is more attractive to a consumer than Product X in one respect but is more attractive than Product Y in both respects.

(D) Product Z is more attractive to a consumer than Product Y in one respect but is more attractive than Product X in both respects.

CONTINUE

13 ☐ Mark for Review

In 2017, researchers in South Africa began tracking the migration of white sharks after the arrival of a pair of killer whales in the sharks' territory. After observing both the appearance of shark carcasses along the shoreline and increased activity from the killer whales, researchers used telemetry data to find that the white sharks began leaving their traditional aggregation site. Although the aggregation site had been a reliable gathering point for white sharks for many years, the team's shark sightings steadily dropped over the next two years. Analysis of the patterns of shark sightings showed that migrations coincided with killer whale arrival. The team concluded that white sharks respond rapidly to the risk presented by a novel predator in their environment and will not return to a habitat they believe is unsafe.

Which finding, if true, would most directly support the team's conclusion?

(A) Near the aggregation site, the populations of prey normally consumed by the white sharks experienced a notable increase.

(B) The killer whales had been established as predators of white sharks in other areas before the South African study.

(C) Over the next two years, sharks begin to risk a return to the aggregation site despite evidence that the pair of killer whales still inhabits the area.

(D) The telemetry sensors that the team used accounted for the movements of the white sharks but not the killer whales.

14 ☐ Mark for Review

Subjective age is a metric for how old one feels, in contrast to one's actual chronological age. Based on nearly 300 studies conducted by various research groups over time, middle-age and older individuals who reported a younger subjective age had fewer physical maladies and improved mental health when compared to individuals of those age groups who did not report a younger subjective age. However, although a younger subjective age brings these benefits, a new study indicates that feeling younger may be an advantage only up to a point. Those who feel younger may take on greater risks, which can lead to increased exposure to disease and injury. Additionally, a younger subjective age may lead to age-group dissociation, in which an individual stops identifying herself in the same age group as her peers, which can lead to personal and social conflicts. Therefore, _____

Which choice most logically completes the text?

(A) although there are mental and physical benefits to having a younger subjective age, these benefits are entirely offset by the disadvantages of identifying as younger than one's chronological age.

(B) although the subjective age of middle-aged people is more likely to be younger than the subjective age of older people, the benefits are the same for both groups.

(C) although a psychological phenomenon may confer several types of advantages, there are certain consequences to the phenomenon that must be considered.

(D) although it would be wiser for individuals to resist the urge to see themselves as younger than they are, middle-aged and older folks are unlikely to accept their biological ages.

CONTINUE ▶

15 ☐ Mark for Review

For 21 years, American pilot Nicole Malachowski served as an officer in the United States Air Force (USAF), including a tour as a member of the USAF Air Demonstration Squadron, also known as the Thunderbirds. Advocating for those impacted by tick-borne illnesses _____ a new mission for Malachowski, whose own tick-borne illness led to her retirement from the military.

Which choice completes the text so that it conforms to the conventions of Standard English?

(A) have been

(B) were

(C) has been

(D) are

16 ☐ Mark for Review

Delta wings, which are triangular-shaped, are used for aircraft that travel at subsonic and supersonic speeds. Delta wings allow for the performance of advanced _____ and reduce the possibility of a stall.

Which choice completes the text so that it conforms to the conventions of Standard English?

(A) maneuvers, provide increased lift,

(B) maneuvers: provide increased lift

(C) maneuvers, provide increased lift;

(D) maneuvers provide increased lift,

17 ☐ Mark for Review

The Cubist-style paintings of Oswaldo Guayasamín, which depict the struggles of Latin American people, were influenced by the Ecuadorian painter's experiences with other _____ of them Mexican muralists, such as José Clemente Orozco and Diego Rivera.

Which choice completes the text so that it conforms to the conventions of Standard English?

(A) artists some

(B) artists. Some

(C) artists, some

(D) artists; some

18 ☐ Mark for Review

Low traffic neighborhoods, or LTNs, are neighborhoods where side roads are closed to cars but remain open to bicycles and _____ reduced presence of cars in multiple neighborhoods in Lambeth, a district in South London, resulted in LTN residents driving less throughout the year.

Which choice completes the text so that it conforms to the conventions of Standard English?

(A) pedestrians, the

(B) pedestrians; with the

(C) pedestrians with the

(D) pedestrians. The

CONTINUE →

19 ⬚ Mark for Review

Bullet ant stings are incredibly unpleasant. In fact, American entomologist Justin Schmidt rated bullet ant stings as the most painful of all insect stings. Why _____ The ant's sting contains a neurotoxin that keeps sodium channels open in sensory neurons, resulting in a long-lasting pain signal.

Which choice completes the text so that it conforms to the conventions of Standard English?

Ⓐ is this particular sting so painful.

Ⓑ this particular sting is so painful!

Ⓒ is this particular sting so painful?

Ⓓ this particular sting is so painful.

20 ⬚ Mark for Review

After attending the Central School of Speech and Drama in London, where both Judi Dench and Maggie Smith studied, Josette Simon joined the Royal Shakespeare Company in 1982, performing in several Shakespearean plays—*Love's Labour's Lost* (1984), *A Midsummer Night's Dream* (1999), and *Antony and Cleopatra* _____ in the leading female role.

Which choice completes the text so that it conforms to the conventions of Standard English?

Ⓐ (2017),

Ⓑ (2017)—

Ⓒ (2017,)

Ⓓ (2017)

21 ⬚ Mark for Review

Known for both his songs and his political activism, Chilean folk singer Víctor Jara started his career on stage, studying _____ wrote songs in the *Nueva Canción Chilena* movement, blending traditional Chilean folk music with political themes; and supported the leftist Popular Unity candidate and later president Salvador Allende.

Which choice completes the text so that it conforms to the conventions of Standard English?

Ⓐ theater during university;

Ⓑ theater, during university

Ⓒ theater during university,

Ⓓ theater, during university,

22 ⬚ Mark for Review

Many scientists and organizations are devoted to saving endangered species, but the methods used are not always universally beneficial to all local species. When endangered animals are captured to promote breeding, they are often exposed to anti-parasitic procedures that can aid in the longevity and health of that specific species. _____ these methods are harmful to the parasites themselves and may unintentionally cause the extinction of a different species.

Which choice completes the text with the most logical transition?

Ⓐ As a result,

Ⓑ However,

Ⓒ In addition,

Ⓓ In effect,

CONTINUE ➤

23 ☐ Mark for Review

A team of researchers at the University of Central Florida created a paint based on structural coloration instead of pigments. Pigments are made from pulverized minerals, chemicals, or heavy metals. Structural coloration, on the other hand, creates color when light is manipulated by microscopic surface structures. A peacock's feathers, _____ have a microscopic structure that reflects blue, turquoise, and green light. The researchers used tiny aluminum flakes and tinier aluminum nanoparticles to diffract light and create different colors.

Which choice completes the text with the most logical transition?

(A) for example,

(B) though,

(C) however,

(D) moreover,

24 ☐ Mark for Review

While there has been much research performed to improve agriculture in outer space, the research surrounding food preparation for astronauts on missions is still very minimal. _____ researchers recently performed experiments in a parabolic flight campaign conducted by the European Space Agency to try to mimic the process of frying french fries safely and satisfactorily while in zero gravity conditions.

Which choice completes the text with the most logical transition?

(A) By comparison,

(B) Consequently,

(C) Furthermore,

(D) In conclusion,

25 ☐ Mark for Review

While researching a topic, a student has taken the following notes:

- Rabindranath Tagore was a writer and social activist from India.
- His written work includes fiction, non-fiction, and poetry.
- He received the Nobel Prize in Literature for his English version of *Gitanjali*, a collection of 157 poems originally written in Bengali.
- *Gitanjali* was first published in 1910 and was later translated into English.
- His novel *Ghare Baire* was first published in 1916 and was originally written in Bengali.

The student wants to emphasize the order in which two of Rabindranath Tagore's works were published. Which choice most effectively uses relevant information from the notes to accomplish this goal?

(A) Rabindranath Tagore received the Nobel Prize in Literature for his English version of *Gitanjali*, a collection of poetry first published in 1910.

(B) Rabindranath Tagore's *Ghare Baire* is a novel originally written in Bengali, while another of his works is a collection of 157 poems.

(C) After writing *Gitanjali*, a collection of poetry, in 1910, Rabindranath Tagore published his novel *Ghare Baire* six years later.

(D) Rabindranath Tagore's written work, some of which first appeared in print in 1910 and 1916, includes fiction, non-fiction, and poetry.

CONTINUE ➤

26 ☐ Mark for Review

While researching a topic, a student has taken the following notes:

- Chemical elements are placed into groups based on their properties.
- Alkali metals are highly reactive with most other elements.
- There are six alkali metals on the periodic table.
- Noble gases usually do not react with other elements.
- There are seven noble gases on the periodic table.

The student wants to emphasize a difference between alkali metals and noble gases. Which choice most effectively uses relevant information from the notes to accomplish this goal?

(A) Alkali metals are highly reactive, whereas noble gases usually do not react with other elements.

(B) Chemical elements are placed into groups; two of these are the alkali metals and the noble gases.

(C) Chemical elements are placed into groups based on their properties (such as whether they are reactive or unreactive).

(D) There are six alkali metals on the periodic table; some other elements are classified as noble gases.

27 ☐ Mark for Review

While researching a topic, a student has taken the following notes:

- Radio telescopes use an array of antennas to detect specific frequencies of electromagnetic radiation from faraway astronomical objects.
- Radio telescopes can be used to observe pulsars and quasars.
- Pulsars and quasars are invisible to optical telescopes, which were used before radio telescopes were developed.
- Pulsars were discovered by astronomer Jocelyn Bell Burnell using a radio telescope called the Interplanetary Scintillation Array.
- This telescope was built in England and covered an area of 4 acres.

The student wants to emphasize the size of the radio telescope used to discover pulsars. Which choice most effectively uses relevant information from the notes to accomplish this goal?

(A) Pulsars and quasars are invisible to optical telescopes but can be observed with radio telescopes.

(B) Radio telescopes use an array of antennas to detect specific frequencies of electromagnetic radiation and can be used to observe pulsars and quasars.

(C) The Interplanetary Scintillation Array, the radio telescope used by astronomer Jocelyn Bell to discover pulsars, was built in England.

(D) The radio telescope used to observe pulsars for the first time, the Interplanetary Scintillation Array, covered an area of 4 acres.

STOP

**If you finish before time is called, you may check your work on this module only.
Do not turn to any other module in the test.**

575+ PSAT Practice Questions Test 1—Math
Module 1

Turn to Section 2 of your answer sheet to answer the questions in this section.

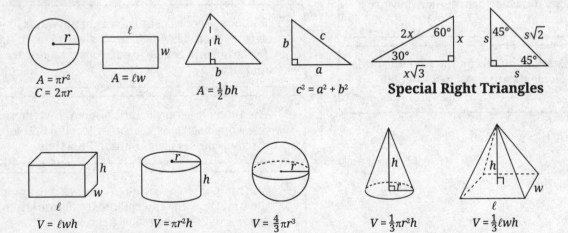
CONTINUE

‒ ‒

For multiple-choice questions, solve each problem, choose the correct answer from the choices provided, and then circle your answer in this book. Circle only one answer for each question. If you change your mind, completely erase the circle. You will not get credit for questions with more than one answer circled or for questions with no answers circled.

For student-produced response questions, solve each problem and write your answer next to or under the question in the test book as described below.

- Once you've written your answer, circle it clearly. You will not receive credit for anything written outside the circle or for any questions with more than one circled answer.

- If you find **more than one correct answer**, write and circle only one answer.

- Your answer can be up to 5 characters for a **positive** answer and up to 6 characters (including the negative sign) for a **negative** answer, but no more.

- If your answer is a **fraction** that is too long (over 5 characters for positive, 6 characters for negative), write the decimal equivalent.

- If your answer is a **decimal** that is too long (over 5 characters for positive, 6 characters for negative), truncate it or round at the fourth digit.

- If your answer is a **mixed number** (such as $3\frac{1}{2}$), write it as an improper fraction (7/2) or its decimal equivalent (3.5).

- Don't enter **symbols** such as a percent sign, comma, or dollar sign in your circled answer.

CONTINUE ➤

1 ▢ Mark for Review

The parking lot of a large retail store has a total of 900 parking spaces. At 10:00 A.M. on a Tuesday, 10% of the parking spaces have cars in them. How many parking spaces have cars in them at this time?

(A) 9

(B) 90

(C) 100

(D) 890

2 ▢ Mark for Review

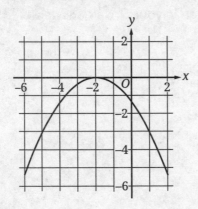

The *x*-intercept of the graph shown is (*x*, 0). What is the value of *x*?

(A) −5

(B) −3

(C) −2

(D) 2

3 ▢ Mark for Review

If $a = 30$, what is the value of $a - 9$?

(A) 12

(B) 21

(C) 30

(D) 39

4 ▢ Mark for Review

A team of zookeepers can clean 28 animal habitats in 4 days. At this rate, how many animal habitats will the team of zookeepers clean in 12 days?

(A) 3

(B) 7

(C) 40

(D) 84

CONTINUE

5 ☐ Mark for Review

$$4y - 44y$$

Which of the following expressions is equivalent to the given expression?

Ⓐ $-176y$

Ⓑ $-48y$

Ⓒ $-40y$

Ⓓ $-11y$

6 ☐ Mark for Review

$$4, 5, 5, 9, 9, 9, 11, 13, 19$$

Data set B has the same range as the data set shown. Which of the following could be the values in data set B?

Ⓐ $3, 5, 5, 5, 9, 11, 13, 19$

Ⓑ $4, 6, 6, 8, 10, 12, 14, 20$

Ⓒ $5, 5, 9, 9, 11, 13, 15, 19$

Ⓓ $5, 5, 9, 9, 11, 11, 11, 20$

7 ☐ Mark for Review

$$y = \frac{3}{2}x - 4$$

Line s is defined by the given equation. In the xy-plane, line t is perpendicular to line s. What is the slope of line t?

8 ☐ Mark for Review

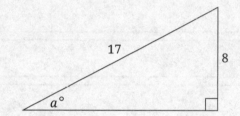

What is the value of $\sin a°$ in the triangle shown?

Ⓐ $\frac{8}{17}$

Ⓑ $\frac{9}{17}$

Ⓒ $\frac{17}{8}$

Ⓓ $\frac{25}{9}$

CONTINUE ➡

9 🔖 Mark for Review

The scatterplot shows the relationship between two variables, x and y. A line of best fit is also shown.

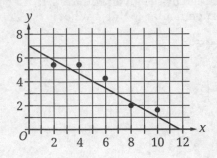

Which of the following equations best represents the line of best fit shown?

Ⓐ $y = -2.2x + 6.2$

Ⓑ $y = -0.51x + 6.2$

Ⓒ $y = 0.51x + 6.2$

Ⓓ $y = 2.2x + 6.2$

10 🔖 Mark for Review

$$f(x) = 12x - 6$$

The function f is defined by the given equation. What is the value of x when $f(x) = 30$?

Ⓐ 2

Ⓑ 3

Ⓒ 36

Ⓓ 354

11 🔖 Mark for Review

Which of the following expressions is a factor of $-18x^3 + 6x^2 - 24x$?

Ⓐ 4

Ⓑ $4x$

Ⓒ $6x$

Ⓓ $6x^2$

12 🔖 Mark for Review

On its first of 12 weekly missions, a remotely operated vehicle (ROV) dives into the ocean to a depth of 630 meters. On each mission after the first, the ROV dives to a depth that is 120% of the depth it reached during its previous mission. Which equation defines d, where $d(w)$ is the estimated depth, in meters, that the ROV dives after w weeks and w is a whole number greater than 1 and less than 12?

Ⓐ $d(w) = 120(1.20)^w$

Ⓑ $d(w) = 120(6.30)^w$

Ⓒ $d(w) = 630(1.20)^w$

Ⓓ $d(w) = 630(6.30)^w$

CONTINUE

13 | Mark for Review

$$3d - 8f = g$$

The given equation relates the distinct positive numbers d, f, and g. Which equation correctly expresses f in terms of d and g?

(A) $f = \dfrac{3d - g}{8}$

(B) $f = \dfrac{3}{8}d - g$

(C) $f = 8(3d - g)$

(D) $f = 24d - g$

14 | Mark for Review

What is the side length, in inches, of a square with an area of 144 square inches?

(A) 5

(B) 12

(C) 1,728

(D) 20,736

15 | Mark for Review

$$2 = x - 3$$
$$y = x^2 - 15x + 36$$

What is the value of y in the solution to the given system of equations?

16 | Mark for Review

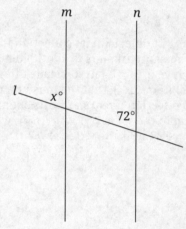

Note: Figure not drawn to scale

In the figure, line l intersects parallel lines m and n. What is the value of y if $x = 6y - 12$?

CONTINUE →

---

17 ☐ Mark for Review

The ratio c to 15 is equivalent to the ratio a to b. In terms of a, what is the value of c when $b = 14$?

(A) $\dfrac{a}{15}$

(B) $\dfrac{a}{14}$

(C) $\dfrac{14a}{15}$

(D) $\dfrac{15a}{14}$

---

18 ☐ Mark for Review

A museum has 371 objects in its collection the year it opens. The museum intends to add 10 items to its collection each year for the first decade after it opens. The number of items, $c(y)$, that the museum predicts having in its collection y years after its opening is given by an equation in the form $c(y) = n + my$, where m and n are constants. What is the value of m?

[____]

---

19 ☐ Mark for Review

$$y - 7 = 5x - 21$$
$$y + 7 = -5x + 13$$

What is the value of $2y$ for the given system of equations with the solution (x, y)?

(A) -16

(B) -8

(C) -4

(D) 2

---

20 ☐ Mark for Review

If y is at least 14 more than 12 times x, what is the least possible value of y when $x = 5$?

[____]

CONTINUE →

21 ☐ Mark for Review

Function f is defined by the equation $f(x) = \frac{13 + k}{x} - 7$, where k is a constant. The graph of function h in the xy-plane, where $y = h(x)$, is the result of translating the graph of $y = f(x)$ 6 units up and 8 units to the left. Which of the following equations defines function h?

Ⓐ $h(x) = \frac{13 + k}{x + 8} - 1$

Ⓑ $h(x) = \frac{13 + k}{x - 8} - 1$

Ⓒ $h(x) = \frac{21 + k}{x + 8} - 7$

Ⓓ $h(x) = \frac{21 + k}{x - 8} - 7$

22 ☐ Mark for Review

The function g is defined by the equation $g(x) = -(x - 3)^2 - 5$. If the graph of function g in the xy-plane reaches its maximum at (x, y), what is the value of x?

☐
‾‾‾‾

YIELD

Once you've finished (or run out of time for) this section, use the answer key to determine how many questions you got right. If you got fewer than 14 questions right, move on to Module 2—Easier, otherwise move on to Module 2—Harder.

575+ PSAT Practice Questions Test 1—Math
Module 2—Easier

Turn to Section 2 of your answer sheet to answer the questions in this section.

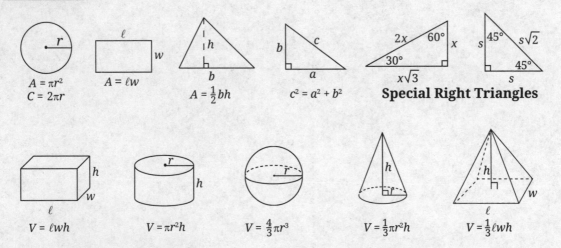
CONTINUE

For multiple-choice questions, solve each problem, choose the correct answer from the choices provided, and then circle your answer in this book. Circle only one answer for each question. If you change your mind, completely erase the circle. You will not get credit for questions with more than one answer circled or for questions with no answers circled.

For student-produced response questions, solve each problem and write your answer next to or under the question in the test book as described below.

- Once you've written your answer, circle it clearly. You will not receive credit for anything written outside the circle or for any questions with more than one circled answer.

- If you find **more than one correct answer**, write and circle only one answer.

- Your answer can be up to 5 characters for a **positive** answer and up to 6 characters (including the negative sign) for a **negative** answer, but no more.

- If your answer is a **fraction** that is too long (over 5 characters for positive, 6 characters for negative), write the decimal equivalent.

- If your answer is a **decimal** that is too long (over 5 characters for positive, 6 characters for negative), truncate it or round at the fourth digit.

- If your answer is a **mixed number** (such as $3\frac{1}{2}$), write it as an improper fraction (7/2) or its decimal equivalent (3.5).

- Don't enter **symbols** such as a percent sign, comma, or dollar sign in your circled answer.

CONTINUE

1 Mark for Review

Inflation needs to be at most 1.5% for a nation's economy to be considered healthy. If the current rate of inflation for a certain nation is 4%, what is the minimum decrease needed in order for the nation's economy to be considered healthy?

(A) 0.5%

(B) 1.5%

(C) 2.5%

(D) 5.5%

2 Mark for Review

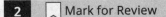

The 9 values in a data set are summarized in the box plot shown. Which of the following is the median of the data set?

(A) 4

(B) 6

(C) 8

(D) 10

3 Mark for Review

A generator starts with a full tank of 10 gallons of gas. The line shown represents the amount of gas, y, in gallons, in the generator after x hours have passed.

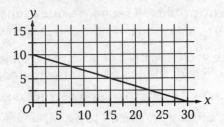

How many hours have passed when the generator has 5 gallons of gas remaining?

(A) 5

(B) 15

(C) 25

(D) 30

4 Mark for Review

A painter is working on identical townhouses and has 70 gallons of paint. Each townhouse uses 13 gallons of paint, and there are 4 townhouses. The painter uses the leftover paint to paint doors, using one-third of a gallon per door. How many doors can the painter paint?

(A) 6

(B) 18

(C) 54

(D) 210

CONTINUE

---

5 ☐ Mark for Review

$$f(x) = \frac{x}{16}$$

The function f is defined by the given equation. What is the value of $f(x)$ when $x = 32$?

Ⓐ 2

Ⓑ 8

Ⓒ 16

Ⓓ 32

---

6 ☐ Mark for Review

What is the value of $5x$ if $3x = 21$?

---

7 ☐ Mark for Review

A bakery currently has 6 apple pies for sale. If the bakery has 31 pies for sale and one pie is selected at random, what is the probability of selecting an apple pie?

Ⓐ $\frac{1}{31}$

Ⓑ $\frac{3}{31}$

Ⓒ $\frac{6}{31}$

Ⓓ $\frac{25}{31}$

---

8 ☐ Mark for Review

$$3(2r + s) = 8t$$

The given equation relates the distinct numbers r, s, and t, where r is not equal to 0. Which equation correctly represents s in terms of r and t?

Ⓐ $s = \frac{8}{3}t - 2r$

Ⓑ $s = \frac{8t}{2r}$

Ⓒ $s = 3(2r) + 8t$

Ⓓ $s = 8t - 3 - 2r$

---

9 ☐ Mark for Review

In the xy-plane, the graph of $y = g(x)$ passes through the point $(0, 2)$ and has a slope of -4. Which equation represents function g?

Ⓐ $g(x) = -4x - 4$

Ⓑ $g(x) = -4x - 2$

Ⓒ $g(x) = -4x$

Ⓓ $g(x) = -4x + 2$

CONTINUE ➡

10 ☐ Mark for Review

A grocery store stocks a total of 1,290 ounces of tuna in a 6-ounce cans of tuna and b 15-ounce cans of tuna. Which of the following equations represents this situation?

(A) $6a + 6b = 1,290$

(B) $6a + 15b = 1,290$

(C) $15a + 6b = 1,290$

(D) $15a + 15b = 1,290$

11 ☐ Mark for Review

$$y = \sqrt{16}$$
$$x = y^2 - 2$$

When graphed in the xy-plane, the given equations intersect at the point (x, y). What is the value of x?

(A) 2

(B) 12

(C) 14

(D) 254

12 ☐ Mark for Review

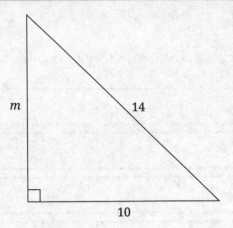

Note: Figure not drawn to scale

For the given triangle, what equation correctly represents the relationship among the side lengths?

(A) $10 + m = 14$

(B) $10m = 14$

(C) $10^2 - m^2 = 14^2$

(D) $10^2 + m^2 = 14^2$

13 ☐ Mark for Review

In quadrilateral $ABCD$, the measure of angle A is 83°, the measure of angle C is 116°, and the measure of angle D is 90°. What is the measure of angle B?

(A) 71°

(B) 90°

(C) 97°

(D) 289°

CONTINUE ➡

14 Mark for Review

An industrial scale is used to measure sacks of grain. What is the weight, in <u>pounds</u>, of a sack of grain that measures 112 stone on the scale? (1 stone = 14 pounds)

---

15 Mark for Review

$$y = \frac{1}{2}x - 6$$

In which of the following tables are all of the values of x and their corresponding values of y solutions to the given equation?

Ⓐ

x	y
0	6
1	$\frac{13}{2}$
2	7

Ⓑ

x	y
0	0
1	$\frac{1}{2}$
2	1

Ⓒ

x	y
0	−6
1	$-\frac{1}{2}$
2	−1

Ⓓ

x	y
0	−6
1	$-\frac{11}{2}$
2	−5

16 Mark for Review

Triangle XYZ is similar to triangle $X'Y'Z'$, where X, Y, and Z correspond to X', Y', and Z', respectively. The measure of angle X' is 74°, the measure of angle Y' is 28°, and the length of each side of XYZ is half the length of each corresponding side of $X'Y'Z'$. What is the measure of angle Z?

Ⓐ 39°

Ⓑ 46°

Ⓒ 78°

Ⓓ 102°

CONTINUE ➡

17 ☐ Mark for Review

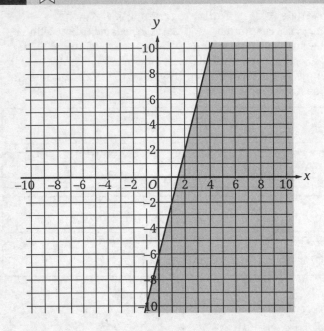

The solutions to an inequality are represented by the shaded region of the graph shown. Which ordered pair (x, y) is a solution to this inequality?

(A) $(-5, 0)$

(B) $(5, 0)$

(C) $(0, -5)$

(D) $(0, 5)$

18 ☐ Mark for Review

$$y = -2$$
$$x = 3 - y$$

Which ordered pair (x, y) is the solution to the given system of equations?

(A) $(-2, 3)$

(B) $(1, -2)$

(C) $(3, -2)$

(D) $(5, -2)$

19 ☐ Mark for Review

In the Fall semester, a third-grade classroom had 84 books. In the following Spring semester, the same third-grade classroom had 25% fewer books than it had in the Fall semester. How many books did the classroom have in the Spring semester?

20 ☐ Mark for Review

What is the solution to the equation $\frac{3}{z} = -4$?

CONTINUE ➡

---

21 ☐ Mark for Review

An equation describes the path that a volleyball takes after being bumped upward by a player. On impact with the player's arms, the ball is 4.2 feet above the surface of the court. If it takes the ball a total of 3.2 seconds to return to its starting height after the initial impact, how long after impact, in seconds, does it take for the ball to reach its maximum height of 10 feet?

Ⓐ 1.6

Ⓑ 3.2

Ⓒ 4.2

Ⓓ 6.4

22 ☐ Mark for Review

$$y = -15.5x^2 + 0.5x + 1600$$

The number of fungi, y, remaining in a dish x hours after a solution is introduced is expressed by the given equation, where $0 \le x \le 10$. Which of the following is the best interpretation of $(x, y) = (10, 55)$ in this context?

Ⓐ 10 hours after the solution was added, there were 55 fungi remaining in the dish.

Ⓑ 55 hours after the solution was added, there were 10 fungi remaining in the dish.

Ⓒ The number of fungi decreased by 10 every hour after the solution was added.

Ⓓ The number of fungi decreased by 55 every 10 hours after the solution was added.

STOP

If you finish before time is called, you may check your work on this module only.
Do not turn to any other module in the test.

575+ PSAT Practice Questions Test 1—Math
Module 2—Harder

Turn to Section 2 of your answer sheet to answer the questions in this section.

DIRECTIONS

The questions in this section address a number of important math skills.
Use of a calculator is permitted for all questions.

NOTES

Unless otherwise indicated:

- All variables and expressions represent real numbers.
- Figures provided are drawn to scale.
- All figures lie in a plane.
- The domain of a given function f is the set of all real numbers x for which $f(x)$ is a real number.

REFERENCE

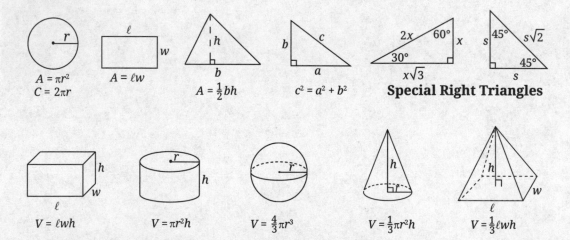

$A = \pi r^2$
$C = 2\pi r$

$A = \ell w$

$A = \frac{1}{2}bh$

$c^2 = a^2 + b^2$

Special Right Triangles

$V = \ell wh$

$V = \pi r^2 h$

$V = \frac{4}{3}\pi r^3$

$V = \frac{1}{3}\pi r^2 h$

$V = \frac{1}{3}\ell wh$

The number of degrees of arc in a circle is 360.
The number of radians of arc in a circle is 2π.
The sum of the measures in degrees of the angles of a triangle is 180.

CONTINUE

For multiple-choice questions, solve each problem, choose the correct answer from the choices provided, and then circle your answer in this book. Circle only one answer for each question. If you change your mind, completely erase the circle. You will not get credit for questions with more than one answer circled or for questions with no answers circled.

For student-produced response questions, solve each problem and write your answer next to or under the question in the test book as described below.

- Once you've written your answer, circle it clearly. You will not receive credit for anything written outside the circle or for any questions with more than one circled answer.

- If you find **more than one correct answer**, write and circle only one answer.

- Your answer can be up to 5 characters for a **positive** answer and up to 6 characters (including the negative sign) for a **negative** answer, but no more.

- If your answer is a **fraction** that is too long (over 5 characters for positive, 6 characters for negative), write the decimal equivalent.

- If your answer is a **decimal** that is too long (over 5 characters for positive, 6 characters for negative), truncate it or round at the fourth digit.

- If your answer is a **mixed number** (such as $3\frac{1}{2}$), write it as an improper fraction (7/2) or its decimal equivalent (3.5).

- Don't enter **symbols** such as a percent sign, comma, or dollar sign in your circled answer.

CONTINUE →

---

1 ☐ Mark for Review

$$3x - 4y = 16$$

When graphed in the xy-plane, the given equation has a y-intercept at $(0, y)$. What is the value of y?

2 ☐ Mark for Review

A roadside stand sells only apples and peaches. The owner of the stand hopes to sell at least 26 pieces of fruit today. Which inequality represents this situation, where a is the number of apples and p is the number of peaches?

Ⓐ $a + p \leq 26$

Ⓑ $a + p \geq 26$

Ⓒ $a - p \leq 26$

Ⓓ $a - p \geq 26$

3 ☐ Mark for Review

In the equation $2x - 6 = cx + 4$, c is a constant. If the equation has no real solutions, what is the value of c?

4 ☐ Mark for Review

Based on a random sample of eligible voters, political consultants predict that 60.8 percent of the electorate will support a particular referendum, with a margin of error of 3 percent. Which of the following is the most appropriate conclusion?

Ⓐ Exactly 60.8 percent of the electorate will support the referendum.

Ⓑ It is plausible that between 57.8 percent and 63.8 percent of the electorate is eligible to vote.

Ⓒ It is plausible that between 57.8 percent and 63.8 percent of the electorate will support the referendum.

Ⓓ It is not possible that less than 57.8 percent or more than 63.8 percent of the electorate will support the referendum.

CONTINUE →

5 ☐ Mark for Review

Value	Frequency
3	8
7	13
9	5
10	8
12	2

The table shows the frequency of values in a data set. What is the mode of the data set?

6 ☐ Mark for Review

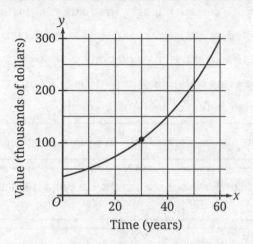

The graph shows the future value of an investment that earns interest at an annual rate of 3.6%. Which statement is the best interpretation of the point (30, 104.015) in this context?

(A) The initial value of the investment is $30,000.

(B) In approximately 104 years, the value of the investment will be $30,000.

(C) In 30 years, the value of the investment will be approximately $104.

(D) In 30 years, the value of the investment will be approximately $104,000.

CONTINUE

---

7 ☐ Mark for Review

The area of a certain triangle, in square centimeters, is represented by a, where $a > 0$. The base of the triangle is 3 times its height. If the equation $a = \frac{1}{2}(3h)(h)$ represents this situation, which of the following is the best interpretation of $3h$ in this context?

(A) The area of the triangle, in square centimeters

(B) The difference between the base and the height of the triangle, in centimeters

(C) The height of the triangle, in centimeters

(D) The base of the triangle, in centimeters

---

8 ☐ Mark for Review

$$S = 5(bc + 1) - 9$$

In the given equation, which of the following is equivalent to bc?

(A) $\dfrac{S-4}{5}$

(B) $S - 4$

(C) $\dfrac{S+4}{5}$

(D) $\dfrac{S+14}{5}$

---

9 ☐ Mark for Review

Which table gives three values of x and their corresponding values of $g(x)$ for the linear function $g(x) = -7$?

(A)

x	$g(x)$
−1	−14
0	−7
1	0

(B)

x	$g(x)$
−1	7
0	0
1	−7

(C)

x	$g(x)$
−1	−7
0	−7
1	−7

(D)

x	$g(x)$
−1	0
0	−7
1	−14

CONTINUE

10 ☐ Mark for Review

When positive quantity q is decreased by 14%, which of the following expressions represents the result?

Ⓐ $0.14q$

Ⓑ $0.86q$

Ⓒ $1.14q$

Ⓓ $86q$

11 ☐ Mark for Review

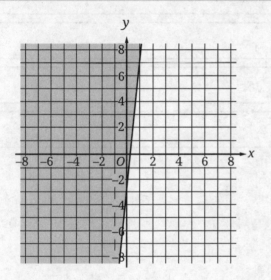

The graph of $y = f(x)$ is shown. Which of the following inequalities defines function f?

Ⓐ $f(x) \leq 10x - 3$

Ⓑ $f(x) \leq 10x + 3$

Ⓒ $f(x) \geq 10x - 3$

Ⓓ $f(x) \geq 10x + 3$

12 ☐ Mark for Review

An ampere (amp) is the unit of measurement for the rate at which electrical current flows through a circuit. The number of amps is found by dividing the number of watts by the number of volts. What is the total power, in watts, of a circuit with a voltage of 24 volts if a current of 2 amps is applied to it?

_____

13 ☐ Mark for Review

An ice cream shop charges $2.60 for a sundae with 2 toppings and $4.00 for a sundae with 4 toppings. There is a linear relationship between the number of toppings, t, and the total cost, $c(t)$, of each sundae. Which equation represents this relationship?

Ⓐ $c(t) = 0.70t + 1.20$

Ⓑ $c(t) = 1.20t + 0.70$

Ⓒ $c(t) = 1.30t$

Ⓓ $c(t) = 1.40t + 1.20$

CONTINUE ➡

14 ☐ Mark for Review

$$14x + 4y = -26$$

The first of two equations in a system of linear equations is given. Which of the following could represent the system's second equation if the system has no real solutions?

Ⓐ $-21x + 6y = 39$

Ⓑ $-21x + 6y = -39$

Ⓒ $21x + 6y = -39$

Ⓓ $21x + 6y = 39$

15 ☐ Mark for Review

$$6x^2 + 11x - 35 = 0$$

Which of the following is the negative solution to the given equation?

Ⓐ -11

Ⓑ $-\frac{7}{2}$

Ⓒ $-\frac{11}{6}$

Ⓓ $-\frac{5}{3}$

16 ☐ Mark for Review

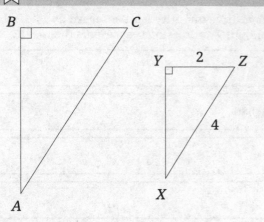

In the figure, triangle ABC is similar to triangle XYZ. What is the value of $\cos(A)$?

Ⓐ $\frac{1}{2}$

Ⓑ $\frac{\sqrt{3}}{2}$

Ⓒ $\sqrt{3}$

Ⓓ 2

CONTINUE

17 ☐ Mark for Review

A student in a writing class completed two assignments that required writing a total of 45 pages. The total amount of time the student spent writing the assignments was 15 hours. The student wrote pages for a research paper at an average rate of 2 pages per hour and wrote pages for creative stories at an average rate of 3 pages per hour. Which of the following systems of equations represents this scenario if a is the number of hours the student spent writing research paper pages and b is the number of hours the student spent writing creative story pages?

(A) $a + b = 15$
$2a + 3b = 45$

(B) $a + b = 15$
$3a + 2b = 45$

(C) $a + b = 45$
$2a + 3b = 15$

(D) $a + b = 45$
$3a + 2b = 15$

18 ☐ Mark for Review

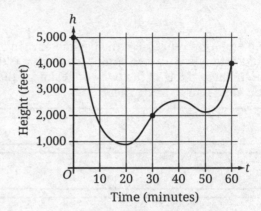

The graph displays the height h, in feet, above sea level of a weather balloon t minutes after it reaches its maximum height. In feet per minute, what is the weather balloon's average change in height above sea level from 30 minutes after it reaches its maximum height to 60 minutes after it reaches its maximum height?

☐☐☐
——

19 ☐ Mark for Review

Function h is defined by the equation $h(x) = |7x - 33|$. For which of the following values of c does $h(c) = 2c$?

(A) $\dfrac{33}{7}$

(B) $\dfrac{33}{5}$

(C) $\dfrac{66}{5}$

(D) 33

CONTINUE ▶

20 ☐ Mark for Review

$$p = 16 + s$$

The given equation represents the perimeter p, in inches, of a triangle with two equal sides. What is the length, in inches, of one of the two equal sides if the third side has a length of s inches?

Ⓐ 2

Ⓑ 4

Ⓒ 8

Ⓓ 16

21 ☐ Mark for Review

$$27x^2 - (3c + 9d)x + cd = 0$$

In the given equation, c and d are positive constants. What is the value of the constant h if the sum of the solutions to the equation is $h(c + 3d)$?

☐

22 ☐ Mark for Review

Angle W in triangle WXY measures 90°. The length of $\overline{WX}$ is 21 units, which is 25 units shorter than the length of $\overline{WY}$. What is the value of $\frac{XZ}{WZ}$ if $\overline{WZ}$ is an altitude of triangle WXY?

Ⓐ $\frac{21}{46}$

Ⓑ $\frac{21}{25}$

Ⓒ $\frac{25}{21}$

Ⓓ $\frac{46}{21}$

STOP

**If you finish before time is called, you may check your work on this module only.
Do not turn to any other module in the test.**

Chapter 61
Practice Test 1: Answers and Explanations

PRACTICE TEST 1 ANSWER KEY

Reading and Writing			Math		
Module 1	Module 2 (Easier)	Module 2 (Harder)	Module 1	Module 2 (Easier)	Module 2 (Harder)
1. B	1. C	1. D	1. B	1. C	1. −4
2. A	2. C	2. B	2. C	2. B	2. B
3. C	3. B	3. D	3. B	3. B	3. 2
4. D	4. D	4. B	4. D	4. C	4. C
5. A	5. B	5. D	5. C	5. A	5. 7
6. B	6. A	6. A	6. D	6. 35	6. D
7. B	7. D	7. D	7. $-\frac{2}{3}$	7. C	7. D
8. A	8. C	8. C	8. A	8. A	8. C
9. C	9. D	9. A	9. B	9. D	9. C
10. B	10. A	10. A	10. B	10. B	10. B
11. D	11. B	11. A	11. C	11. C	11. C
12. B	12. B	12. B	12. C	12. D	12. 48
13. B	13. A	13. A	13. A	13. A	13. A
14. D	14. A	14. C	14. B	14. 1568	14. D
15. C	15. B	15. C	15. −14	15. D	15. B
16. C	16. D	16. A	16. 14	16. C	16. B
17. D	17. B	17. C	17. D	17. B	17. A
18. C	18. D	18. D	18. 10	18. D	18. $\frac{200}{3}$
19. D	19. A	19. C	19. B	19. 63	19. B
20. A	20. D	20. B	20. 74	20. $-\frac{3}{4}$ or -0.75	20. C
21. B	21. C	21. A	21. A	21. A	21. $\frac{1}{9}$ or .1111
22. B	22. A	22. B	22. 3	22. A	22. A
23. C	23. B	23. A			
24. C	24. D	24. B			
25. A	25. D	25. C			
26. A	26. A	26. A			
27. D	27. C	27. D			

PRACTICE TEST 1—READING AND WRITING EXPLANATIONS

Module 1

1. **B** This is a Vocabulary question, as it asks what "haggard" *most nearly means*. Treat "haggard" as if it were a blank—the blank describes the lodge-keeper's face, so look for and highlight clues in the text about the lodge-keeper. The text states that the lodge-keeper's face *bore the reflection of some great disaster.* Since the lodge-keeper is also described as *old* in addition to dealing with some stressful event, a good word to enter in the annotation box would be "worn out" or "upset."

    • (A) is wrong because *Dull* is **Recycled Language**—it misuses *bore* from the text.

    • (B) is correct because *Exhausted* matches "worn out."

    • (C) and (D) are wrong because *Friendly* and *Simple* don't match "worn out."

2. **A** This is a Vocabulary question, as it asks for a *logical and precise word or phrase*. The blank describes what Ahimbisibwe does with aspects of digital art, painting, or photography, so look for and highlight clues in the text about Ahimbisibwe's work. The text states that Ahimbisibwe *integrates a variety of elements* and has *diversity* in his work, so a good word to enter into the annotation box would be "incorporating" or "using."

    • (A) is correct because *utilizing* matches "incorporating" or "using."

    • (B) and (C) are wrong because *masking* and *ignoring* are the **Opposite** of what Ahimbisibwe does with the aspects mentioned.

    • (D) is wrong because *measuring* doesn't match "incorporating."

3. **C** This is a Vocabulary question, as it asks for a *logical and precise word or phrase*. The blank describes what scholars can say about Shakespeare's motivations, so look for and highlight clues in the text about those motivations. Because *few resources of that nature are available for interpreting the motivations* behind Shakespeare's works, a good word to enter in the annotation box would be that the scholars can only "guess" about Shakespeare's motivations.

    • (A) and (B) are wrong because *imply* and *insinuate* don't match "guess"—these words mean to hint at something a person knows without directly stating it, but the scholars in the text do not actually know Shakespeare's motivations and therefore cannot hint at them, even indirectly.

    • (C) is correct because *speculate* matches "guess."

    • (D) is wrong because *regulate* doesn't match "guess."

4. **D**   This is a Vocabulary question, as it asks for a *logical and precise word or phrase*. The blank describes the tennis champion's assessment of her ability, so look for and highlight clues in the text about the champion's feelings towards her ability. The text states that *her attitude and posture* indicated *doubt rather than assuredness*. Because of the transition word *rather*, the blank should go in the opposite direction of the clue, so a good word to enter in the annotation box would be "certain" or "sure."

- (A) and (B) are wrong because *ingenious* (clever) and *methodical* (systematic) don't match "certain."

- (C) is wrong because *hesitant* is the **Opposite** of "certain"—this answer doesn't account for the idea that what the champion felt and what the observers saw were contradictory.

- (D) is correct because *confident* matches "certain."

5. **A**   This is a Purpose question, as it asks for the *main purpose of the text*. Read the text and highlight who or what is focused on. The text focuses on *the lawyer*, and his assessment of *Nazimoff's family*. The text goes on to say that although the lawyer was *not acquainted* with the family, he *guessed at once that the general's home life was not happy*. Therefore, a good main purpose of the text to enter in the annotation box would be "describe what lawyer learns about family."

- (A) is correct because it's consistent with the highlighting and annotation.

- (B) is wrong because it goes **Beyond the Text**—neither the lawyer's nor the general's *interpretation of the will* is discussed.

- (C) is wrong because it goes **Beyond the Text**—the text only describes the lawyer's interactions with one client, so no conclusion can be made about how he *conducts his research on new clients* in general.

- (D) is wrong because it's **Extreme Language**—just because the lawyer knows the general by *repute*, or reputation, does not mean the lawyer has *great respect* for the general.

6. **B**   This is a Purpose question, as it asks for the *main purpose of the text*. Read the text and highlight who or what is focused on. The text focuses on the work of *Australian artist Patricia Piccinini*. The text goes on to say that *Though her work has drawn criticism for its perceived brashness, she was recognized in 2016 as one of the most popular artists in the world*. Therefore, a good main purpose of the text to enter in the annotation box would be "explain Patricia's work and how it's received."

- (A) is wrong because it's **Recycled Language**—it misuses *criticism* and *environmental* from different parts of the text.

- (B) is correct because it's consistent with the highlighting and annotation.

- (C) is wrong because it's **Extreme Language**—while Piccinini's work may sound unusual, the author does not go as far as to call her a *true innovator*.

- (D) is wrong because it goes **Beyond the Text**—it's not discussed in the text how long it takes for Piccinini to create one of her installations.

7. **B** This is a Purpose question, as it asks for the *function of the underlined question in the text as a whole*. Read the text and focus on the lines after the underlined question to understand its function. The underlined sentence asks a question commonly posed to actors, and the lines after indicate that while *audience members marvel at actors' abilities to commit such large amounts of text to memory...most actors believe that memorizing lines for a play is not the most challenging of the technical and creative demands of performing*. A good function of the underlined portion to enter in the annotation box would be "ask a question that audience and actors feel differently about."

- (A) is wrong because it goes **Beyond the Text**—while actors may keep audiences in mind when they create their roles, this is not related to the underlined question.

- (B) is correct because it's consistent with the highlighting and annotation—the text implies that actors don't find memorization as hard as audiences think it to be.

- (C) is wrong because it's the **Opposite** of the text—while the actors don't state that memorizing lines is easy, they don't describe it as the hardest part of their job or as being a source of *hesitation*.

- (D) is wrong because it's **Recycled Language**—it misuses *technical and creative* from the text to make an unsupported criticism of audience members.

8. **A** This is a Retrieval question, as it asks what the text would *most strongly suggest* about a detail. Look for and highlight information about *the chemical signatures reported by Will and her team*. The text states that *Will and her team claim* that their findings regarding the signatures *support what is known as the synestia theory*, while the text goes on to say that the findings *would contradict what is known as the accretion theory*. The correct answer should be as consistent as possible with these details.

- (A) is correct because it's consistent with the highlighting—Will and her team's findings support the synestia theory and go against the accretion theory.

- (B), (C), and (D) are wrong because they each go **Beyond the Text**—it's unknown from the text whether the chemical signatures are the *first known evidence*, another team recorded them *first*, or *the distance between the moon and the Earth* made them *difficult to record*.

9. **C** This is a Retrieval question, as it asks for a detail *based on the text*. Look for and highlight information about how *DNA methylation* was *involved in the process of hibernation*. The text says the study showed that *periods of hibernation were correlated with DNA methylation activity* and that this activity ultimately prevented *the production of proteins that lead to aging in bats*. The correct answer should be as consistent as possible with these details.

- (A) and (D) are wrong because they're each **Recycled Language**—they misuse either *energy conservation* or *torpor* from one part of the text along with *DNA methylation* from a different part of the text.

- (B) is wrong because it's the **Opposite** of what's stated in the text—DNA methylation ultimately *prevents* the production of proteins rather than *allows for increased protein production*.

- (C) is correct because it's consistent with the highlighted details.

10. **B** This is a Charts question, as it asks for *data from the table* that will *complete the text*. Read the title, variables, and units from the table. Then, read the text and highlight the claim or statement that references the information from the table. The incomplete sentence focuses on the depth of *The highest number of Abelisaurus fossils that were recovered from the Argentinian site*. The correct answer should offer accurate information from the table that completes the sentence.

   - (A), (C), and (D) are wrong because it's inconsistent with the data in the table—the highest number of *Abelisaurus* fossils was at 3–5 feet.

   - (B) is correct because it's consistent with the statement and the table.

11. **D** This is a Charts question, as it asks for *data from the graph* that will *complete the statement*. Read the title, key, variables, and units from the graph. Then, read the text and highlight the claim or statement that references the information from the graph. The meteorologist is *comparing the data* for *January*. The correct answer should offer accurate information from the graph that completes the statement.

   - (A) is wrong because it's **Half-Right**—while the January average snowfalls for Vermont and Michigan are fairly close, there's a considerable gap between the average snowfalls of Colorado and Maine.

   - (B) and (C) are wrong because they're the **Opposite** of what can be seen in the graph—Vermont has one of the lowest snowfalls in January, rather than the greatest amount, and Michigan's average snowfall is nowhere near 25 inches.

   - (D) is correct because it's consistent with the graph.

12. **B** This is a Claims question, as it asks which choice would *best support the critic's claim*. Look for and highlight the claim in the text, which is that *Waterhouse had an exquisite talent for using color to represent the personal characteristics of his subjects*. The correct answer should address and be consistent with each aspect of this claim.

   - (A), (C), and (D) are wrong because while they all praise Waterhouse or at least describe his work, none of them makes any reference to *color*.

   - (B) is correct because it's consistent with the highlighted claim—saying that Waterhouse *masterfully conveys* something is a reference to his *exquisite talent* and the *bright red dress* is a reference to *color*.

13.   **B**   This is a Charts question, as it asks for *data from the table* that will *illustrate the claim*. Read the title and variables from the table. Then, read the text and highlight the claim or argument that references the information from the table. The text states that *cheap generic grocery brands became popular, but only for foods that were more expensive, such as complete meals or luxury items like chocolates* rather than for *inexpensive pantry staples such as flour and rice.* The correct answer should offer accurate information from the table that illustrates this contrast.

- (A), (C), and (D) are wrong because they're each not relevant to the claim—comparing a grocery item to itself or comparing one expensive item to another expensive item will not illustrate the difference between how much of a generic expensive item and a generic inexpensive item that consumers will purchase.

- (B) is correct because it's consistent with the argument and the table—by noting that consumers purchased a generic item for 55% of all frozen dinner sales but only for 9% of uncooked rice sales, the data shows that people bought generic versions of expensive items with more frequency than they bought generic versions of inexpensive items.

14.   **D**   This is a Conclusions question, as it asks what *most logically completes the text*. Look for and highlight the main focus of the text, which is that *Florida has a distinctly different culture from those of the other states of the American South.* Then, highlight the main point made regarding this focus, which is that *large numbers of northerners began settling in Florida seeking a subtropical climate and good farmland, and the twentieth century provided a similarly large influx of migrants.* Therefore, Florida's different culture is due to the influence of northerners moving there. The correct answer should be as consistent as possible with this conclusion.

- (A) is wrong because it goes **Beyond the Text**—it's not stated in the text to what extent residents of US states understand each other's cultural practices.

- (B) is wrong because it's the **Opposite** of the text—the text specifically discusses a group from one region, the North, affecting the culture of another region, Florida.

- (C) is wrong because it's **Recycled Language**—it misuses *customs, practices, speech patterns, and accents* to make a logical but unsupported claim.

- (D) is correct because it's consistent with what the highlighted sentences say about how people moving to Florida affected Florida's culture.

15.   **C**   This is a Conclusions question, as it asks what *most logically completes the text*. Look for and highlight the main focus of the text, which is the disparity between the quality of *Civil War* writing and *modern American* writing. Then, highlight the main point made regarding this focus, which is that *Civil War-era writers of all backgrounds placed a stronger emphasis on clarity of speech than modern Americans do because the technological limitations of the nineteenth century often made it impossible to interact with one's audience and clarify writings in person.* Therefore, the disparity in writing quality is due to a specific

reason that Civil War-era writers believed they had to write carefully, rather than anything to do with class distinctions. The correct answer should be as consistent as possible with this conclusion.

- (A) is wrong because it's the **Opposite** of what's stated by the text—the opening and closing sentences of the text imply that the two groups write differently.

- (B) is wrong because it goes **Beyond the Text**—no *other countries* besides the US are mentioned.

- (C) is correct because it's consistent with what the highlighted sentences say about why Civil War-era writers wrote as clearly as they did.

- (D) is wrong because it's **Recycled Language**—it misuses *wealthy* and *educated* from the text to make an unsupported prediction about modern American writers.

16. **C** In this Rules question, apostrophes with nouns are changing in the answer choices. Determine whether each word possesses anything. The dancers do not possess *wear*, and the masks don't possess anything. Eliminate any answer that doesn't match this.

- (A), (B), and (D) are wrong because *dancers* shouldn't be possessive.

- (C) is correct because *dancers* and *masks* are plural but not possessive.

17. **D** In this Rules question, verbs are changing in the answer choices, so it's testing consistency with verbs. Find and highlight the subject, *a team*, which is singular, so a singular verb is needed. All of the answers work with a singular subject, so look for a clue regarding tense. This sentence begins with *Over the next 50 years* and refers to the period starting after 1801, so the answer should be in past tense. Highlight those words and write an annotation that says "past." Eliminate any answer not in past tense.

- (A) is wrong because it's in future tense.

- (B) and (C) are wrong because they're in present tense.

- (D) is correct because it's in past tense.

18. **C** In this Rules question, punctuation is changing in the answer choices. The main meaning of the sentence is *Día de los Muertos includes visiting the graves of the deceased…*. The phrase *also known as the Day of the Dead* is a describing phrase that has a long dash after it, so it must have a long dash before it to show that it is Extra Information. Eliminate answers that do not have a long dash before the describing phrase.

- (A), (B), and (D) are wrong because they don't use a long dash.

- (C) is correct because it uses a long dash before the Extra Information.

19.   **D**   In this Rules question, punctuation is changing in the answer choices. Look for independent clauses. The first part of the sentence says *While completing a 1996 mission for the National Aeronautics and Space Administration (NASA)*, which is a dependent clause. The second part of the sentence says *astronaut Shannon W. Lucid celebrated the Fourth of July holiday by wearing patriotic socks as the only American aboard the Russian space station*, which is an independent clause. Eliminate any option that doesn't correctly connect a dependent + an independent clause.

- (A) and (C) are wrong because a FANBOYS word (*and*) can't be used with a dependent clause, with or without a comma.

- (B) is wrong because a comma is needed in this case to connect the two clauses.

- (D) is correct because dependent + independent can be connected with a comma.

20.   **A**   In this Rules question, punctuation is changing in the answer choices. Look for independent clauses. The first part of the sentence says *From 1956 to 1960 Sabin worked with Russian scientists to develop an oral poliovirus vaccine that prevented initial intestinal infection*, which is an independent clause. The second part says *in 1961 his first oral poliovirus vaccine was licensed and administered in the United States*, which is also an independent clause. Eliminate any answer that can't correctly connect two independent clauses.

- (A) is correct because it connects the independent clauses with a comma + a coordinating conjunction (FANBOYS), which is acceptable.

- (B) is wrong because some type of punctuation is needed in order to connect two independent clauses.

- (C) is wrong because a coordinating conjunction (*and*) without a comma can't connect two independent clauses.

- (D) is wrong because a comma without a coordinating conjunction (FANBOYS) can't connect two independent clauses.

21.   **B**   In this Rules question, the subjects of the answers are changing, which suggests it may be testing modifiers. Look for and highlight a modifying phrase: *Upon investigating the origin and spread of the fire*. Whoever is *investigating the origin* of the fire needs to come immediately after the comma. Eliminate any answer that doesn't start with someone who is investigating the fire.

- (A) is wrong because the *workers* didn't investigate the fire.

- (B) is correct because *the fire marshal* can investigate the fire.

- (C) and (D) are wrong because *escape* and *locked factory doors* cannot investigate.

22. **B** This is a transition question, so follow the basic approach. Highlight ideas that relate to each other. The preceding sentence states that Cheechoo *struggled with a lack of self-assurance as a young person*, and this sentence describes the result that *she provides opportunities for students to build confidence and self-esteem*. These ideas agree, so a same-direction transition is needed. Make an annotation that says "agree." Eliminate any answer that doesn't match.

- (A) is wrong because this sentence isn't providing a separate thing that is similar to the previously mentioned topic.

- (B) is correct because *Thus* indicates the result based on the previous sentence.

- (C) is wrong because *In the end* suggests a summary, which isn't the case here.

- (D) is wrong because *As a rule* indicates something that usually happens, not a direct result.

23. **C** This is a transition question, so follow the basic approach. Highlight ideas that relate to each other. This sentence describes a common belief regarding who wrote the scrolls, and the following sentence says that *Subsequent research and analysis…has challenged…our understanding of the texts' origins*. These ideas disagree, so an opposite-direction transition is needed. Make an annotation that says "disagree." Eliminate any answer that doesn't match.

- (A) is wrong because this sentence doesn't contrast with the one before.

- (B) is wrong because this sentence doesn't contain an example.

- (C) is correct because *Initially* contrasts with the *Subsequent research* in the following sentence.

- (D) is wrong because this sentence represents the earlier view, not the eventual one.

24. **C** This is a transition question, so follow the basic approach. Highlight ideas that relate to each other. The preceding sentence states that *The microbiome existing in the human body can benefit and harm a person*, and this sentence says that *the microbes in the gut help digest food and support the immune system*. These ideas agree, so a same-direction transition is needed. Make an annotation that says "agree." Eliminate any answer that doesn't match.

- (A) is wrong because this sentence isn't a conclusion.

- (B) is wrong because the sentences don't indicate a sequence of events.

- (C) is correct because *On one hand* indicates one side of an idea and sets up a contrasting view-point, as stated in the following sentence.

- (D) is wrong because *In any case* means "regardless," and this sentence isn't contrasting with the one before.

25. **A** This is a Rhetorical Synthesis question, so follow the basic approach. Highlight the goal(s) stated in the question: *emphasize a similarity in the imagery of the poems from this collection*. Eliminate any answer that doesn't fulfill this purpose.

- (A) is correct because it states that *colors are a recurring theme* in the collection, which suggests a *similarity* among different poems.

- (B) is wrong because it contrasts two poems in the collection rather than showing a *similarity*.

- (C) and (D) are wrong because they don't mention any similarities in imagery.

26. **A** This is a Rhetorical Synthesis question, so follow the basic approach. Highlight the goal(s) stated in the question: *make and support a generalization about dental insurance*. Eliminate any answer that doesn't fulfill this purpose.

- (A) is correct because the *generalization* is the causal effect between having insurance and generally having less tooth decay and the *support* is the reasoning that *insurance allows them to receive regular teeth cleanings*.

- (B) is wrong because it doesn't mention *dental insurance*.

- (C) is wrong because it provides specific data rather than making a *generalization*.

- (D) is wrong because it focuses on children's likelihood of having tooth decay, not on dental insurance.

27. **D** This is a Rhetorical Synthesis question, so follow the basic approach. Highlight the goal(s) stated in the question: *emphasize the different categories in which the Morgan-Keenan system classifies stars*. Eliminate any answer that doesn't fulfill this purpose.

- (A), (B), and (C) are wrong because they each mention only one category of stars.

- (D) is correct because it mentions *O-type* and *M-type* stars.

Module 2—Easier

1. **C** This is a Vocabulary question, as it asks what "fill" *most nearly means*. Treat "fill" as if it were a blank—the blank describes what happens to the fruit, so look for and highlight clues in the text about the fruit. The text mentions *fruitfulness* and that the season and sun are looking to *bless / With fruit the vines*, so a good word to enter in the annotation box would be "provide" or "give."

- (A), (B), and (D) are wrong because *Weaken, Steal,* and *Rot* are the **Opposite** of "provide."

- (C) is correct because *Supply* matches "provide."

2.   **C**   This is a Vocabulary question, as it asks for a *logical and precise word or phrase*. The blank describes what the evidence in the text does to the historians' determination, so look for and highlight clues in the text about this interaction. The text states that the *Art historians have dated* the painting to the *late 1800s*, and the canvas and paints used in the painting date to the same time. Therefore, a good word to enter into the annotation box would be "confirms" or "backs up."

- (A) and (B) are wrong because *declines* and *dissolves* are the **Opposite** of "confirms."

- (C) is correct because *supports* matches "confirms."

- (D) is wrong because *analyzes* doesn't match "confirms."

3.   **B**   This is a Vocabulary question, as it asks what "plainly" *most nearly means*. Treat "plainly" as if it were a blank—the blank describes how the narrator wishes to describe the events in his life, so look for and highlight clues in the text about how he wants to do that. The text mentions that he wants to discuss *mere household events* and do so *without comment*, which implies that he wants to keep things as straightforward as possible. Therefore, a good word to enter in the annotation box would be "clearly" or "straightforwardly."

- (A), (C), and (D) are wrong because *Boringly*, *Loudly*, and *Quickly* don't match "clearly" and there is no support that the narrator wants to speak in any of these fashions.

- (B) is correct because *Simply* matches "clearly."

4.   **D**   This is a Vocabulary question, as it asks for a *logical and precise word or phrase*. The blank describes the extent to which the pledge made by J. P. Morgan *alleviated* (lessened) the economic damage caused by the Knickerbocker Crisis, so look for and highlight clues in the text about that interaction. The text states that the pledges made by J. P Morgan were *vital in solidifying the weakened banking system*, so a good word to enter in the annotation box would be that the pledges "greatly" or "mostly" helped to lessen the economic damage from the Crisis.

- (A) and (C) are wrong because *uncommonly* and *abruptly* (suddenly) don't match "greatly."

- (B) is wrong because *needlessly* is the **Opposite** of the text—the pledges made by J. P. Morgan were *vital* rather than not needed.

- (D) is correct because *largely* matches "greatly."

5.   **B**   This is a Purpose question, as it asks for the *function of the underlined sentence in the text as a whole*. Read the text and focus on the lines before the underlined sentence to understand its function. The lines before discuss the creation of a *hydrogel* meant to replace *disintegrated cartilage*, and the underlined sentence explains one of the advantages of the hydrogel. A good function of the underlined portion to enter in the annotation box would be "explain benefits of hydrogel."

- (A) is wrong because there's no mention of *traditional treatments* in the text.

- (B) is correct because it's consistent with the highlighting and annotation.

- (C) is wrong because it's the **Opposite** of the text—the underlined sentence does not question the benefits of the hydrogel; it explains its benefits.

- (D) is wrong because it's **Extreme Language**—it's not possible to know from the text whether combining crystallized polyvinyl alcohol and cellulose is the *only* way to make a hydrogel.

6. **A** This is a Purpose question, as it asks for the *main purpose of the text*. Read the text and highlight who or what is focused on. The text focuses on the argument between de Berault and M. l'Anglais. The dialogue between the men indicates that M. l'Anglais believes de Berault has used *Marked cards*, but de Berault reveals he has been looking at M. l'Anglais's cards using a mirror located behind M. l'Anglais. Therefore, a good main purpose of the text to enter in the annotation box would be "describe the two men's argument."

    - (A) is correct because it's consistent with the highlighting and annotation.

    - (B) is wrong because it's the **Opposite** of the text—M. l'Anglais does not have *respect* for his opponent, as he considers de Berault a cheater.

    - (C) is wrong because it goes **Beyond the Text**—while both men probably enjoy playing cards, it's not stated whether they do or don't in the text.

    - (D) is wrong because it also goes **Beyond the Text**—while de Berault is probably upset at being caught, the text instead focuses on how he attempts to outmaneuver M. l'Anglais during their argument.

7. **D** This is a Purpose question, as it asks for the *function of the underlined sentence in the text as a whole*. Read the text and focus on the lines before the underlined sentence to understand its function. The lines before introduce Stephen Graham Jones and mention his *dark and playful* writing style as well as his focus on *the ethics of hunting wild animals*. The underlined sentence compares Jones to David Foster Wallace by stating that they *both balance elements of morality and humor in their works*. A good function of the underlined portion to enter in the annotation box would be "state that Jones and Wallace focus on similar things."

    - (A) is wrong because it's **Extreme Language**—the author does not suggest that *other authors* should do what Jones does.

    - (B) is wrong because it goes **Beyond the Text**—as likely as it is that one's heritage informs their writing choices, the text does not establish this link.

    - (C) is wrong because no *other famous works that have advocated for animal rights* are discussed.

    - (D) is correct because it's consistent with the highlighting and annotation.

8. **C** This is a Dual Texts question, as it asks how *the scientists at the University of Illinois Urbana-Champaign* in Text 2 would *respond to the underlined potion of Text 1*. Read Text 1 and highlight the underlined portion, which is that *the behaviors of others have a greater influence on an individual's behaviors and attitudes than do that individual's specific personality traits*. Then, read Text 2 and highlight what the scientists at the University of Illinois Urbana-Champaign say about the same topic. The scientists state that *a person will acknowledge and even give an advantage to behavior that is consistent with the person's baseline personality traits…even when doing so negatively impacted their own situations*. Therefore, the scientists in Text 2 think that personality traits play a stronger role in behavior than Text 1 does. Enter "Text 2 disagrees—personality traits do matter" into the annotation box.

    - (A) is wrong because it's the **Opposite** of Text 2's argument—*herd mentality and perceived social norms* affecting behavior were part of Text 1's argument, not Text 2's.

    - (B) is wrong because it goes **Beyond the Text**—not only would the scientists in Text 2 disagree that herd mentality and perceived social norms are necessarily the major factor in competitions, but also neither text mentions *collaborations*, or partnerships.

    - (C) is correct because it's consistent with the highlighting and annotation—by stating that the factors from Text 1 *are not necessarily the dominant factor*, this answer implies that other factors, such as personality traits, may matter just as much, if not more.

    - (D) is wrong because it's **Extreme Language**—Text 1 never claims that people *always* adapt to social norms, only that it happens *often* and to *most people*.

9. **D** This is a Retrieval question, as it asks for a detail *according to the text*. Look for and highlight information about *which gases are present in the interior of the Moon*. The text mentions that the samples from the Moon's interior contain helium, neon, and in the next sentence, argon. The correct answer should be as consistent as possible with these details.

    - (A), (B), and (C) are wrong because they're each **Half-Right**—all three of the gases mentioned in the text were found in samples from the Moon's interior, not just one or two of them.

    - (D) is correct because it's consistent with the highlighted details.

10. **A** This is a Main Idea question, as it asks for the *main idea of the text*. Look for and highlight information that can help identify the main idea. The text talks about *the height above mean sea level* but then the last sentence explains that this calculation can change over time due to *climate change*. Since the middle sentence only offers details regarding height above mean sea level, the first and last sentences serve as the main idea. The correct answer should be as consistent as possible with this portion of the text.

    - (A) is correct because it's consistent with the highlighted portions of the text, incorporating concepts from both the first and last sentences.

    - (B) is wrong because it's the **Opposite** of what is stated in the text—the text indicates that the height above mean sea level has changed over time due to climate change.

- (C) is wrong because it goes **Beyond the Text**—the text never mentions that there has been any discussion of a *universal method* for measuring the height of objects and locations above mean sea level.

- (D) is wrong because it's **Extreme Language**—while it's stated that the height above mean sea level does change, it's not said to *only* decrease.

11. **D** This is a Charts question, as it asks for *data from the table* that will *complete the example*. Read the title and variables from the table. Then, read the text and highlight the claim or statement that references the information from the table. The text states that *France supplemented its own populations of these animals by importing them from other countries*. The correct answer should offer accurate information from the table that supports this claim and completes the example.

- (A), (B), and (C) are wrong because they are numbers for England, the United States, and Spain, respectively, but the example is referencing animals that *actually came from France*. (C) is additionally wrong because 35% refers to *mules*, when the correct answers should be a percentage of *horses*.

- (D) is correct because it's consistent with the highlighted claim and the table.

12. **B** This is a Charts question, as it asks for *data from the table* that will *complete the example*. Read the title and variables from the table. Then, read the text and highlight the claim or statement that references the information from the table. The text states that the researcher is looking at the *shyest male albatrosses*. The correct answer should offer accurate information from the table that refers to this group of albatrosses and completes the example.

- (A), (C), and (D) are wrong because they're each the **Opposite** of the data presented in the table—(A) is wrong because those same albatrosses were *least* likely, not *most* likely, to find a new mate, and (C) and (D) are wrong because the shyest male albatrosses were the *most* likely, not the *least* likely, to separate from their mates.

- (B) is correct because it's consistent with what the table says about the shyest male albatrosses.

13. **A** This is a Claims question, as it asks which quotation would be the *most effective for the student to include in support of this claim*. Look for and highlight the claim in the text, which is that *American art entered a new era largely due to the influence of the exhibition*. The correct answer should address and be consistent with each aspect of this claim.

- (A) is correct because it's consistent with the highlighted claim—*the dawn of Modernism* could be the *new era*, and the *exhibition* referenced is *The International Exhibition of Modern Art*."

- (B), (C), and (D) are wrong because they're each **Half-Right**—they all mention some aspect of the International Exhibition of Modern Art, but none of them refers to anything that could be *a new era* for American art.

14. **A** This is a Conclusions question, as it asks what *most logically completes the text*. Look for and highlight the main focus of the text, which is *lithium-ion* and *sodium-ion batteries*. Then, highlight the main point made regarding this focus, which is that sodium-ion batteries are meant to be a *high-performance, low-cost* alternative to lithium-ion batteries, but their performance depends on the transport of *ions across a carbon lattice*. Therefore, sodium-ion batteries may work as an alternative to lithium-ion batteries, assuming their lattice structure can continue to be improved upon. The correct answer should be as consistent as possible with this conclusion.

- (A) is correct because it's consistent with what the highlighted sentences say about the comparison between lithium-ion and sodium-ion batteries and what must happen to further improve the performance of sodium-ion batteries.

- (B), (C), and (D) are wrong because they're each **Recycled Language**—the *ability to store large amounts of energy*, used in a *wide range of products*, and used in *smartphones* and *electric cars* are all mentioned as features of lithium-ion batteries, not sodium-ion batteries.

15. **B** In this Rules question, verbs are changing in the answer choices, so it's testing consistency with verbs. Find and highlight the subject, *formations*, which is plural, so a plural verb is needed. All of the answers work with a plural subject, so look for a clue regarding tense. The sentence says *since the Precambrian age*. Highlight this phrase and write an annotation that says "past." Eliminate any answer not in past tense.

- (A) and (C) are wrong because they're in future tense.

- (B) is correct because it's in past tense.

- (D) is wrong because it's in present tense.

16. **D** In this Rules question, verb forms are changing in the answer choices, so it's testing sentence structure. The phrase after the comma describes what Mash *wanted*. Eliminate any answer that does not make the phrase clear and correct.

- (A) is wrong because it does not say who or what Mash *wanted*.

- (B) and (C) are wrong because these forms do not provide a clear and correct meaning.

- (D) is correct because it states that Mash *wanted to study ibogaine*, which provides a clear and correct meaning.

17. **B** In this Rules question, verbs are changing in the answer choices, so it's testing consistency with verbs. Find and highlight the subject, *The acidic precipitation*, which is singular, so a singular verb is needed. Write an annotation saying "singular." Eliminate any answer that is not singular.

- (A), (C), and (D) are wrong because they are plural.

- (B) is correct because it's singular.

18. **D** In this Rules question, verb forms are changing in the answer choices, so it's testing sentence structure. The sentence already contains an independent clause followed by a comma. Thus, the phrase after the comma must be a phrase that describes Ivan and his *existential dilemmas*. Eliminate any answer that does not correctly form this phrase.

    - (A), (B), and (C) are wrong because these forms do not provide a clear and correct meaning.

    - (D) is correct because it correctly describes Ivan as *navigating* several things.

19. **A** In this Rules question, periods and question marks are changing in the answer choices, so it's testing questions versus statements. The beginning of the sentence starts with the word *How*, so the sentence should be a question. Eliminate answers that aren't correctly written as questions.

    - (A) is correct because it's correctly written as a question.

    - (B), (C), and (D) are wrong because they are statements.

20. **D** In this Rules question, pronouns are changing in the answer choices, so it's testing consistency with pronouns. Find and highlight the word the pronoun refers back to, *scenario*, which is singular, so a singular pronoun is needed. Write an annotation saying "singular." Eliminate any answer that isn't singular or doesn't clearly refer back to the *theoretical scenario*.

    - (A), (B), and (C) are wrong because they are plural.

    - (D) is correct because *it* is singular and is consistent with the *theoretical scenario*.

21. **C** In this Rules question, punctuation is changing in the answer choices. Look for independent clauses. The first part of the sentence says *Upon noticing the resemblance*, which is a describing phrase that is not an independent clause. The second part of the sentence says *explorers named the bird "penguin" after the auk's Latin name*, which is an independent clause. Eliminate any option that doesn't correctly connect the describing phrase to the independent clause.

    - (A) is wrong because a colon can only be used after an independent clause.

    - (B) is wrong because a semicolon connects two independent clauses.

    - (C) is correct because a comma is appropriate after this describing phrase.

    - (D) is wrong because it opens parentheses but doesn't close them.

22. **A** This is a transition question, so follow the basic approach. Highlight ideas that relate to each other. The preceding sentence says, *First, the Earth does exhibit various feedback mechanisms*, and this sentence describes another observation regarding the stable conditions on Earth. These ideas agree, so a same-direction transition is needed. Make an annotation that says "agree." Eliminate any answer that doesn't match.

    - (A) is correct because *Second* is consistent with *First*.

- (B) and (D) are wrong because *Conversely* and *Still* are opposite-direction transitions.

- (C) is wrong because this sentence isn't a more specific version of the previous sentence.

23. **B** In this Rules question, punctuation is changing in the answer choices. The main meaning of the sentence is *Several species of cuttlefish exhibit unique camouflage abilities*. The blank comes between the subject and the verb, and there is no other punctuation. A single punctuation mark can't separate a subject and a verb, so eliminate answers with punctuation.

- (A), (C), and (D) are wrong because a single punctuation mark can't come between a subject and a verb.

- (B) is correct because no punctuation should be used here.

24. **D** In this Rules question, punctuation is changing in the answer choices. The main meaning of the sentence is *Kreutz sungrazers are comets that are thought to have originated from one large comet that fragmented several hundred years ago*. The phrase *as first proposed by German astronomer Heinrich Kreutz* is a describing phrase that has a comma after it, so it must have a comma before it to show that it is Extra Information. Eliminate answers that do not have a comma before the describing phrase.

- (A), (B), and (C) are wrong because they don't use a comma.

- (D) is correct because it uses a comma before the Extra Information.

25. **D** This is a transition question, so follow the basic approach. Highlight ideas that relate to each other. The preceding sentence states that *she first selected ribosomal material isolated from particularly robust bacterial strains*, and this sentence describes the next step Yonath took in her research. These ideas agree, so a same-direction transition is needed. Make an annotation that says "agree." Eliminate any answer that doesn't match.

- (A) and (B) are wrong because this sentence isn't an additional point building upon the previous sentence.

- (C) is wrong because this sentence isn't making a similar point to the previous sentence.

- (D) is correct because *Next* is consistent with *first*.

26. **A** This is a transition question, so follow the basic approach. Highlight ideas that relate to each other. The preceding sentence states that *Paul writes about her experience as a member of an Indigenous tribe*, and this sentence describes more detail regarding how she wrote about her experience. These ideas agree, so a same-direction transition is needed. Make an annotation that says "agree." Eliminate any answer that doesn't match.

- (A) is correct because *Specifically* is consistent with providing more detail based on the information in the previous sentence.

- (B) is wrong because this sentence isn't a conclusion.

- (C) and (D) are wrong because *Though* and *Besides* are opposite-direction transitions.

27. **C**   This is a transition question, so follow the basic approach. Highlight ideas that relate to each other. The preceding sentence states that *Shostakovich met the challenge, composing Tahiti Trot in under an hour*, and this sentence describes an additional detail about the information. These ideas agree, so a same-direction transition is needed. Make an annotation that says "agree." Eliminate any answer that doesn't match.

    - (A) and (B) are wrong because *Still* and *Nonetheless* are opposite-direction transitions.

    - (C) is correct because *Moreover* is consistent with providing an additional detail about the previous sentence.

    - (D) is wrong because this sentence doesn't introduce another thing that is similar to something previously discussed.

Module 2—Harder

1. **D**   This is a Vocabulary question, as it asks for a *logical and precise word or phrase*. The blank describes the interaction between the study and the gene variant, so look for and highlight clues in the text about that interaction. The text states that the *cause of hypertension…is unknown*, but the transitional word *but* indicates that the blank should go in the opposite direction of that clue. Therefore, a good word to enter in the annotation box would be "found" or "identified."

    - (A) and (C) are wrong because they each go **Beyond the Text**—a study cannot publish a gene variant, only information about a gene variant, and it's not supported in the text that the study *affected*, or influenced, the gene variant in any way.

    - (B) is wrong because *measured* doesn't match "found."

    - (D) is correct because *discovered* matches "found."

2. **B**   This is a Vocabulary question, as it asks what "conveyed" *most nearly means*. Treat "conveyed" as if it were a blank—the blank describes something that happens to the narrator in his travels, so look for and highlight clues in the text about those travels. The text mentions that the narrator was *to be met by one of the Dumbleton carriages* and taken *across the remaining nine miles of country*, so a good word to enter in the annotation box would be "carried" or "driven."

    - (A) and (C) are wrong because *Explained* and *Communicated* are **Right Answer, Wrong Question**—they are normal definitions of "conveyed" that don't fit the context of this text.

    - (B) is correct because *Transported* matches "carried."

    - (D) is wrong because *Questioned* doesn't match "conveyed"—if anything, it's the **Opposite** meaning, as *Questioned* means asked and "conveyed" can mean explained or answered.

3. **D** This is a Vocabulary question, as it asks for a *logical and precise word or phrase*. The blank describes how the improvements to the oxcart wheel design interacted with a more seamless transportation of goods, so look for and highlight clues in the text about that interaction. The text states that the new wheel design *could withstand the country's rugged paths and roadways* in a way the old wheel design could not, so a good word to enter in the annotation box would be "allowed" or "made possible."

- (A) and (C) are wrong because *conspired against* and *contended with* are the **Opposite** of "allowed" or "made possible."

- (B) is wrong because it's the **Opposite** of the relationship between the oxcart wheels and the seamless transportation. The improved wheel design is what made the seamless transportation possible, but the wheel design did not rely on seamless transportation.

- (D) is correct because *provided for* matches "allowed."

4. **B** This is a Purpose question, as it asks for the *main purpose of the text*. Read the text and highlight who or what is focused on. The text focuses on Sarah Margaret Fuller and her contributions as a member of the transcendentalist movement. The text mentions that Fuller *advocated for women's rights* and that *her influence inspired the likes of Ralph Waldo Emerson and Susan B. Anthony*. Therefore, a good main purpose of the text to enter in the annotation box would be "explain Fuller's goals and contributions."

- (A) and (C) are wrong because they each go **Beyond the Text**—only one journalist, Fuller, is discussed, and the text only focuses on Fuller's activism, not the details of her journalism career.

- (B) is correct because it's consistent with the highlighting and annotation.

- (D) is wrong because it also goes **Beyond the Text**—while men and women probably faced different challenges during the transcendentalist movement, none of the specific issues facing men are discussed in the text.

5. **D** This is a Purpose question, as it asks for the *main purpose of the text*. Read the text and highlight who or what is focused on. The text focuses on debt relief and states that *some of the ancient practices of debt relief came to form modern debt relief practices* and then offers examples of both ancient and modern debt relief practices before and after this sentence. Therefore, a good main purpose of the text to enter in the annotation box would be "discuss old and modern debt relief."

- (A) is wrong because it's **Recycled Language**—*modern American* and *modern European* debt relief practices are not compared to each other in the text but rather to *ancient Roman practices*.

- (B) is wrong because it's **Extreme Language**—the history of debt relief given in the text is not *comprehensive*, nor does the text speculate on the *future* of debt relief.

- (C) is wrong because it's **Half-Right**—while the author does not advocate for modern debt relief to include things such as labor or imprisonment, this answer directly contradicts the highlighted sentence about how ancient Roman practices influenced modern debt relief.

- (D) is correct because it's consistent with the highlighting and annotation.

6. **A** This is a Purpose question, as it asks for the *main purpose of the text*. Read the text and highlight who or what is focused on. The text focuses on the reaction by Irene to the quantity of food delivered to her by another woman. The dialogue between the women indicates that Irene thinks she and Klea do *not have enough to satisfy* themselves. Therefore, a good main purpose of the text to enter in the annotation box would be "Irene believes she and Klea don't get enough food."

    - (A) is correct because it's consistent with the highlighting and annotation.

    - (B) is wrong because it goes **Beyond the Text**—it is the quantity of food rather than the *quality* of the food that Irene objects to.

    - (C) is wrong because no *disagreement* between Irene and Klea is referenced in the text, only one between Irene and the woman delivering the food.

    - (D) is wrong because it also goes **Beyond the Text**—while it's easy to imagine that Klea could be disdainful toward Irene's behavior, there's no support for such a conclusion in the text, as none of Klea's thoughts or reactions are included.

7. **D** This is a Dual Texts question, as it asks how *Crane* in Text 2 would *respond to the conclusion* reached by Oshri in Text 1. Read Text 1 and highlight the conclusion, which is that *individuals who experienced low-to-moderate stress levels had increased neural activity...while individuals who experienced chronically high stress levels had decreased activity*. Then, read Text 2 and highlight what M. F. Crane says about the same topic. He argues that *systemic self-reflection...can improve an individual's resilience to stress, reducing the impact of high stress levels on working memory in the future*. Therefore, while Crane doesn't disagree that high stress levels affect working memory, he believes this impact can be reduced. Enter "Text 2 expands discussion—self-reflection can reduce impact of stress" into the annotation box.

    - (A) is wrong because Text 2 makes no comment on a lack of *detailed information* in Text 1, nor does Crane take issue with how Oshri's participants were asked to report.

    - (B) is wrong because it's **Recycled Language**—Crane focuses only on *resilience to stress* and not *brain function*, which is only addressed in Text 1.

    - (C) is wrong because it goes **Beyond the Text**—neither author claims that there isn't a *quantifiable way* to measure the impact of stressful events.

    - (D) is correct because it's consistent with the relationship between the texts—*reducing the impact of high-stress levels on working memory* is a good thing, so Crane believes that some positive may come out of exposure to higher stress levels.

8. **C** This is a Main Idea question, as it asks for the *main idea of the text*. Look for and highlight information that can help identify the main idea. The text states that *Titan's anti-greenhouse effect, which cools Titan by 9 degrees Kelvin (K), is countered by a greenhouse effect, which warms Titan by 21 K.* Since the other sentences explain what an anti-greenhouse effect should do, and the last sentence explains what actually

happens on Titan through the use of the transition word *However*, the last sentence serves as the main idea. The correct answer should be as consistent as possible with this portion of the text.

- (A) and (D) are wrong because they each go **Beyond the Text**—*other planets* and the evolution of the *understanding of stratospheric particles* are not discussed in the text.

- (B) is wrong because it's **Right Answer, Wrong Question**—this is a detail stated by the text but not the text's *main idea*.

- (C) is correct because it's consistent with the highlighted portion of the text—the greenhouse and anti-greenhouse effects both exist on Titan and have contradictory effects.

9. **A** This is a Retrieval question, as it asks for a detail *Based on the text*. Look for and highlight information about *the 2021 Suez Canal obstruction*. Since the entire text discusses this obstruction, go to the answers and use the process of elimination. The correct answer should be as consistent as possible with the text.

- (A) is correct because it's consistent with the second and third sentences' descriptions of how *Ever Given* became stuck in the canal.

- (B) is wrong because it's the **Opposite** of what happens in the text—*the stern moved in towards the closer bank* rather than being forced *away from the nearer bank*.

- (C) is wrong because it's **Extreme Language**—the quality of the ship's navigation is not discussed in the text, much less described as *poor*.

- (D) is wrong because it's **Recycled Language**—it misuses *ship propeller action*, *bank shape*, *canal*, and *hull* from different parts of the text to make an unsupported conclusion.

10. **A** This is a Main Idea question, as it asks for the *main idea of the text*. Look for and highlight information that can help identify the main idea. The last sentence states that *Çelebi's focus on the entertainment of his readership rather than strict adherence to historical accuracy helped to spread awareness of Ottoman culture in a more readily digestible fashion*. Since the other sentences introduce Çelebi and discuss his work, the last sentence serves as the main idea. The correct answer should be as consistent as possible with this portion of the text.

- (A) is correct because it's consistent with the highlighted portion of the text, paraphrasing each of its key points.

- (B) is wrong because it's **Half-Right**—while Çelebi's work definitely included *comedy*, it's not stated in the text that writings by other Arab travelers were usually *somber*, or gloomy.

- (C) is wrong because it goes **Beyond the Text**—it's not stated in the text how successful Çelebi *would have been* if he had focused on historical accuracy over entertainment.

- (D) is wrong because it's the **Opposite** of the last sentence of the text, which states that Çelebi's work was actually successful because it focused on *entertainment* rather than *historical accuracy*, not the other way around.

11.   **A**   This is a Claims question, as it asks which finding *would most challenge the conclusion in the underlined sentence*. Look for and highlight the underlined claim in the text, which is that *the team concluded that the presence of birdsong is strongly linked with positive feelings*. The correct answer should be as contradictory as possible to this claim, offering an alternative conclusion or a differing explanation for the results found by the team.

- (A) is correct because the sunny versus overcast weather is a possible alternative explanation for the differences in reports of positive emotions rather than the presence or absence of birdsong—this is also consistent with the idea that the team tried to *account for…appealing environmental factors,* as it presents an environmental factor that was perhaps not accounted for.

- (B) and (D) are wrong because they're not relevant to the claim—the number of reports completed by each participant and the locations visited by each participant are not part of the team's conclusion.

- (C) is wrong because it would do the **Opposite** of the question task—it would strengthen, not *challenge,* the team's conclusion regarding the connection between the presence of birdsong and positive emotions.

12.   **B**   This is a Charts question, as it asks for *data from the table* that will *support the team's marketing plan*. Read the title, variables, and units from the table. Then, read the text and highlight the claim or statement that references the information from the table. The text states that *when the decoy product is only partially unattractive, that is, only one of its parameters is inferior to a competitor's product, consumers will often be swayed away from the competitor's product.* This is the goal the marketing team wants to accomplish by suggesting that *the company introduce decoy Product Z* instead of decoy Product Y. The correct answer should offer accurate information from the table that supports this recommendation.

- (A) and (D) are wrong because they're each the **Opposite** of the data presented in the table—Product Y and Product Z are not more attractive than Product X in either respect, as both products cost more and have shorter lifespans than Product X.

- (B) is correct because it's consistent with the highlighted text and the table—although Product Z is both more expensive and has a shorter lifespan than Product X, the fact that Product Z is at least cheaper than Product W means it's more likely that consumers will be swayed away from Product W, which is the competitor's product.

- (C) is wrong because it's consistent with the table but irrelevant to the claim—the team's plan specifically references *decoy Product Z*, so the correct information from the table must mention decoy Product Z also.

13.   **A**   This is a Claims question, as it asks which finding *would most directly support the team's conclusion*. Look for and highlight the team's conclusion in the text, which is that *white sharks respond rapidly to the risk*

presented by a novel predator in their environment and will not return to a habitat they believe is unsafe. The correct answer should be as consistent as possible with this conclusion.

- (A) is correct because it's consistent with the highlighted conclusion—if sharks have abandoned their aggregation site because they believe it to be unsafe, the *food resources* preyed upon by those sharks should *experience a notable increase*, since the sharks are not there to feed on those resources.

- (B) and (D) are wrong because they're not relevant to the claim—knowing that *killer whales had been established as predators of white sharks in other areas* or which of the two species had *telemetry sensors* on it would not affect the team's conclusion regarding this particular shark site, at which killer whales have only recently arrived.

- (C) is wrong because it would do the **Opposite** of the question task—it would weaken, not *support* the team's conclusion if sharks returned to the aggregation site despite the danger of the killer whales.

14. **C**   This is a Conclusions question, as it asks what *most logically completes the text*. Look for and highlight the main focus of the text, which is *subjective age*. Then, highlight the main point made regarding this focus, which is that a younger subjective age is associated with *fewer physical maladies and improved mental health* but can also lead to negatives such as *increased exposure to disease and injury* as well as *personal and social conflicts*. Therefore, there are positives and negatives associated with having a younger subjective age. The correct answer should be as consistent as possible with this conclusion.

- (A) is wrong because it's **Extreme Language**—while the negative aspects of younger subjective age are discussed, it's not stated that they *entirely offset* the benefits of having a younger subjective age.

- (B) is wrong because it's **Recycled Language**—while *middle-age people* and *older people* are discussed in the text, the actual subjective ages they have are neither discussed nor compared.

- (C) is correct because it's consistent with what the highlighted sentences say regarding the positives and negatives of having a younger subjective age.

- (D) is wrong because it goes **Beyond the Text**—while people in the real world do sometimes struggle with accepting *their biological ages*, this struggle isn't mentioned in the text.

15. **C**   In this Rules question, verbs are changing in the answer choices, so it's testing consistency with verbs. Find and highlight the subject, *Advocating*, which is singular, so a singular verb is needed. Write an annotation saying "singular." Eliminate any answer that is not singular.

- (A), (B), and (D) are wrong because they are plural.

- (C) is correct because it's singular.

16. **A** In this Rules question, commas are changing in the answer choices. The sentence describes what the benefits of delta wings are and contains the word *and* toward the end, so look for a list. The list consists of 1) *allow for the performance of advanced maneuvers*, 2) *provide increased lift*, and 3) *reduce the possibility of a stall*. Eliminate any answer that doesn't put commas between the list items.

- (A) is correct because it has a comma after each of the first two items.

- (B) and (C) are wrong because they don't have a comma after *lift*.

- (D) is wrong because it doesn't have a comma after *maneuvers*.

17. **C** In this Rules question, punctuation is changing in the answer choices. The main meaning of the sentence is *The Cubist-style paintings…were influenced by the Ecuadorian painter's experiences with other artists*. The phrase *some of them Mexican muralists* is a describing phrase that has a comma after it, so it must have a comma before it to show that it is Extra Information. Eliminate answers that do not have a comma before the describing phrase.

- (A), (B), and (D) are wrong because they don't use a comma before the Extra Information.

- (C) is correct because it uses a comma before the Extra Information.

18. **D** In this Rules question, punctuation is changing in the answer choices. Look for independent clauses. The first part of the sentence says *Low traffic neighborhoods…are neighborhoods where side roads are closed to cars but remain open to bicycles and pedestrians*, which is an independent clause. The second part says *The reduced presence of cars in multiple neighborhoods in Lambeth…resulted in LTN residents driving less throughout the year*, which is also an independent clause. Eliminate any answer that can't correctly connect two independent clauses.

- (A) is wrong because a comma without a coordinating conjunction (FANBOYS) can't connect two independent clauses.

- (B) is wrong because a semicolon links two independent clauses, but adding the word *with* to the second part of the sentence makes the second part no longer an independent clause.

- (C) is wrong because adding the word *with* makes the second part of the sentence lack a subject for the verb *resulted*.

- (D) is correct because the period makes each independent clause its own sentence, which is fine.

19. **C** In this Rules question, periods and question marks are changing in the answer choices, so it's testing questions versus statements. The beginning of the sentence starts with *Why*, so the sentence should be a question. Eliminate answers that aren't correctly written as questions.

- (A), (B), and (D) are wrong because they are statements.

- (C) is correct because it's correctly written as a question.

20. **B** In this Rules question, punctuation is changing in the answer choices. The main meaning of the sentence is *Josette Simon joined the Royal Shakespeare Company in 1982, performing in several Shakespearean plays…in the leading female role.* The phrase *Love's Labour's Lost (1984), A Midsummer Night's Dream (1999), and Antony and Cleopatra (2017)* is a describing phrase that has a long dash before it, so it must have a long dash after it to show that it is Extra Information. Eliminate answers that do not have a long dash after the describing phrase.

- (A), (C), and (D) are wrong because they don't use a long dash after the Extra Information.

- (B) is correct because it uses a long dash after the Extra Information.

21. **A** In this Rules question, commas and semicolons are changing in the answer choices. The sentence already contains a semicolon near the end, and the part after it is not an independent clause, which suggests that the sentence contains a list separated by semicolons. Use the second example to determine the structure of each item: Action, Comma, Description. Make an annotation of this pattern and eliminate any answer that doesn't follow it.

- (A) is correct because it follows the pattern of the second item.

- (B), (C), and (D) are wrong because they don't have a semicolon after the first item.

22. **B** This is a transition question, so follow the basic approach. Highlight ideas that relate to each other. The preceding sentence states that endangered animals are *often exposed to anti-parasitic procedures that can aid in the longevity and health of that specific species*, and this sentence states that *these methods are harmful to the parasites themselves and may unintentionally cause the extinction of a different species.* These ideas disagree, so an opposite-direction transition is needed. Make an annotation that says "disagree." Eliminate any answer that doesn't match.

- (A), (C), and (D) are wrong because they are all same-direction transitions.

- (B) is correct because *However* is an opposite-direction transition.

23. **A** This is a transition question, so follow the basic approach. Highlight ideas that relate to each other. The preceding sentence says that *Structural coloration…creates color when light is manipulated by microscopic surface structures,* and this sentence says *A peacock's feathers…have a microscopic structure that reflects blue, turquoise, and green light.* These ideas agree, so a same-direction transition is needed. Make an annotation that says "agree." Eliminate any answer that doesn't match.

- (A) is correct because *for example* is a same-direction transition, and this sentence is an example of the preceding sentence.

- (B) and (C) are wrong because *though* and *however* are opposite-direction transitions.

- (D) is wrong because this sentence is an example of the previous claim rather than an additional point.

24. **B**   This is a transition question, so follow the basic approach. Highlight ideas that relate to each other. The preceding sentence states that *research surrounding food preparation for astronauts on missions is still very minimal*, and this sentence describes research intended to find out about frying in space. These ideas agree, so a same-direction transition is needed. Make an annotation that says "agree." Eliminate any answer that doesn't match.

- (A) is wrong because *By comparison* is an opposite-direction transition.

- (B) is correct because this sentence is a consequence of the preceding sentence: because there's a lack of information on the topic, researchers are trying to find out more.

- (C) is wrong because this sentence is a consequence rather than an additional point.

- (D) is wrong because this sentence is not a summary of the preceding sentence.

25. **C**   This is a Rhetorical Synthesis question, so follow the basic approach. Highlight the goal stated in the question: *emphasize the order in which two of Rabindranath Tagore's works were published*. Eliminate any answer that doesn't fulfill this purpose.

- (A) is wrong because it mentions only one of Tagore's works.

- (B) is wrong because it doesn't state the *order* of the two works.

- (C) is correct because it states which work came before and which came after.

- (D) is wrong because it doesn't mention any specific *works*.

26. **A**   This is a Rhetorical Synthesis question, so follow the basic approach. Highlight the goal stated in the question: *emphasize a difference between alkali metals and noble gases*. Eliminate any answer that doesn't fulfill this purpose.

- (A) is correct because it uses the contrast word *while*, and the words *reactive* and *do not react* demonstrate a *difference*.

- (B) and (D) are wrong because they don't mention a *difference* between alkali metals and noble gases.

- (C) is wrong because it doesn't mention alkali metals or noble gases.

27. **D**   This is a Rhetorical Synthesis question, so follow the basic approach. Highlight the goal stated in the question: *emphasize the size of the radio telescope used to discover pulsars*. Eliminate any answer that doesn't fulfill this purpose.

- (A), (B), and (C) are wrong because they don't mention anything related to *the size of the radio telescope*.

- (D) is correct because *covered an area of 4 acres* shows *the size of the radio telescope*.

PRACTICE TEST 1—MATH EXPLANATIONS

Module 1

1. **B** The question asks for a value based on a percentage. Translate the English to math in bite-sized pieces.

   The question states that *10% of the parking spaces have cars in them. Percent* means out of 100, so translate 10% as $\frac{10}{100}$. Translate *of* as times. Thus, 10% of the 900 parking spaces becomes $\frac{10}{100}$ (900) = 90 of the parking spaces are occupied by cars. The correct answer is (B).

2. **C** The question asks for a value based on a graph. Specifically, the question asks for the value of the *x*-intercept on the graph of a parabola. This is the point at which $y = 0$ and the graph intersects the *x*-axis. Look on the graph for the point on the parabola at which the *y* coordinate equals 0 and the graph touches the *x*-axis. This point is (–2, 0). The correct answer is (C).

3. **B** The question asks for the value of an expression. Plug in 30 for *a* in the expression $a - 9$ to get 30 – 9, which becomes 30 – 9 = 21. The correct answer is (B).

4. **D** The question asks for a value given a rate. Begin by reading the question to find information about the rate. The question states that the zookeepers can clean animal habitats at a rate of *28 habitats in 4 days*.

   Set up a proportion to determine how many habitats they can clean in 12 days at this rate. The proportion is $\frac{28 \text{ habitats}}{4 \text{ days}} = \frac{x \text{ habitats}}{12 \text{ days}}$. Cross-multiply to get (28)(12) = (4)(x), which becomes 336 = 4x. Divide both sides of the equation by 4 to get 84 = x. The correct answer is (D).

5. **C** The question asks for an equivalent form of an expression. Both terms include *y* multiplied by a different coefficient. Subtract the coefficients to get 4 – 44 = –40. Thus, $4y - 44y = -40y$. The correct answer is (C).

6. **D** The question asks for a list of numbers that has the same range as the list shown. The range of a list of numbers is the difference between the greatest and least numbers in the list. Start by finding the range of the list of numbers given. The greatest number in the list is 19. The least number in the list is 4. The range is 19 – 4 = 15.

   Next, find the ranges of the lists in the answer choices, and eliminate any that do not have a range of 15. All of the lists in the answer choices contain numbers in order, so the range will be the difference between the first and last numbers in the list. The range of the list in (A) is 19 – 3 = 16. This is not 15, so eliminate (A). The range of the list in (B) is 20 – 4 = 16; eliminate (B). The range of the list in (C) is 19 – 5 = 14; eliminate (C). The range of the list in (D) is 20 – 5 = 15. This is the same range as the range in the list of numbers in the question, so stop here. The correct answer is (D).

7. $-\dfrac{2}{3}$ The question asks for the slope of a line. The question states that *line t is perpendicular to line s*, which means the lines have slopes that are negative reciprocals. The question gives the equation of line *s*, so find the slope of that line. The equation is in slope-intercept form, $y = mx + b$, where *m* is the slope and *b* is the *y*-intercept. In the equation of line *s*, $m = \dfrac{3}{2}$, so the slope of line *t* is $-\dfrac{2}{3}$. The decimal forms $-.6666$, $-.6667$, and -0.666 would also be accepted as correct. The correct answer is $-\dfrac{2}{3}$ or equivalent forms.

8. **A**   The question asks for the value of a trigonometric function based on a geometric figure. First, redraw the figure and labels on the scratch paper. Next, write down SOHCAHTOA to remember the trig functions. The SOH part of the acronym defines the sine as $\dfrac{opposite}{hypotenuse}$. The side opposite angle *a* is 8, and the hypotenuse is 17, so $\sin a° = \dfrac{8}{17}$. The correct answer is (A).

9. **B**   The question asks for the slope of the line of best fit of a scatterplot. The equations in the answer choices are all in standard form, $y = mx + b$, in which *m* is the slope and *b* is the *y*-intercept. All of the equations have a *y*-intercept of 6.2, so work with the slope. The line is descending from left to right, so it has a negative slope. Eliminate (C) and (D) because they have positive slopes. Use two points on the line of best fit to calculate the slope of the line using the formula $slope = \dfrac{y_2 - y_1}{x_2 - x_1}$. The line of best fit passes through a point close to (6, 4) and through another point at (8, 3). Plug those values into the slope formula to get $slope = \dfrac{4 - 3}{6 - 8}$, which becomes $slope = \dfrac{1}{-2}$ or $slope = -0.5$. Eliminate (D) because the slope is not close to -0.5. The slope of the line in (B), -0.51, is close to -0.5, so keep (B). The correct answer is (B).

10. **B**   The question asks for a value given a function. In function notation, the number inside the parentheses is the *x*-value that goes into the function, or the input, and the value that comes out of the function is the *y*-value, or the output. The question provides an output value of 30, and the answers have numbers that could represent the input value, so use the values in the answers. Start with one of the middle numbers and try (C), 36. Plug 36 into the function for *x* to get $30 = 12(36) - 6$, which becomes $30 = 432 - 6$, or $30 = 426$. This is not true, so eliminate (C). The result was too large, so also eliminate (D). Now try (B), 3. Plug 3 into the function for *x* to get $30 = 12(3) - 6$, which becomes $30 = 36 - 6$, or $30 = 30$. The correct answer is (B).

11. **C**   The question asks for a factor of a quadratic. The correct answer must be a value that all three terms of the expression can be divided by without leaving a remainder. The first and second terms, $-18x^2$ and $6x^2$, cannot be evenly divided by 4, so eliminate (A) and (B). The last term, $24x$, cannot be divided by x^2. Eliminate (D) because it includes x^2. All three terms can be divided by 6 and by *x*, so $6x$ is a factor of the expression. The correct answer is (C).

12. **C** The question asks for an equation that represents a specific situation. The depth of the ROV is increasing by a certain percent over time, so this question is about exponential growth. Write down the growth and decay formula, which is *final amount* = (*original amount*)(*multiplier*)$^{number\ of\ changes}$. The question states that the initial depth was 630 meters, so that is the *original amount*. Eliminate (A) and (B) because they do not have 630 as the original amount in front of the parentheses. The depth after each subsequent dive is 120% of the depth after the previous dive, so the *multiplier* is 120%. *Percent* means out of 100, so translate 120% as $\dfrac{120}{100}$, or 1.20. Eliminate (D) because it does not have 1.20 as the multiplier. The correct answer is (C).

13. **A** The question asks for an equation in terms of specific variables. The question asks about the relationship among variables and there are variables in the answer choices, so plugging in is an option. However, that might get messy with three variables, and all of the answer choices have f on the left side of the equation, so the other option is to solve for f. To begin to isolate f and make it positive, add $8f$ to both sides of the equation to get $3d = 8f + g$. Subtract g from both sides of the equation to get $3d - g = 8f$. Divide both sides of the equation by 8 to get $\dfrac{3d - g}{8} = f$. Flip the two sides of the equation to get $f = \dfrac{3d - g}{8}$. The correct answer is (A).

14. **B** The question asks for a measure on a geometric figure. Start by drawing a square on the scratch paper. Next, label the figure with information from the question. Label each side as s inches. Next, write out the formula for the area of a square, either from memory or after looking it up on the reference sheet. The formula is *Area* = *side*^{2}, or $A = s^2$. Plug in the value for the area given in the question to get $144 = s^2$. Take the positive square root of both sides of the equation to get $12 = s$. The correct answer is (B).

15. **−14** The question asks for the value of the y-coordinate of the solution to a system of equations. The quickest method is to enter both equations into the built-in graphing calculator, then scroll and zoom as needed to find the point of intersection. The graphs intersect at $(5, -14)$, so the y-coordinate is -14.

To solve the system for the y-coordinate algebraically, first isolate x in the first equation. Add 3 to both sides of the equation to get $x = 5$. Now, plug in 5 for x in the second equation to get $y = 5^2 - 15(5) + 36$. Simplify the right side of the equation to get $y = 25 - 75 + 36$, which becomes $y = -14$.

Using either method, the correct answer is -14.

16. **14** The question asks for a value based on a figure. Redraw the figure and labels on the scratch paper. When a line intersects two parallel lines, two kinds of angles are created: big and small. All of the small angles are equal to each other, all of the big angles are equal to each other, and any small angle plus any big angle = 180°. The angle labeled $x°$ is a small angle, and the angle labeled 72° is a small angle. Thus,

angle x also measures 72°. Plug in 72 for x in the given equation to get $72 = 6y - 12$. Add 12 to both sides of the equation to get $84 = 6y$. Divide both sides of the equation by 6 to get $14 = y$. The correct answer is 14.

17. **D** The question asks for the value of one variable in terms of another. The question asks about the relationship among variables and there is a variable in the answer choices, so one option is to plug in. However, that might get messy with three variables. The question gives the value of b, so the other option is to translate the English to math in bite-sized pieces and solve for c. A ratio can be written as a fraction, so translate *the ratio a to b* as $\dfrac{a}{b}$, and translate *the ratio c to 15* as $\dfrac{c}{15}$. The question states that the two ratios are equivalent, so set the two fractions equal to each other: $\dfrac{a}{b} = \dfrac{c}{15}$. Next, plug in 14 for b, and the equation becomes $\dfrac{a}{14} = \dfrac{c}{15}$ Cross-multiply to get $(a)(15) = (14)(c)$, or $15a = 14c$. Divide both sides of the equation by 14 to get $\dfrac{15a}{14} = c$. The correct answer is (D).

18. **10** The question asks for the value of a constant in an equation that models a specific situation. Start by reading the final question, which asks for the meaning of the constant m. Rewrite the equation and label it with information from the question. One piece of information says that the model predicts that *a museum has 371 objects in its collection in the year it opens*. The term n is alone on the right side of the equation, so it must be the initial number of objects: label n as 371. The question also states that $c(y)$ is the predicted *number of items*, and that y represents the number of years after the museum's opening: label the equation with this information. The equation is now labeled as follows:

number of items after y years = 371 + m(*number of years after opening*)

Finally, the question states that *the museum intends to add 10 items to its collection each year for the first decade after it opens*. The only remaining term is m, and it is multiplied by the number of years. Therefore, m must equal the number of items to be added each year, which is 10. The correct answer is 10.

19. **B** The question asks for the value of an expression given a system of equations. When a PSAT question asks for the value of an expression, there is usually a straightforward way to solve for the expression without needing to completely isolate either variable. Try stacking and adding the two equations.

$$\begin{array}{rcl} y - 7 &=& 5x - 21 \\ +\ \ y + 7 &=& -5x + 13 \\ \hline 2y &=& -8 \end{array}$$

The question asks for the value of $2y$, so stop here. The correct answer is (B).

20. **74** The question asks for the least possible value based on a specific situation. Translate the English to math in bite-sized pieces. Translate *is at least* as greater than or equal to, or ≥. Translate *14 more than* as + 14. Translate *12 times x* as 12x. The inequality becomes $y \geq 12x + 14$. Plug in 5 for x to get $y \geq 12(5) + 14$. Simplify the right side of the inequality to get $y \geq 60 + 14$, and then $y \geq 74$. The question asks for the least possible value of y, which is 74. The correct answer is 74.

21. **A** The question asks for the equation of a function that is a translation of another function. In function notation, $f(x) = y$. The number inside the parentheses is the x-value that goes into the function, or the input, and the value that comes out of the function is the y-value, or the output. When a function is translated, up or down, the y-value changes. Add 6 to both sides of the equation to translate the graph up 6 units. The equation becomes $f(x) + 6 = \left(\dfrac{13 + k}{x}\right) - 7 + 6$, or $f(x) + 6 = \left(\dfrac{13 + k}{x}\right) - 1$. Eliminate (C) and (D) because they have − 7 instead of − 1. To translate the graph 8 units to the left, add 8 to the x-value in the function to get $f(x + 8) + 6 = \left(\dfrac{13 + k}{x + 8}\right) - 1$. Now both translations have been applied, and the equation for function h is $h(x) = \left(\dfrac{13 + k}{x + 8}\right) - 1$. The correct answer is (A).

22. **3** The question asks for the value of x when the graph of a function reaches its maximum. A parabola reaches its minimum or maximum value at its vertex, so find the x-coordinate of the vertex. One method is to enter the equation into the built-in graphing calculator, then scroll and zoom as needed to find the vertex. The vertex is at (3, −5), so the x-coordinate is 3.

Another approach is to know the vertex form of a parabola. That form is $y = a(x - h)^2 + k$, where (h, k) is the vertex. In this quadratic, $(x - h) = (x - 3)$, so $-h = -3$. Divide both sides of this equation by −1 to get $h = 3$.

Using either method, the correct answer is 3.

Module 2—Easier

1. **C** The question asks for a minimum change in value given a specific situation. The question states that *inflation needs to be at most 1.5% for a nation's economy to be considered healthy*. It also states that *the current rate of inflation for a certain nation is 4%*. Find the difference between the two rates to determine the minimum decrease. To reach a healthy rate of inflation of 1.5%, the rate must decrease by 4 − 1.5 = 2.5 percent. The correct answer is (C).

2. **B** The question asks for a value based on a box plot. In a box plot, the median is the value at the vertical line inside the box. The line representing the median of the 9 values is at 6. The correct answer is (B).

3. **B** The question asks for a value based on a graph. First, check the units on each axis of the line graph. According to the question, the x-axis shows the number of hours, and the y-axis shows the number of gallons of gas. The question asks about the number of hours that have passed when the generator has 5 gallons remaining, so find 5 on the y-axis. Move to the right from there—using the mouse pointer or the edge of the scratch paper—to the point on the line where $y = 5$. Move down from there to find the value on the x-axis. The value is 15. The correct answer is (B).

4. **C** The question asks for a value given a specific situation. Translate the information in bite-sized pieces. The question states that a painter *has 70 gallons of paint*, and that *Each townhouse uses 13 gallons of paint*. The amount of paint used for 4 townhouses is $(4)(13) = 52$ gallons. The question also states that *the painter uses the leftover paint to paint doors, using one-third of a gallon per door*. After using 52 gallons of paint, the remaining amount is $70 - 52 = 18$ gallons. To determine the number of doors that the painter can paint, divide the remaining amount of paint by the amount used per door to get $\frac{18}{\left(\frac{1}{3}\right)} = 54$. The correct answer is (C).

5. **A** The question asks for the value of a function. In function notation, the number inside the parentheses is the x-value that goes into the function, or the input, and the value that comes out of the function is the y-value, or the output. The question provides an input value of 32, so plug $x = 32$ into the function to get $f(32) = \frac{32}{16}$, which becomes $f(32) = 2$. The correct answer is (A).

6. **35** The question asks for the value of an expression based on an equation. There isn't a straightforward way to get from $3x$ to $5x$, so start by isolating x. Divide both sides of the equation by 3 to get $x = 7$. Next, substitute 7 for x in the expression $5x$ to get $5(7) = 35$. The correct answer is 35.

7. **C** The question asks for a probability based on a situation. Probability is defined as $\frac{\text{\# of outcomes that fit requirements}}{\text{total \# of possible outcomes}}$. Read carefully to find the numbers that make up the probability. The questions states that there are *31 pies for sale*, so 31 is the total # of possible outcomes. There are *6 apples pies*, so the # of outcomes that fit requirements is 6. Therefore, the probability of selecting an apple pie is $\frac{6}{31}$. The correct answer is (C).

8. **A** The question asks for an equation in terms of a specific variable. The question asks about the relationship among variables and there are variables in the answer choices, so plugging in is an option. However, that might get messy with three variables, and all of the answer choices have s on the left side of the equation, so the other option is to solve for s. To begin to isolate s, divide both sides of the equation by 3 to get $2r + s = \frac{8}{3}t$. Subtract $2r$ from both sides of the equation to get $s = \frac{8}{3}t - 2r$. The correct answer is (A).

9. **D** The question asks for the equation that represents a line. Translate the information in bite-sized pieces and eliminate after each piece. In function notation, $g(x) = y$, so the answer choices are all in slope-intercept form, $y = mx + b$, in which m is the slope and b is the y-intercept. All of the answers have the correct slope of -4, so focus on the y-intercept. The y-intercept is the point where the graph crosses the y-axis, which happens when $x = 0$. Thus, the point $(0, 2)$ is the y-intercept, and b in slope-intercept form is 2. Eliminate (A), (B), and (C) because they have the wrong value for the y-intercept.

Another option is to plug $x = 0$ and $g(x) = 2$ into each answer choice and eliminate any that don't work, which eliminates every answer except (D).

Using either method, the correct answer is (D).

10. **B** The question asks for an equation that represents a given situation. Translate the information in bite-sized pieces. One piece of information says that a represents *6-ounce cans of tuna*, and another piece says that b represents *15-ounce cans of tuna*. All of the answer choices have 1,290 on the right side of the equation, which correctly translates the total number of ounces of tuna. The left side of the equation must also represent the total number of ounces of tuna. If a and b represent the numbers of cans, the coefficients of a and b must represent the numbers of ounces per can. Therefore, the coefficient of a must be 6 and the coefficient of b must be 15. Eliminate (A), (C), and (D) because they have different values for the coefficients of a and b. The correct answer is (B).

11. **C** The question asks for the x-coordinate of the point of intersection of a system of equations. The most efficient method is to enter both equations into the built-in graphing calculator, then scroll and zoom as needed to find the point of intersection. Click on the gray dot to see that the coordinates of the point are $(14, 4)$. The x-value is 14, which is (C).

To solve algebraically, first simplify the first equation by taking the square root of 16 to get $y = 4$. Next, substitute 4 for y in the second equation to get $x = 4^2 - 2$. Simplify the right side of the equation get $x = 16 - 2$, and then $x = 14$.

Using either method, the correct answer is (C).

12. **D** The question asks for an equation that represents the relationship among the side lengths of a triangle. Start by redrawing the figure and the labels. One of the angles is marked with the 90-degree symbol, so

this is a right triangle. Write down the Pythagorean Theorem: $a^2 + b^2 = c^2$. Plug in the given values to get $10^2 + m^2 = 14^2$. This is (D), so stop here. The correct answer is (D).

13.   **A**   The question asks for a value based on a geometric figure. Draw a quadrilateral on the scratch paper and label the vertices A, B, C, and D. Label angle A as 83°, label angle C as 116°, and label angle D as 90°. All quadrilaterals contain 360°, so the measurement of the fourth angle in the quadrilateral, B, is $360° - 83° - 116° - 90° = 71°$. The correct answer is (A).

14.   **1568**   The question asks for a measurement and gives conflicting units. The question provides the conversion that 1 stone = 14 pounds. Set up a proportion, being sure to match up units. The proportion is $\frac{1 \text{ stone}}{14 \text{ pounds}} = \frac{112 \text{ stone}}{x \text{ pounds}}$. Cross-multiply to get $(14)(112) = (1)(x)$, or $1,568 = x$. Leave out the comma when entering the answer in the fill-in box. The correct answer is 1568.

15.   **D**   The question asks for the table that contains values that are solutions to an equation. When given an equation and asked for a table of values, plug values from the table into the equation to see which ones work. Plugging in 0 or 1 is likely to make more than one answer work, so start with the third row of the tables in the answer choices. Plug $x = 2$ into the equation to get $y = \frac{1}{2}(2) - 6$, which becomes $y = 1 - 6$, and then $y = -5$. Eliminate (A), (B), and (C) because they have a value other than -5 when $x = 2$. The correct answer is (D).

16.   **C**   The question asks for the value of the measure of an angle on a geometric figure. Start by drawing two triangles that are similar to each other, meaning they have the same angle measures but are different sizes. It doesn't matter whether the figures have the exact angle measures given in the question as long as the two triangles are similar. Be certain to match up the corresponding vertices that are given in the question. The drawing could look something like this:

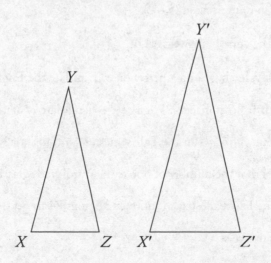

Next, label the figure with the given information. Label angle X' as 74° and angle Y' as 28°. Because the triangles are similar, corresponding angle measures are the same, so also label angle X as 74° and angle Y as 28°. The drawing now looks like this:

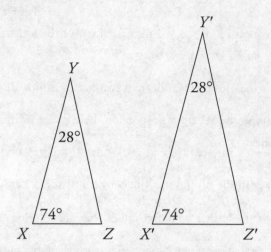

There are 180° in a triangle, so the measure of angle Z is 180° − 74° − 28° = 78°. The correct answer is (C).

17. **B** The question asks which point is a solution to an inequality shown by a graph. The shaded region of the graph represents the solutions to the inequality. The answers contain specific points that could be a solution to the inequality, so find each point from the answer choices on the graph and eliminate any that are not in the shaded area. Only (B), (5, 0), is within the shaded area of the graph. The correct answer is (B).

18. **D** The question asks for the solution to a system of equations. One approach is to enter both equations into the built-in graphing calculator, then scroll and zoom as needed to find the point of intersection. Click on the gray dot to see that the point is at (5, −2), which is (D).

To solve algebraically, plug in −2 for y in the second equation to get $x = 3 − (−2)$, or $x = 5$. Thus, when $x = 5$, $y = −2$, and the lines intersect at (5, −2).

Using either method, the correct answer is (D).

19. **63** The question asks for a value based on a percentage. Translate the English to math in bite-sized pieces. *Percent* means out of 100, so translate 25% as $\frac{25}{100}$. Translate *of* as times. The question states that *a third-grade classroom had 84 books* in the Fall semester, so translate 25% of 84 to get $\frac{25}{100}(84) = 21$. The question also states that the number of books the third-grade classroom had in the Spring semester is *25% fewer than* in the Fall semester, so subtract 21 from 84 to get 84 − 21 = 63 books in the Spring semester. The correct answer is 63.

20. $-\dfrac{3}{4}$ **or –0.75**

The question asks for the solution to an equation. To isolate z, first multiply both sides of the equation by z to get $3 = -4z$. Divide both sides of the equation by -4 to get $-\dfrac{3}{4} = z$. The correct answer is $-\dfrac{3}{4}$ or 0.75.

21. **A** The question asks for a value based on a specific situation. A quadratic function that models the height of a volleyball from impact will form a parabola when graphed. The question states that the volleyball will be *4.2 feet above the surface of the court* when hit. It also states that it will take *3.2 seconds to return to its starting height after the initial impact* and the volleyball will reach a *maximum height of 10 feet*, which is the vertex.

Use the information to determine some points on the graph. When no time had elapsed and the ball was hit, $x = 0$, and $y = 4.2$. Therefore, the parabola contains a point at (0, 4.2). After 3.2 seconds, the volleyball returned to its starting height, which can be graphed at (3.2, 4.2). Between those two times, it reached its maximum height of 10 feet. Sketch a graph of the parabola on the scratch paper, which should look something like this:

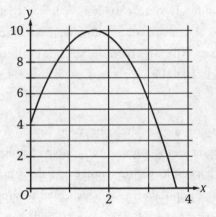

The vertex of a parabola is on the axis of symmetry, which is a vertical line exactly halfway between the point of initial impact and the point at which the volleyball returns to its starting height. Take the average of the two x-coordinates when the height $y = 4.2$ to find the axis of symmetry: $\dfrac{3.2 - 0}{2} = 1.6$. Thus, the x-coordinate of the vertex, which represents the time when the volleyball reached its maximum height, is 1.6. The correct answer is (A).

22. **A** The question asks for the interpretation of a feature of the graph of an equation. Start by reading the final question, which asks for the best interpretation of the equation $(x, y) = (10, 55)$. It may help to enter the equation in the built-in calculator to see that it is a parabola that opens downward and has a vertex of (0, 1,600). The given point, (10, 55), is a single point on the graph, not a change per hour.

Eliminate (C) and (D) because they refer to a change over time rather than a single point. The question states that x is the number of hours and y is the number of fungi. Since 10 is the x-value and 55 is the corresponding y-value, 10 is the number of hours and 55 is a number of fungi. Eliminate (B) because it reverses the two values. The correct answer is (A).

Module 2—Harder

1. **−4** The question asks for the y–coordinate of the y-intercept of a graph. The question provides a y-intercept of $(0, y)$, so plug in 0 for x and solve for y. The equation becomes $3(0) - 4y = 16$, or $-4y = 16$. Divide both sides of the equation by -4 to get $y = -4$. The correct answer is -4.

2. **B** The question asks for an inequality that models a specific situation. Translate the information in bite-sized pieces and eliminate after each piece. One piece of information says that the roadside stand *sells only apples and peaches.* This means that the number of apples and number of peaches need to be added together. Eliminate (C) and (D) because they subtract the two values instead of adding them. Another piece of information says that the owner of the stand hopes to sell *at least 26 pieces of fruit.* Translate *at least* as greater than or equal to, or $\geq$. Eliminate (A) because the inequality sign is facing the wrong direction. The correct answer is (B).

3. **2** The question asks for a value given an equation. A linear equation has no real solutions when the x-terms are the same and the constants are different. Both sides of the equation have different constants, so focus on the x-terms. The x-term on the left side of the equation, $2x$, must equal the x-term on right side of the equation, cx. Therefore, $2x = cx$. Divide both sides of the equation by x to get $c = 2$. The correct answer is 2.

4. **C** The question asks for the most appropriate conclusion based on a population sample and a margin of error. A margin of error expresses the amount of random sampling error in a survey's results. The margin of error is 3, meaning that results within a range of 3 above and 3 below the estimate are reasonable. The estimated percent of the population that is expected to support the referendum is given as 60.8, so subtract the margin of error to get $60.8 - 3 = 57.8$, and then add the margin of error to get $60.8 + 3 = 63.8$. The most appropriate conclusion is that between 57.8 and 63.8 percent of the electorate will support the referendum. Choice (C) matches the range and says it is plausible that the percent is within that range, so keep (C). Eliminate (A) because it states the opposite of what a margin of error means. Eliminate (B) because it mentions eligibility to vote, not support of a particular referendum. Eliminate (D) because it says that numbers outside the range of values are *not possible,* which also misinterprets the meaning of margin of error. The correct answer is (C).

5. **7** The question asks for the mode of a data set. A frequency table has two columns: the left-hand column contains the values, and the right-hand column contains the number of times each value occurs, or its frequency. The value that appears most frequently is 7, which occurs 13 times, so that is the mode of the data set. The correct answer is 7.

6. **D** The question asks for the interpretation of a feature of the graph of a function. Start by reading the final question, which asks for the best interpretation of the point (30, 104.015). In a graph that represents an amount over time, the x–coordinate represents time, and the y–coordinate represents the amount. In this case, the x–coordinate represents the time, in years, of an investment that earns interest, and the y–coordinate represents the value, in thousands of dollars, of the investment. Therefore, 30 represents the time in years of the investment, and 104.015 represents the value, in thousands of dollars. Eliminate (B) because it reverses the values. Eliminate (A) because the initial value is when $x = 0$ and the question asks about when $x = 30$. Eliminate (C) because the y-coordinate represents the value in thousands of dollars, so the value is approximately $104,000, not $104. The correct answer is (D).

7. **D** The question asks for the interpretation of a term in context. Start by reading the final question, which asks for the meaning of $3h$. Rewrite the equation on the scratch paper. Then label the parts of the equation with the information given, and eliminate answers that do not match the labels. The equation $a = \frac{1}{2}(3h)(h)$ is in the form of the formula for the area of a triangle, which is $Area = \frac{1}{2} base \times height$, or $A = \frac{1}{2}bh$. The question states that a is the area, so the two terms on the right side of the equation must be the base and height. Eliminate (A) because the area of the triangle is represented by a, not by $3h$. Eliminate (B) because $3h$ is either the base or the height, not the difference between them. Compare the remaining answers: the difference is whether $3h$ represents the base or the height of the triangle. The question states that the *base of the triangle is 3 times its height*. Translate *is* as equals and *times* as multiplication, and the equation becomes *base* = (3)(*height*), or *base* = $3h$. Therefore, $3h$ represents the base of the triangle. The correct answer is (D).

8. **C** The question asks for an expression that is equivalent to a term in an equation. The question asks for the product bc, so there is no need to isolate the variables individually. Instead, rearrange the equation to isolate bc. Add 9 to both sides of the equation to get $S + 9 = 5(bc + 1)$. Divide both sides of the equation by 5 to get $\frac{S+9}{5} = bc + 1$. Subtract 1 from both sides of the equation to get $\frac{S+9}{5} - 1 = bc$. To get the left side of the equation into the form of the answer choices, make it into a single fraction. Use 5 as a common denominator and rewrite 1 as $\frac{5}{5}$. The equation becomes $\frac{S+9}{5} - \frac{5}{5} = bc$. Subtract the numerators to get $\frac{S+9-5}{5} = bc$, or $\frac{S+4}{5} = bc$. The correct answer is (C).

9. **C** The question asks for the table that contains values that are solutions to a function. In function notation, $g(x) = y$, so $y = -7$. This will be true for all values of x, which makes (C) correct. To check, enter the equation into the built-in graphing calculator, either as $g(x) = -7$ or as $y = -7$. Scroll and zoom as needed

to see that the graph is a straight horizontal line at $y = -7$. Whether $x = -1$, $x = 0$, or $x = 1$, the value of y is always -7. The correct answer is (C).

10. **B** The question asks for the expression representing a decrease by a percentage. There are variables in the answer choices, so plug in. Make $q = 100$ because 100 works well with percents. *Percent* means out of 100, so translate 14% as $\frac{14}{100}$. Take 14% of 100 to get $\frac{14}{100}(100) = 14$. The question asks for the result of decreasing q by 14%, so subtract 14 from the original value to get $100 - 14 = 86$. This is the target value; write it down and circle it. Next, plug $q = 100$ into each answer choice, and eliminate any that don't match the target value. Choice (A) becomes $0.14(100) = 14$. This does not match the target value, so eliminate (A). Choice (B) becomes $0.86(100) = 86$. This matches the target value, so keep (B), but check the remaining answers just in case. Choice (C) becomes $1.14(100) = 114$; eliminate (C). Choice (D) becomes $86(100) = 8,600$; eliminate (D). The correct answer is (B).

11. **C** The question asks for an inequality that represents a graph. One approach is to enter the inequality from each answer choice into the built-in graphing calculator and see which graph looks most like the graph in the question. The graph of the inequality in (C) looks like the graph in the question, so (C) is correct.

Since there are variables in the answer choices, another approach is to plug in. Pick a point in the shaded area of the graph, plug it into the inequalities in the answer choices, and eliminate any answers that don't work. Try the point $(0, 0)$. Plug $x = 0$ and $f(x) = 0$ into (A) to get $0 \leq 10(0) - 3$, which becomes $0 \leq 0 - 3$, and then $0 \leq -3$. This is not true, so eliminate (A). Plug the same values into (B) to get $0 \leq 10(0) + 3$, which becomes $0 \leq 0 + 3$, and then $0 \leq 3$. This is true, so keep (B), but check the remaining answers. Plug $x = 0$ and $f(x) = 0$ into (C) to get $0 \geq 10(0) - 3$, which becomes $0 \geq 0 - 3$, and then $0 \geq -3$; keep (C). Plug the same values into (D) to get $0 \geq 10(0) + 3$, which becomes $0 \geq 0 + 3$, and then $0 \geq 3$; eliminate (D).

Two answers worked with the first point, so try a second point, such as $(0, 8)$. Plug $x = 0$ and $f(x) = 8$ into (B) to get $8 \leq 10(0) + 3$, which becomes $8 \leq 0 + 3$, and then $8 \leq 3$. This is not true, so eliminate (B). Plug the same values into (C) to get $8 \geq 10(0) - 3$, which becomes $8 \geq 0 - 3$, and then $8 \geq -3$, which is true. Only (C) worked with both points, so it is the correct inequality.

Using either method, the correct answer is (C).

12. **48** The question asks for an amount of power. Other information about the circuit is given, so use the units to determine where to start. The question asks for the total power in watts and gives the voltage in volts and the current in amps. The question states that dividing the number of watts by the number of volts gives the number of amps. Plug in the known values for volts and amps and solve for watts: $\frac{\text{watts}}{24} = 2$. Multiply both sides of the equation by 24 to get watts $= 48$. The question asks for the total power in watts. The correct answer is 48.

13.   **A**   The question asks for an equation that represents a specific situation. The question gives two scenarios for the cost of a sundae, so use the information to plug values into the answers and eliminate functions that don't work. The question states that the cost of a sundae with 2 toppings is $2.60, so plug $t = 2$ and $c(t) = 2.60$ into the answer choices. Choice (A) becomes $2.60 = 0.70(2) + 1.20$, which becomes $2.60 = 1.40 + 1.20$, and then $2.60 = 2.60$. This is true, so keep (A), but check the remaining answers because the correct equation must work for both pairs of values. Choice (B) becomes $2.60 = 1.20(2) + 0.70$, which becomes $2.60 = 2.40 + 0.70$, and then $2.60 = 3.10$. This is not true, so eliminate (B). Choice (C) becomes $2.60 = 1.30(2)$ or $2.60 = 2.60$; keep (C). Choice (D) becomes $2.60 = 1.40(2) + 1.20$, which becomes $2.60 = 2.80 + 1.20$, and then $2.60 = 4.00$; eliminate (D).

Now test the remaining answers with the other piece of information, which is that a sundae with 4 toppings costs $4.00. Plug $t = 4$ and $c(t) = 4.00$ into (A) to get $4.00 = 0.70(4) + 1.20$, which becomes $4.00 = 2.80 + 1.20$, and then $4.00 = 4.00$. This is true, but check (C). Choice (C) becomes $4.00 = 1.30(4)$ or $4.00 = 5.20$. Eliminate (C). The correct answer is (A).

14.   **D**   The question asks for the equation that makes a system of equations have no real solutions. A system of linear equations in two variables has no real solutions when the graphs of the lines are parallel. One method is to recall that parallel lines have the same slope. All of the equations are linear equations in standard form, $Ax + By + C$. In this form, the slope is $-\dfrac{A}{B}$, so this would need to be calculated for all the equations. There is also a good chance that more than one answer has the correct slope, making it necessary to compare y-intercepts as well.

A more efficient method is to use the built-in calculator to graph the first equation and the equations in the answer choices and find the line that is parallel to the first line. Be careful: the lines for (B) and (C) are parallel to each other, but only the line for (D) is parallel to the line in the question. Click on the circular symbol next to the lines for (A), (B), and (C) to hide them and make it easier to see. Since the line for (D) is parallel, it is the second equation that gives the system no real solutions. The correct answer is (D).

15.   **B**   The question asks for the negative solution to a quadratic equation. The equation is a quadratic in standard form, which is $ax^2 + bx + c$. However, this quadratic is difficult to factor, so look for a different approach. One approach is to use the built-in calculator. Enter the expression without "= 0" into the built-in calculator, then scroll and zoom as needed to see the negative x-intercept, which represents the negative solution to the equation. This is at $(-\dfrac{7}{2}, 0)$, making (B) correct.

Another approach is to use the values in the answers: plug in the value for x from each answer choice until one of them makes the equation true. When $x = -\dfrac{7}{2}$, the equation becomes $6\left(-\dfrac{7}{2}\right)^2 + 11\left(-\dfrac{7}{2}\right) - 35 = 0$. Simplify to get $6\left(\dfrac{49}{4}\right) - \dfrac{77}{2} - 35 = 0$, then $\dfrac{147}{2} - \dfrac{77}{2} - 35 = 0$. Continue simplifying to get $\dfrac{70}{2} - 35 = 0$, then $35 - 35 = 0$, and finally $0 = 0$.

Using either method, the correct answer is (B).

16. **B** The question asks for the value of $\cos(A)$ but gives measurements on triangle XYZ. Because the two triangles are similar, the value of corresponding trigonometric functions will be equal. Therefore, $\cos(A) = \cos(X)$. The value of $\cos(X)$ is $\dfrac{\text{adjacent}}{\text{hypotenuse}}$ or $\dfrac{XY}{XZ}$. It is possible to use the Pythagorean Theorem to find XY, but it's easier to use the special right triangle from the reference sheet. Because the hypotenuse is twice one of the legs, this is a 30°-60°-90° triangle. YZ is the shortest side, (x), so XY is $x\sqrt{3}$ or $2\sqrt{3}$. Therefore, $\cos(X) = \dfrac{2\sqrt{3}}{4}$, which reduces to $\dfrac{\sqrt{3}}{2}$. Because $\cos(X) = \cos(A)$, $\cos(A)$ also equals $\dfrac{\sqrt{3}}{2}$. The correct answer is (B).

17. **A** The question asks for a system of equations that represents a specific situation. Translate the English into math in bite-sized pieces and eliminate after each piece. Start with the information about time. The question states that the *total amount of time the student spent writing the assignments was 15 hours* and that a hours were spent writing research paper pages and b hours were spent writing creative story pages. Translate this as $a + b = 15$. Eliminate (C) and (D) because they do not include this equation. Compare the remaining answer choices. Both (A) and (B) correctly translate the total number of pages as = 45, and the difference is the coefficients for a and b. The question states that the student wrote pages for a research paper at an average rate of 2 pages per hour and wrote pages for creative stories at an average rate of 3 pages per hour. Since a is the time spent on writing research paper pages and b is the time spent writing creative story pages, 2 should go with a and 3 should go with b. Eliminate (B) because it has the coefficients on the wrong variables. The correct answer is (A).

18. $\dfrac{200}{3}$ The question asks for a rate given a function that models a specific situation. To calculate the average change in height, divide the change in height, in feet, by the change in time, in minutes. Height in feet is on the y-axis, so find the height when $x = 30$ and $x = 60$ by looking at the y-value for each of the x-coordinates. When $x = 30$ minutes, $y = 2{,}000$ feet, and when $x = 60$ minutes, $y = 4{,}000$ feet. Set up a fraction to determine the average rate of change in feet per minute: $\dfrac{4{,}000 - 2{,}000}{60 - 30} = \dfrac{2{,}000}{30}$. This fraction does not fit in the fill-in box, so reduce it to $\dfrac{200}{3}$. The decimal forms 66.66 and 66.67 would also be accepted as correct. The correct answer is $\dfrac{200}{3}$ or equivalent forms.

19. **B** The question asks for the value of a constant given a function. In function notation, the number inside the parentheses is the x-value that goes into the function, or the input, and the value that comes out of the function is the y-value, or the output. The question states that $h(c) = 2c$, so when the input is c, the output is $2c$. Plug these values into the function to get $2c = |7c - 33|$. With an absolute value, the value inside the absolute value bars can be either positive or negative, so this equation has two possible solutions. To find the solutions, set $7c - 33$ equal to both $2c$ and $-2c$, and solve for c. When $7c - 33 = 2c$, subtract $2c$ from both sides of the equation and add 33 to both sides of the equation to get $5c = 33$. Divide both sides of the equation by 5 to get $c = \dfrac{33}{5}$. Since this value is in the answer choices, there is no need to solve for the other solution. The correct answer is (B).

20. **C** The question asks for a value on a geometric figure. Draw a triangle on the scratch paper, and then label it with information from the question. The question states that the equation represents the perimeter of a *triangle with two equal sides*, so label two sides as x. The question also states that the third side is s, so label this on the figure. The perimeter of a triangle is the sum of all three sides, so the perimeter can be represented by the equation $P = x + x + s$, or $P = 2x + s$. Write the equation and the formula given in the question above each other to see how the terms match up.

$$P = 2x + s$$
$$P = 16 + s$$

Thus, $2x = 16$. Divide both sides of this equation by 2 to get $x = 8$. The correct answer is (C).

21. $\dfrac{1}{9}$ **or .1111**

The question asks for the value of a constant that is part of the sum of the solutions to a quadratic equation. It takes a lot of algebra to answer this question, but a shortcut is to recall that, when a quadratic is in standard form, $ax^2 + bx + c$, the sum of the solutions is $-\dfrac{b}{a}$. Put the quadratic equation into standard form by distributing the negative sign to the x-terms to get $27x^2 + (-3c - 9d)x + cd = 0$. Now that the quadratic is in standard form, $a = 27$ and $b = (-3c - 9d)$, so the sum of the solutions is $-\dfrac{(-3c - 9d)}{27}$. Distribute the negative sign in front of the fraction to the numerator to get $\dfrac{(3c + 9d)}{27}$. Reduce the fraction by dividing all of the terms by 3 to get $\dfrac{(c + 3d)}{9}$. The question states that the sum of the solutions is $h(c + 3d)$, so set the two ways to represent the sum of the solutions equal to each other to get $\dfrac{(c + 3d)}{9} = h(c + 3d)$. Rewrite the left side of the equation as $\dfrac{1}{9}(c + 3d)$ so that the equation can be written as $\frac{1}{9}(c + 3d) = h(c + 3d)$. Finally, divide both sides of the equation by $(c + 3d)$ to get $\frac{1}{9} = h$. The decimal form .1111 would also be accepted as correct. The correct answer is $\frac{1}{9}$ or .1111.

22. **A** The question asks for the value of the proportion of two sides in a geometric figure. Start by drawing a triangle with vertices W, X, and Y. Label angle W with the right angle symbol, label $\overline{WX}$ as 21, and label $\overline{WY}$ as 21 + 25 = 46. An altitude of a triangle is a line that goes from a vertex to the opposite side, so draw a line that starts at W and is perpendicular to $\overline{XY}$ at point Z. The drawing should look something like this:

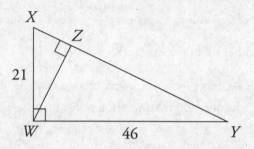

The question asks for the ratio of sides $\overline{XZ}$ and $\overline{WZ}$, which are part of right triangle WXZ. Determine whether triangles WXY and WXZ are similar triangles. Redraw the two right triangles with the right angles in the lower left in order to compare them more easily.

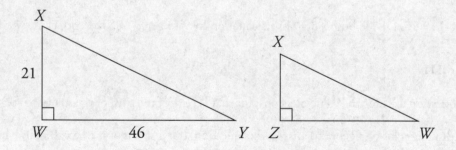

Both triangles have a right angle in the lower left and angle X in the upper left, so the third angles, Y and W, must have the same measure. The triangles are similar, so the sides are proportional. Since $\overline{XZ}$ corresponds to $\overline{WX}$ and $\overline{WZ}$ corresponds to $\overline{WY}$, the proportion $\frac{XZ}{WZ}$ is equal to the proportion $\frac{WX}{WY}$. Plug in the known values for WX and WY to get $\frac{WX}{WY} = \frac{21}{46}$. Thus, $\frac{XZ}{WZ}$ also equals $\frac{21}{46}$. The correct answer is (A).

575+ PSAT/NMSQT Practice Questions
Practice Test

The Princeton Review®

© 2024 by TPR Education IP Holdings, LLC.

YOUR NAME: _____
(Print)   Last   First   M.I.

SIGNATURE: _____ DATE: ___/___/___

HOME ADDRESS: _____
(Print)   Number and Street

_____
                City   State   Zip Code

PHONE NO.: _____
(Print)

DATE OF BIRTH: ___/___/_____
(Print)   Month / Day / Year

For both the Reading and Writing and the Math, be sure to only fill in the bubbles for the version of Module 2 that you took. If you took the Easier Module 2, only fill in the answer in the Easier column. If you took the Harder Module 2, only fill in the answers in the Harder column.

Section 1: Module 1
Reading and Writing

1. Ⓐ Ⓑ Ⓒ Ⓓ
2. Ⓐ Ⓑ Ⓒ Ⓓ
3. Ⓐ Ⓑ Ⓒ Ⓓ
4. Ⓐ Ⓑ Ⓒ Ⓓ
5. Ⓐ Ⓑ Ⓒ Ⓓ
6. Ⓐ Ⓑ Ⓒ Ⓓ
7. Ⓐ Ⓑ Ⓒ Ⓓ
8. Ⓐ Ⓑ Ⓒ Ⓓ
9. Ⓐ Ⓑ Ⓒ Ⓓ
10. Ⓐ Ⓑ Ⓒ Ⓓ
11. Ⓐ Ⓑ Ⓒ Ⓓ
12. Ⓐ Ⓑ Ⓒ Ⓓ
13. Ⓐ Ⓑ Ⓒ Ⓓ
14. Ⓐ Ⓑ Ⓒ Ⓓ
15. Ⓐ Ⓑ Ⓒ Ⓓ
16. Ⓐ Ⓑ Ⓒ Ⓓ
17. Ⓐ Ⓑ Ⓒ Ⓓ
18. Ⓐ Ⓑ Ⓒ Ⓓ
19. Ⓐ Ⓑ Ⓒ Ⓓ
20. Ⓐ Ⓑ Ⓒ Ⓓ
21. Ⓐ Ⓑ Ⓒ Ⓓ
22. Ⓐ Ⓑ Ⓒ Ⓓ
23. Ⓐ Ⓑ Ⓒ Ⓓ
24. Ⓐ Ⓑ Ⓒ Ⓓ
25. Ⓐ Ⓑ Ⓒ Ⓓ
26. Ⓐ Ⓑ Ⓒ Ⓓ
27. Ⓐ Ⓑ Ⓒ Ⓓ

Section 1: Module 2 (Easier)
Reading and Writing

1. Ⓐ Ⓑ Ⓒ Ⓓ
2. Ⓐ Ⓑ Ⓒ Ⓓ
3. Ⓐ Ⓑ Ⓒ Ⓓ
4. Ⓐ Ⓑ Ⓒ Ⓓ
5. Ⓐ Ⓑ Ⓒ Ⓓ
6. Ⓐ Ⓑ Ⓒ Ⓓ
7. Ⓐ Ⓑ Ⓒ Ⓓ
8. Ⓐ Ⓑ Ⓒ Ⓓ
9. Ⓐ Ⓑ Ⓒ Ⓓ
10. Ⓐ Ⓑ Ⓒ Ⓓ
11. Ⓐ Ⓑ Ⓒ Ⓓ
12. Ⓐ Ⓑ Ⓒ Ⓓ
13. Ⓐ Ⓑ Ⓒ Ⓓ
14. Ⓐ Ⓑ Ⓒ Ⓓ
15. Ⓐ Ⓑ Ⓒ Ⓓ
16. Ⓐ Ⓑ Ⓒ Ⓓ
17. Ⓐ Ⓑ Ⓒ Ⓓ
18. Ⓐ Ⓑ Ⓒ Ⓓ
19. Ⓐ Ⓑ Ⓒ Ⓓ
20. Ⓐ Ⓑ Ⓒ Ⓓ
21. Ⓐ Ⓑ Ⓒ Ⓓ
22. Ⓐ Ⓑ Ⓒ Ⓓ
23. Ⓐ Ⓑ Ⓒ Ⓓ
24. Ⓐ Ⓑ Ⓒ Ⓓ
25. Ⓐ Ⓑ Ⓒ Ⓓ
26. Ⓐ Ⓑ Ⓒ Ⓓ
27. Ⓐ Ⓑ Ⓒ Ⓓ

Section 1: Module 2 (Harder)
Reading and Writing

1. Ⓐ Ⓑ Ⓒ Ⓓ
2. Ⓐ Ⓑ Ⓒ Ⓓ
3. Ⓐ Ⓑ Ⓒ Ⓓ
4. Ⓐ Ⓑ Ⓒ Ⓓ
5. Ⓐ Ⓑ Ⓒ Ⓓ
6. Ⓐ Ⓑ Ⓒ Ⓓ
7. Ⓐ Ⓑ Ⓒ Ⓓ
8. Ⓐ Ⓑ Ⓒ Ⓓ
9. Ⓐ Ⓑ Ⓒ Ⓓ
10. Ⓐ Ⓑ Ⓒ Ⓓ
11. Ⓐ Ⓑ Ⓒ Ⓓ
12. Ⓐ Ⓑ Ⓒ Ⓓ
13. Ⓐ Ⓑ Ⓒ Ⓓ
14. Ⓐ Ⓑ Ⓒ Ⓓ
15. Ⓐ Ⓑ Ⓒ Ⓓ
16. Ⓐ Ⓑ Ⓒ Ⓓ
17. Ⓐ Ⓑ Ⓒ Ⓓ
18. Ⓐ Ⓑ Ⓒ Ⓓ
19. Ⓐ Ⓑ Ⓒ Ⓓ
20. Ⓐ Ⓑ Ⓒ Ⓓ
21. Ⓐ Ⓑ Ⓒ Ⓓ
22. Ⓐ Ⓑ Ⓒ Ⓓ
23. Ⓐ Ⓑ Ⓒ Ⓓ
24. Ⓐ Ⓑ Ⓒ Ⓓ
25. Ⓐ Ⓑ Ⓒ Ⓓ
26. Ⓐ Ⓑ Ⓒ Ⓓ
27. Ⓐ Ⓑ Ⓒ Ⓓ

575+ PSAT/NMSQT Practice Questions
Practice Test

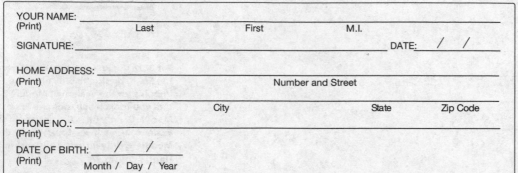

YOUR NAME: _____
(Print)   Last   First   M.I.

SIGNATURE: _____ DATE: __ / __ / __

HOME ADDRESS: _____
(Print)   Number and Street

_____
City   State   Zip Code

PHONE NO.: _____
(Print)

DATE OF BIRTH: __ / __ / _____
(Print)   Month / Day / Year

For both the Reading and Writing and the Math, be sure to only fill in the bubbles for the version of Module 2 that you took. If you took the Easier Module 2, only fill in the answer in the Easier column. If you took the Harder Module 2, only fill in the answers in the Harder column.

Section 2: Module 1 Math

1. (A) (B) (C) (D)
2. (A) (B) (C) (D)
3. (A) (B) (C) (D)
4. (A) (B) (C) (D)
5. (A) (B) (C) (D)
6. (A) (B) (C) (D)
7. _____
8. (A) (B) (C) (D)
9. (A) (B) (C) (D)
10. (A) (B) (C) (D)
11. (A) (B) (C) (D)
12. (A) (B) (C) (D)
13. (A) (B) (C) (D)
14. (A) (B) (C) (D)
15. _____
16. _____
17. (A) (B) (C) (D)
18. _____
19. (A) (B) (C) (D)
20. _____
21. (A) (B) (C) (D)
22. _____

Section 2: Module 2 (Easier) Math

1. (A) (B) (C) (D)
2. (A) (B) (C) (D)
3. (A) (B) (C) (D)
4. (A) (B) (C) (D)
5. (A) (B) (C) (D)
6. _____
7. (A) (B) (C) (D)
8. (A) (B) (C) (D)
9. (A) (B) (C) (D)
10. (A) (B) (C) (D)
11. (A) (B) (C) (D)
12. (A) (B) (C) (D)
13. (A) (B) (C) (D)
14. _____
15. (A) (B) (C) (D)
16. (A) (B) (C) (D)
17. (A) (B) (C) (D)
18. (A) (B) (C) (D)
19. _____
20. _____
21. (A) (B) (C) (D)
22. (A) (B) (C) (D)

Section 2: Module 2 (Harder) Math

1. _____
2. (A) (B) (C) (D)
3. _____
4. (A) (B) (C) (D)
5. _____
6. (A) (B) (C) (D)
7. (A) (B) (C) (D)
8. (A) (B) (C) (D)
9. (A) (B) (C) (D)
10. (A) (B) (C) (D)
11. (A) (B) (C) (D)
12. _____
13. (A) (B) (C) (D)
14. (A) (B) (C) (D)
15. (A) (B) (C) (D)
16. (A) (B) (C) (D)
17. (A) (B) (C) (D)
18. _____
19. (A) (B) (C) (D)
20. (A) (B) (C) (D)
21. _____
22. (A) (B) (C) (D)